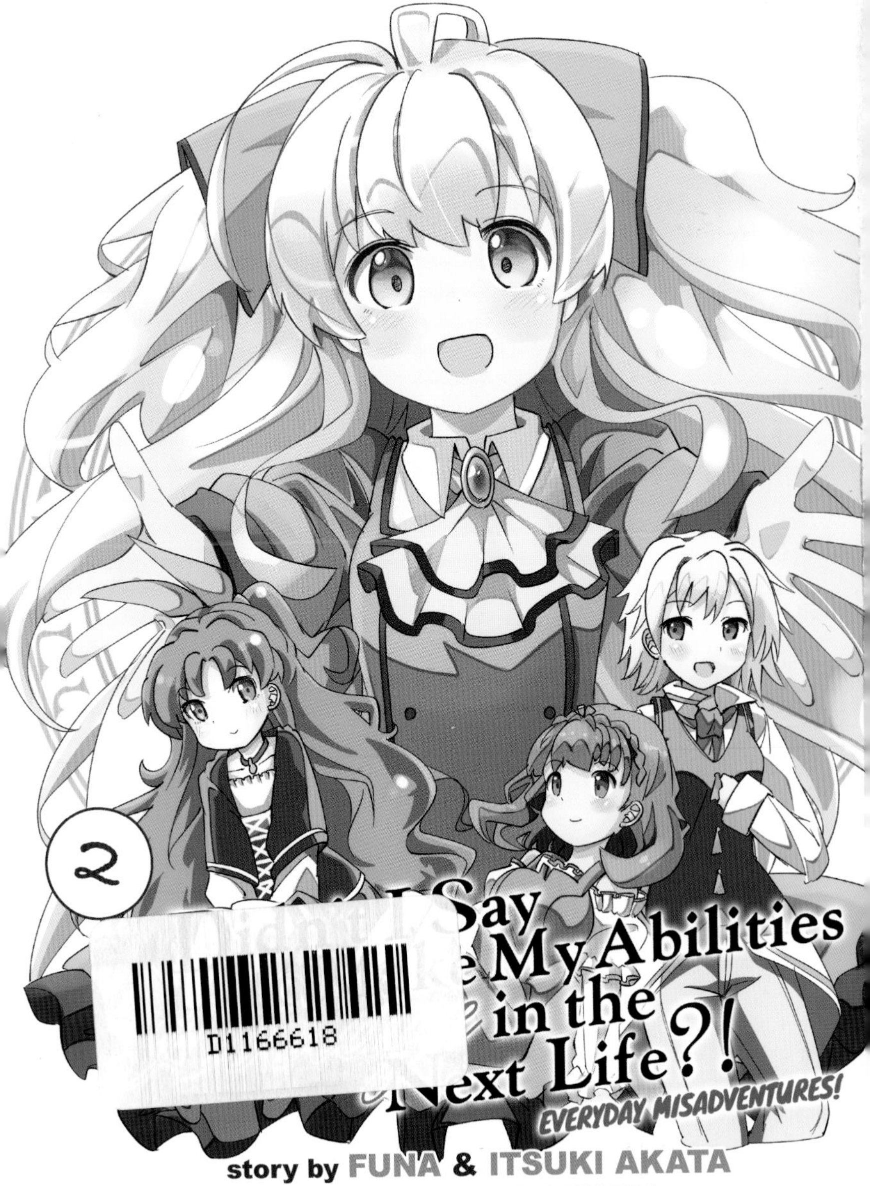
2
Say
My Abilities
in the
Next Life?!
EVERYDAY MISADVENTURES!

story by FUNA & ITSUKI AKATA
art by YUKI MORITAKA

Contents

Chapter 10 ···················· 5

Chapter 11 ···················· 19

Chapter 12 ···················· 33

Chapter 13 ···················· 47

Chapter 14 ···················· 61

Chapter 15 ···················· 75

Chapter 16 ···················· 89

Chapter 17 ···················· 103

Chapter 18 ···················· 117

Bonus Story ················ 133

Characters

MILE (ADELE)

THE MAIN CHARACTER. SHE WISHED TO BE REBORN WITH AVERAGE ABILITIES, BUT INSTEAD WAS GIFTED WITH EXTRAORDINARY ONES. OBSESSED WITH LITTLE BEASTGIRLS.

REINA

A COMBAT MAGIC SPECIALIST KNOWN AS "CRIMSON REINA." FORCEFUL IN PERSONALITY, BUT ALWAYS LOOKS AFTER MILE.

MAVIS

BORN FROM A LONG LINE OF KNIGHTS, HER FAMILY DISAPPROVED WHEN SHE WANTED TO BE A KNIGHT HERSELF, SO SHE RAN AWAY FROM HOME. OSTENSIBLY THE LEADER OF THE CRIMSON VOW.

PAULINE

A SPECIALIST IN HEALING MAGIC. ALWAYS SOOTHES THE OTHERS WITH HER CALMING NATURE, BUT AT TIMES CAN BE QUITE TERRIFYING!!

BEST NOT TO WASTE MONEY.

MARCELLA (CENTER), MONIKA (RIGHT), AUREANA (LEFT)

MILE'S FRIENDS AND CLASSMATES FROM HER TIME AT ECKLAND ACADEMY (WHEN SHE WAS CALLED ADELE). MARCELLA IS A LOWER-RANKING NOBLE, WHILE THE OTHER TWO ARE COMMONERS.

LENNY

INNKEEPERS' DAUGHTER AT THE INN WHERE THE CRIMSON VOW ARE REGULARS. YOUNG, BUT TAKES GREAT PRIDE IN THE INN'S BUSINESS AFFAIRS.

Chapter 10

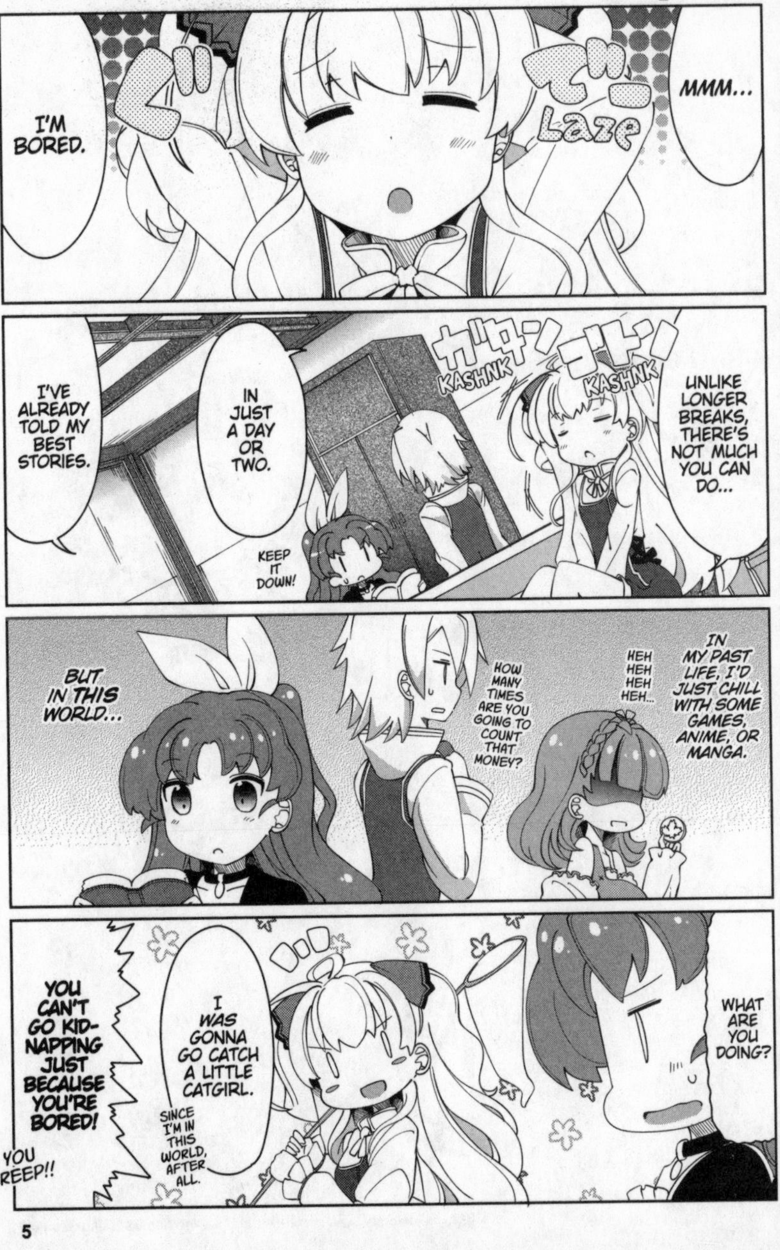

MMM...
Laze
I'M BORED.
UNLIKE LONGER BREAKS, THERE'S NOT MUCH YOU CAN DO...
KASHNK
KASHNK
IN JUST A DAY OR TWO.
I'VE ALREADY TOLD MY BEST STORIES.
KEEP IT DOWN!
IN MY PAST LIFE, I'D JUST CHILL WITH SOME GAMES, ANIME, OR MANGA.
HEH HEH HEH HEH...
HOW MANY TIMES ARE YOU GOING TO COUNT THAT MONEY?
BUT IN *THIS* WORLD...
WHAT ARE YOU DOING?
I *WAS* GONNA GO CATCH A LITTLE CATGIRL.
SINCE I'M IN THIS WORLD, AFTER ALL.
YOU CAN'T GO KID-NAPPING JUST BECAUSE YOU'RE BORED!
YOU CREEP!!

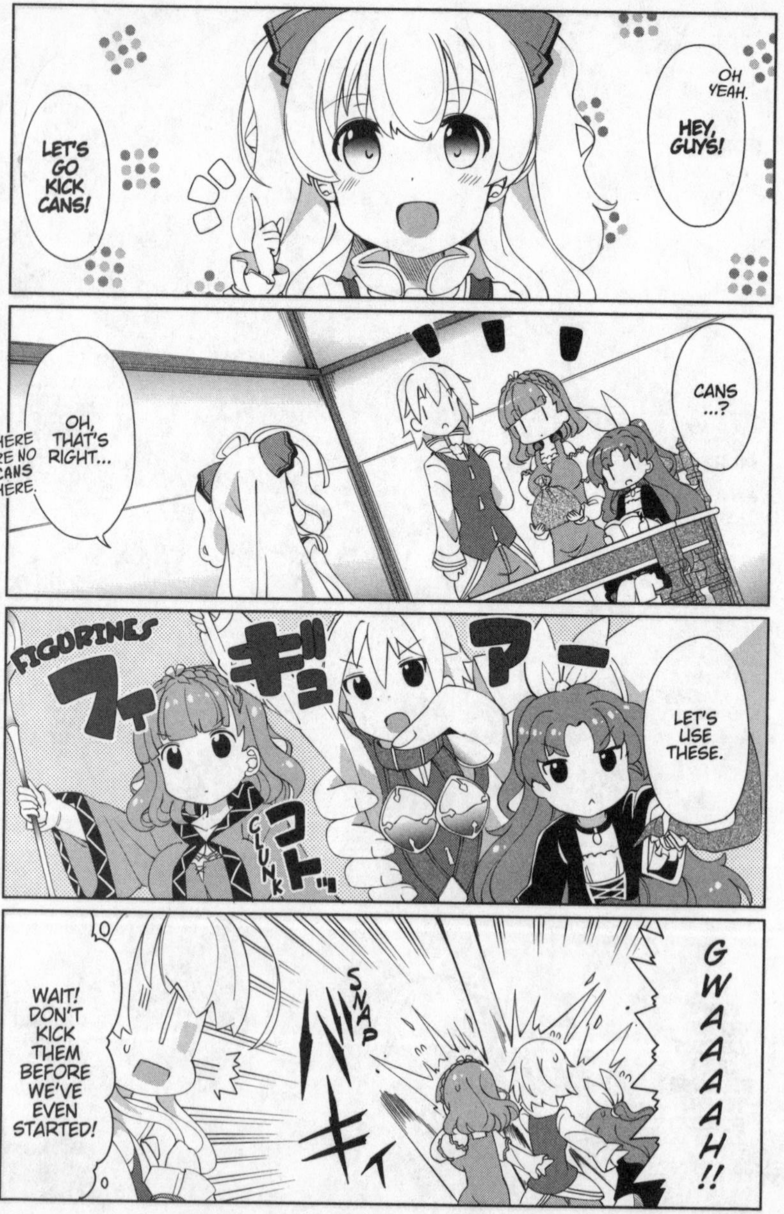
OH YEAH.
HEY, GUYS!
LET'S GO KICK CANS!
CANS ...?
OH, THAT'S RIGHT...
THERE ARE NO CANS HERE.
LET'S USE THESE.
フィギュアー
FIGURINES
ゴトッ
CLUNK
GWAAAAAH!!
SNAP
WAIT! DON'T KICK THEM BEFORE WE'VE EVEN STARTED!

※*A shared dark past of making and selling figures of themselves.*

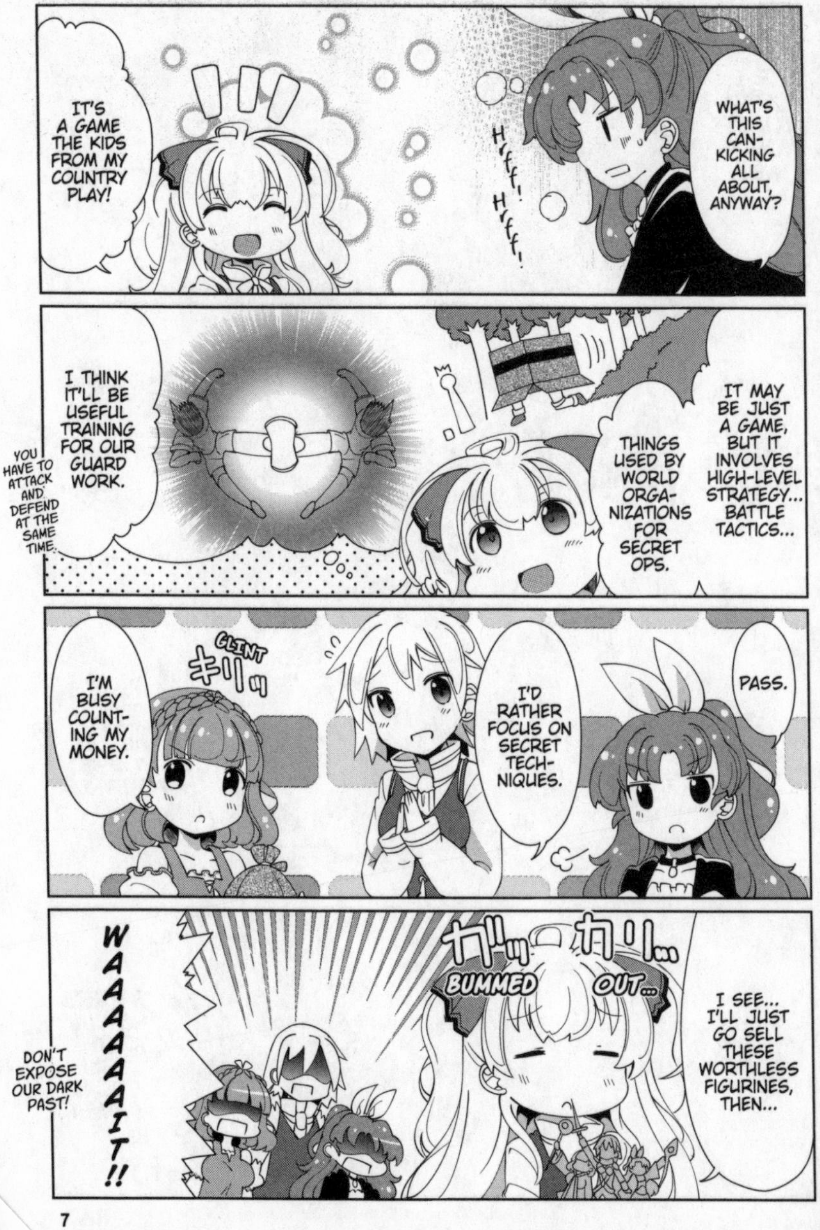
WHAT'S THIS CAN-KICKING ALL ABOUT, ANYWAY?
Hfff! Hfff!
IT'S A GAME THE KIDS FROM MY COUNTRY PLAY!
IT MAY BE JUST A GAME, BUT IT INVOLVES HIGH-LEVEL STRATEGY... BATTLE TACTICS...
THINGS USED BY WORLD ORGANIZATIONS FOR SECRET OPS.
I THINK IT'LL BE USEFUL TRAINING FOR OUR GUARD WORK.
YOU HAVE TO ATTACK AND DEFEND AT THE SAME TIME.
PASS.
I'D RATHER FOCUS ON SECRET TECHNIQUES.
GLINT
I'M BUSY COUNTING MY MONEY.
BUMMED OUT...
I SEE... I'LL JUST GO SELL THESE WORTHLESS FIGURINES, THEN...
WAAAAAAAAIT!!
DON'T EXPOSE OUR DARK PAST!

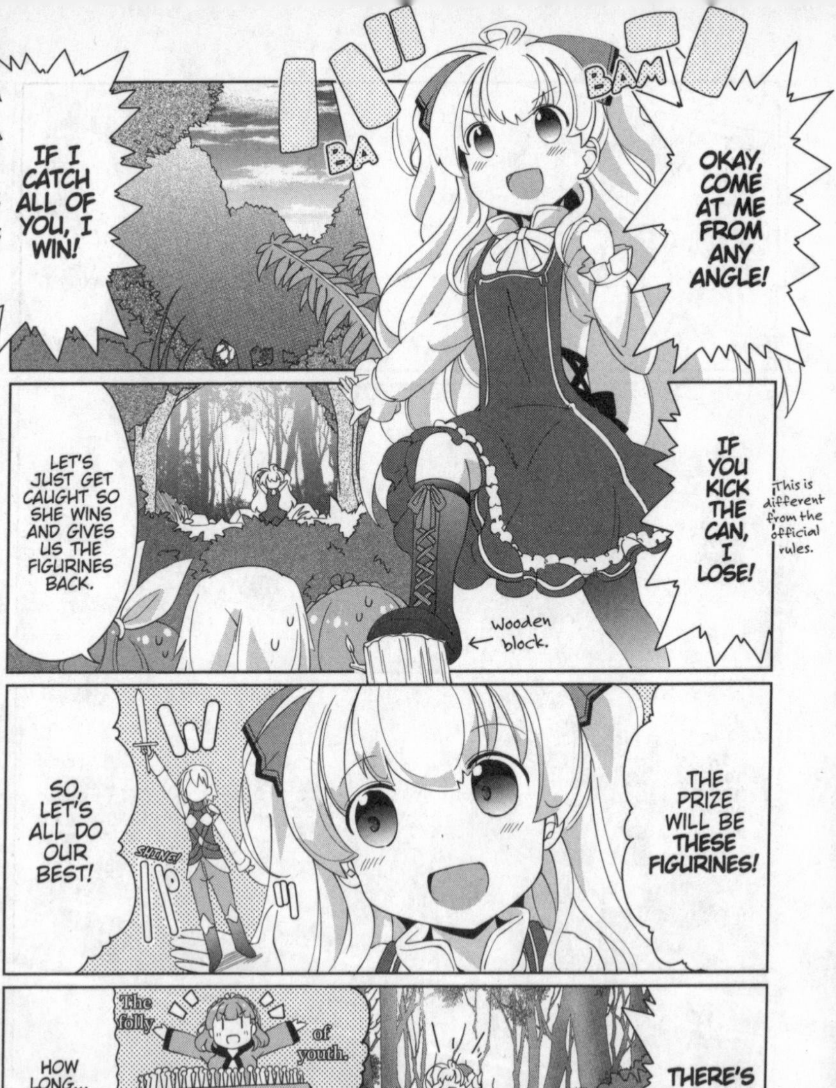
BA
BAM
OKAY, COME AT ME FROM ANY ANGLE!
IF I CATCH ALL OF YOU, I WIN!
IF YOU KICK THE CAN, I LOSE!
This is different from the official rules.
Wooden block.
LET'S JUST GET CAUGHT SO SHE WINS AND GIVES US THE FIGURINES BACK.
THE PRIZE WILL BE THESE FIGURINES!
SO, LET'S ALL DO OUR BEST!
SHINE!
THERE'S NO WAY TO BEAT THIS STUPID GAME!!
The folly of youth.
HOW LONG... HOW LONG WILL THIS DARK PAST HAUNT ME...?
Guhh...

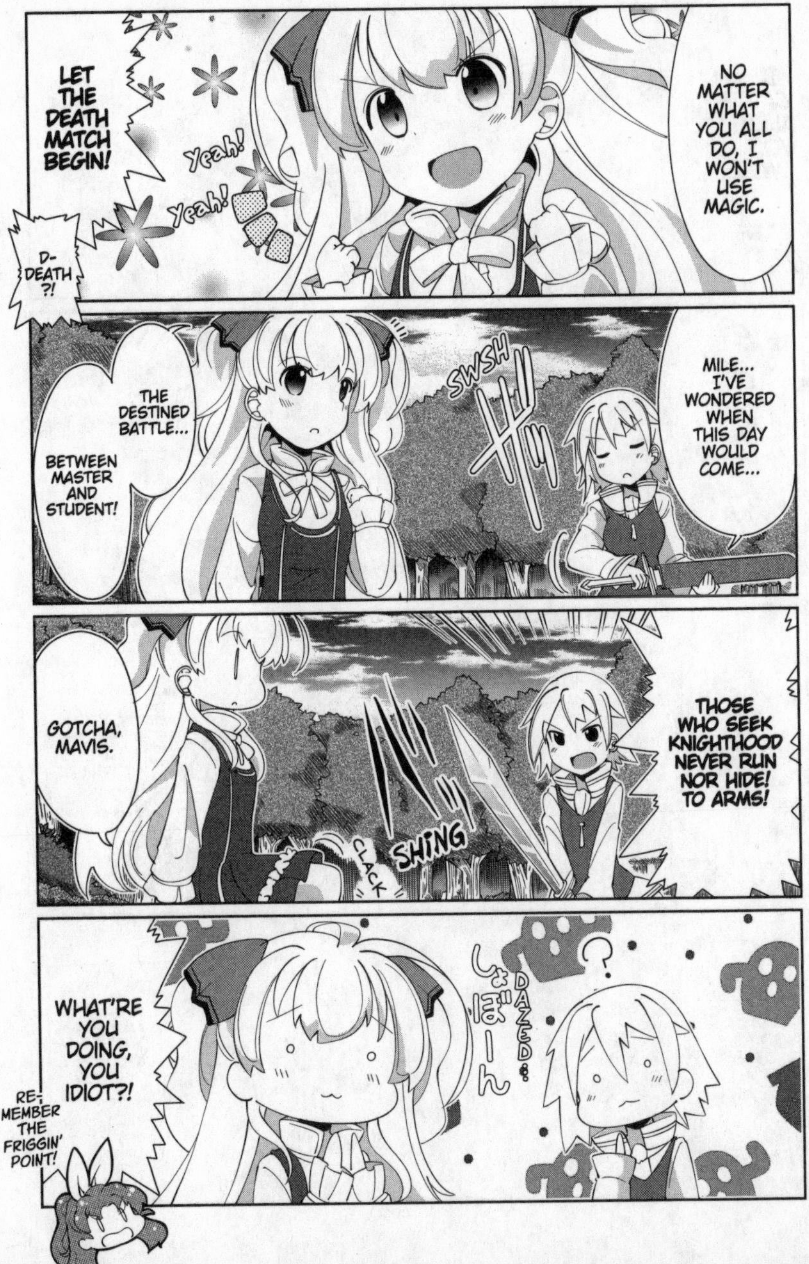
NO MATTER WHAT YOU ALL DO, I WON'T USE MAGIC.
LET THE DEATH MATCH BEGIN!
Yeah!
Yeah!
D-DEATH?!
MILE... I'VE WONDERED WHEN THIS DAY WOULD COME...
SWSH
THE DESTINED BATTLE...
BETWEEN MASTER AND STUDENT!
THOSE WHO SEEK KNIGHTHOOD NEVER RUN NOR HIDE! TO ARMS!
SHING
CLACK
GOTCHA, MAVIS.
しょぼーん
DAZED
WHAT'RE YOU DOING, YOU IDIOT?!
RE-MEMBER THE FRIGGIN' POINT!

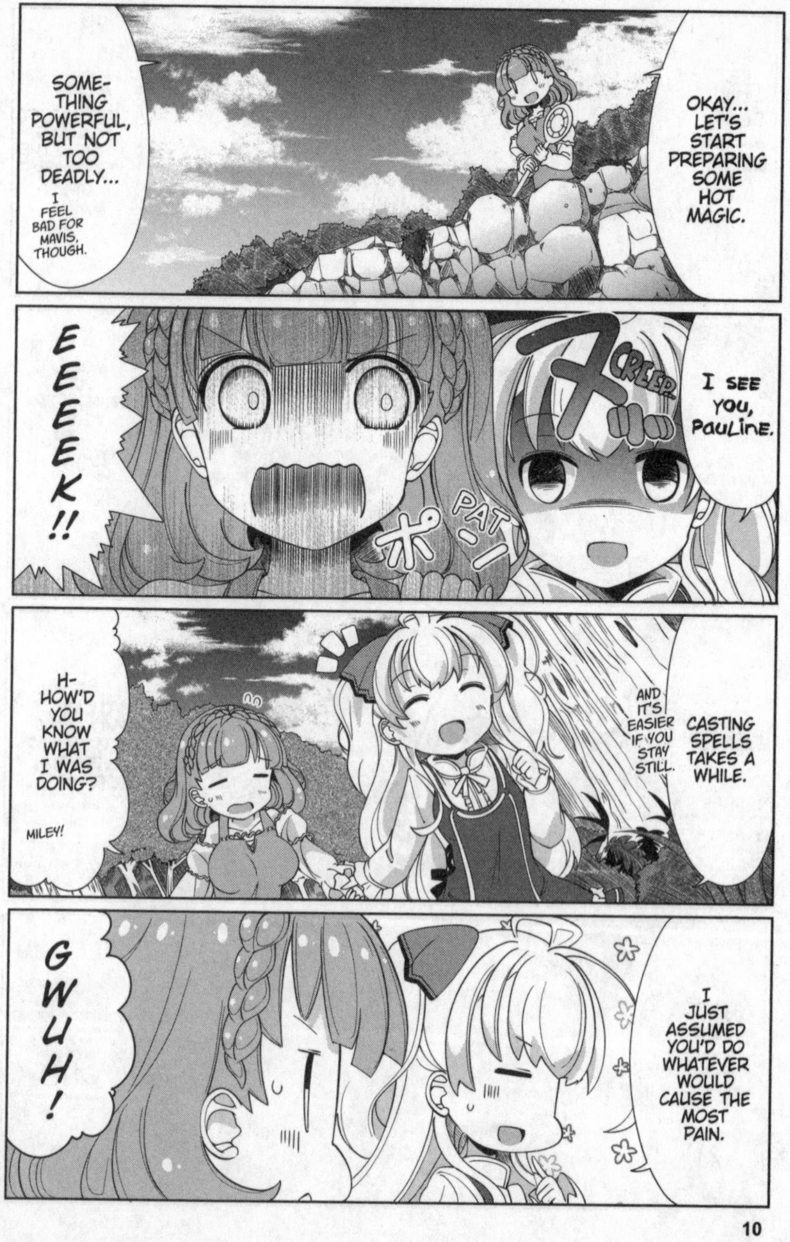
OKAY... LET'S START PREPARING SOME HOT MAGIC.
SOME-THING POWERFUL, BUT NOT TOO DEADLY...
I FEEL BAD FOR MAVIS, THOUGH.
I SEE YOU, PAULINE.
CREEP..
PAT
EEEEEK!!
CASTING SPELLS TAKES A WHILE.
AND IT'S EASIER IF YOU STAY STILL.
H-HOW'D YOU KNOW WHAT I WAS DOING?
MILEY!
I JUST ASSUMED YOU'D DO WHATEVER WOULD CAUSE THE MOST PAIN.
GWUH!

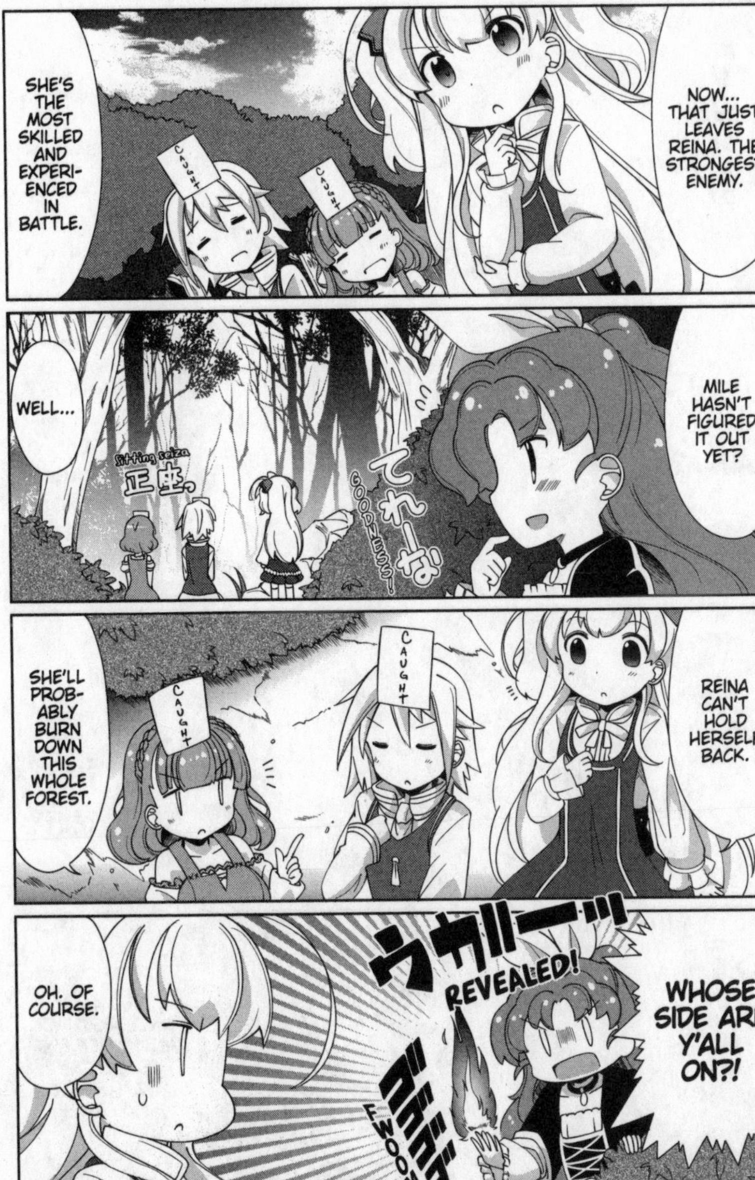
NOW... THAT JUST LEAVES REINA. THE STRONGEST ENEMY.
CAUGHT
CAUGHT
SHE'S THE MOST SKILLED AND EXPERI-ENCED IN BATTLE.
MILE HASN'T FIGURED IT OUT YET?
てれーな
GOODNESS!
正座っ
Sitting seiza
WELL...
REINA CAN'T HOLD HERSELF BACK.
CAUGHT
CAUGHT
SHE'LL PROBABLY BURN DOWN THIS WHOLE FOREST.
WHOSE SIDE ARE Y'ALL ON?!
REVEALED!
FWOOM
OH. OF COURSE.

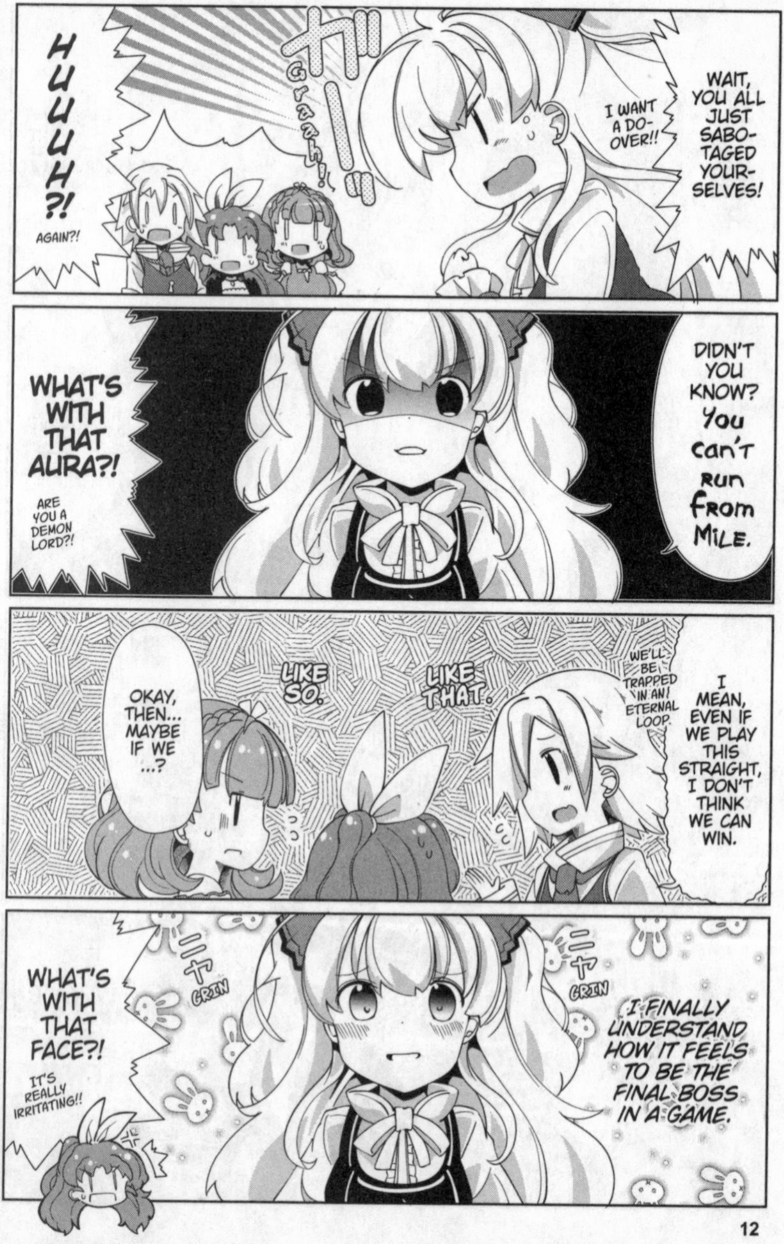
WAIT, YOU ALL JUST SABOTAGED YOURSELVES!
I WANT A DO-OVER!!
ガー
Graaah!!
HUUUUH?!
AGAIN?!
DIDN'T YOU KNOW? You can't run from Mile.
WHAT'S WITH THAT AURA?!
ARE YOU A DEMON LORD?!
I MEAN, EVEN IF WE PLAY THIS STRAIGHT, I DON'T THINK WE CAN WIN.
WE'LL BE TRAPPED IN AN ETERNAL LOOP.
LIKE THAT.
LIKE SO.
OKAY, THEN... MAYBE IF WE ...?
ニヤ
GRIN
I FINALLY UNDERSTAND HOW IT FEELS TO BE THE FINAL BOSS IN A GAME.
ニヤ
GRIN
WHAT'S WITH THAT FACE?!
IT'S REALLY IRRITATING!!

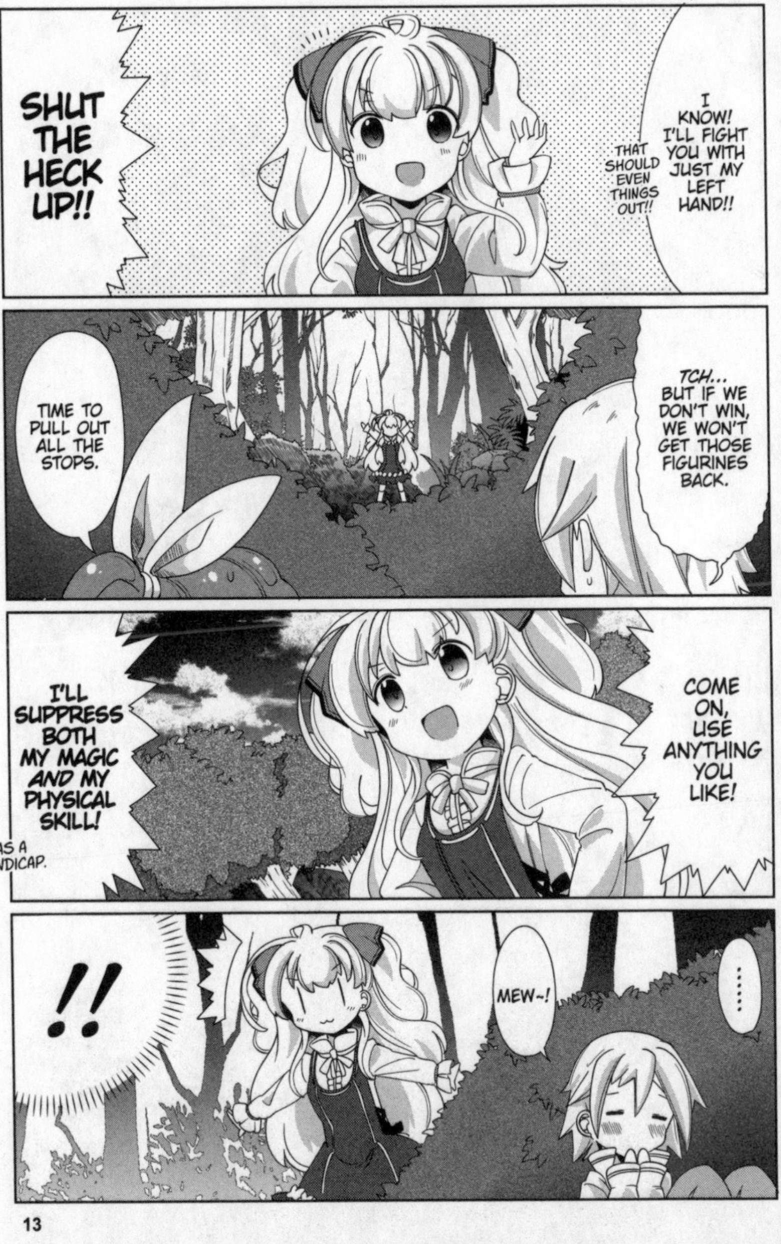
I KNOW! I'LL FIGHT YOU WITH JUST MY LEFT HAND!!
THAT SHOULD EVEN THINGS OUT!!
SHUT THE HECK UP!!
TCH... BUT IF WE DON'T WIN, WE WON'T GET THOSE FIGURINES BACK.
TIME TO PULL OUT ALL THE STOPS.
COME ON, USE ANYTHING YOU LIKE!
I'LL SUPPRESS BOTH MY MAGIC AND MY PHYSICAL SKILL!
AS A HANDICAP.
......
MEW~!
!!

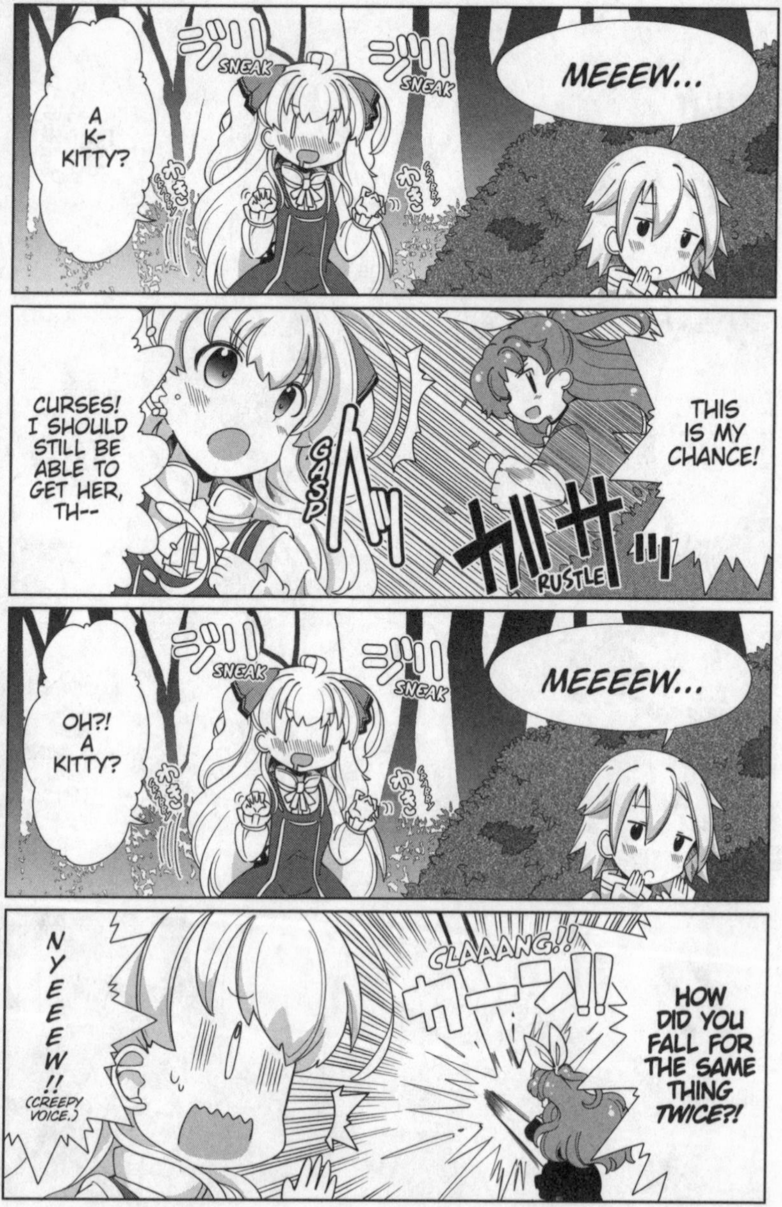
MEEEW...
SNEAK
SNEAK
GRABBY
A K-KITTY?
GRABBY
THIS IS MY CHANCE!
RUSTLE
GASP
CURSES! I SHOULD STILL BE ABLE TO GET HER, TH--
MEEEEW...
SNEAK
SNEAK
GRABBY
OH?! A KITTY?
GRABBY
HOW DID YOU FALL FOR THE SAME THING TWICE?!
CLAAANG!!
NYEEEEW!!
(CREEPY VOICE.)

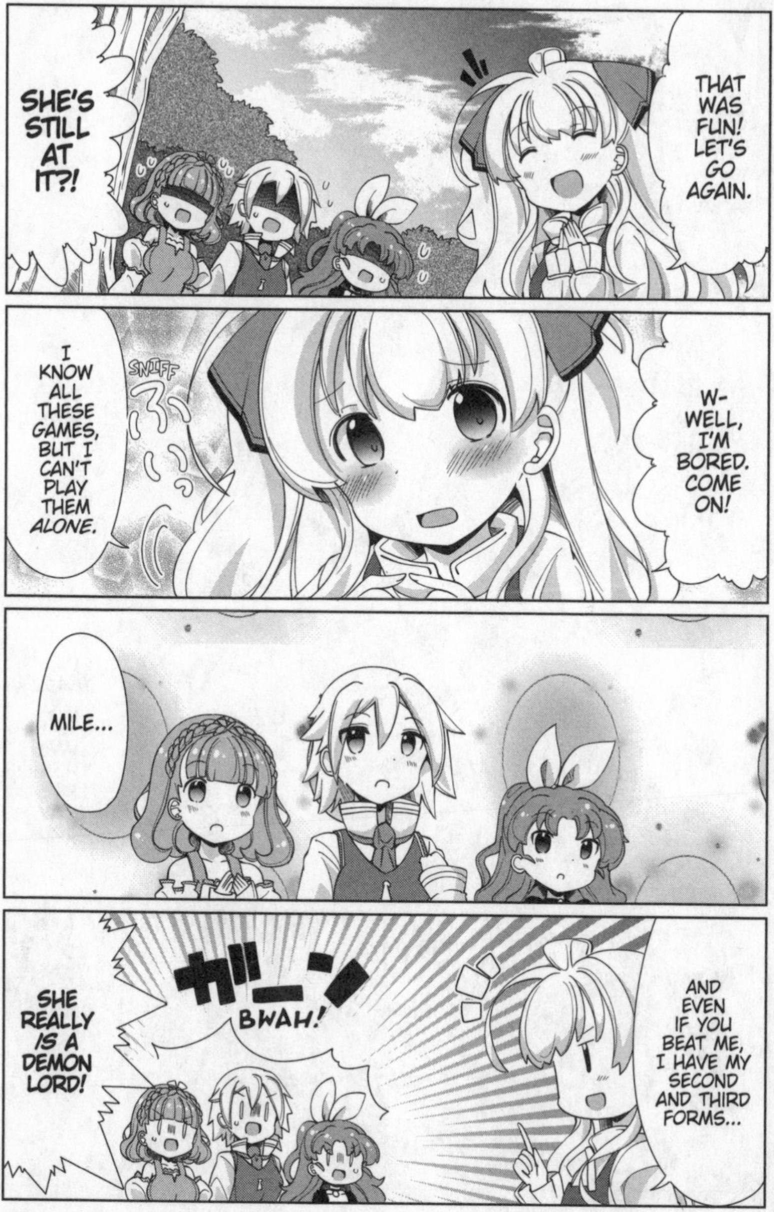
THAT WAS FUN! LET'S GO AGAIN.
SHE'S STILL AT IT?!
W-WELL, I'M BORED. COME ON!
SNIFF
I KNOW ALL THESE GAMES, BUT I CAN'T PLAY THEM *ALONE*.
MILE...
AND EVEN IF YOU BEAT ME, I HAVE MY SECOND AND THIRD FORMS...
BWAH!
SHE REALLY *IS* A DEMON LORD!

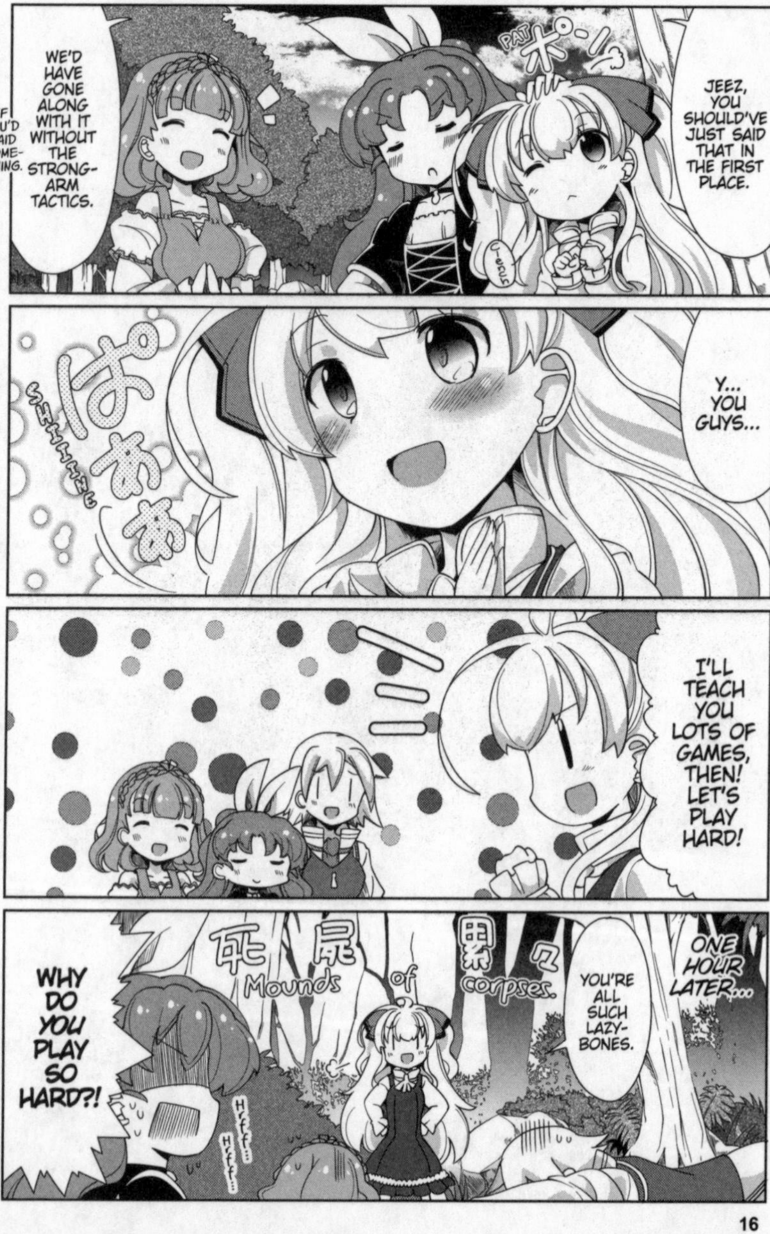
PAT
JEEZ, YOU SHOULD'VE JUST SAID THAT IN THE FIRST PLACE.
WE'D HAVE GONE ALONG WITH IT WITHOUT THE STRONG-ARM TACTICS.
IF YOU'D SAID SOME-THING.
Y... YOU GUYS...
SHIIIINE
I'LL TEACH YOU LOTS OF GAMES, THEN! LET'S PLAY HARD!
ONE HOUR LATER...
YOU'RE ALL SUCH LAZY-BONES.
死屍累々
Mounds of corpses.
WHY DO YOU PLAY SO HARD?!
Hrff... Hrff...

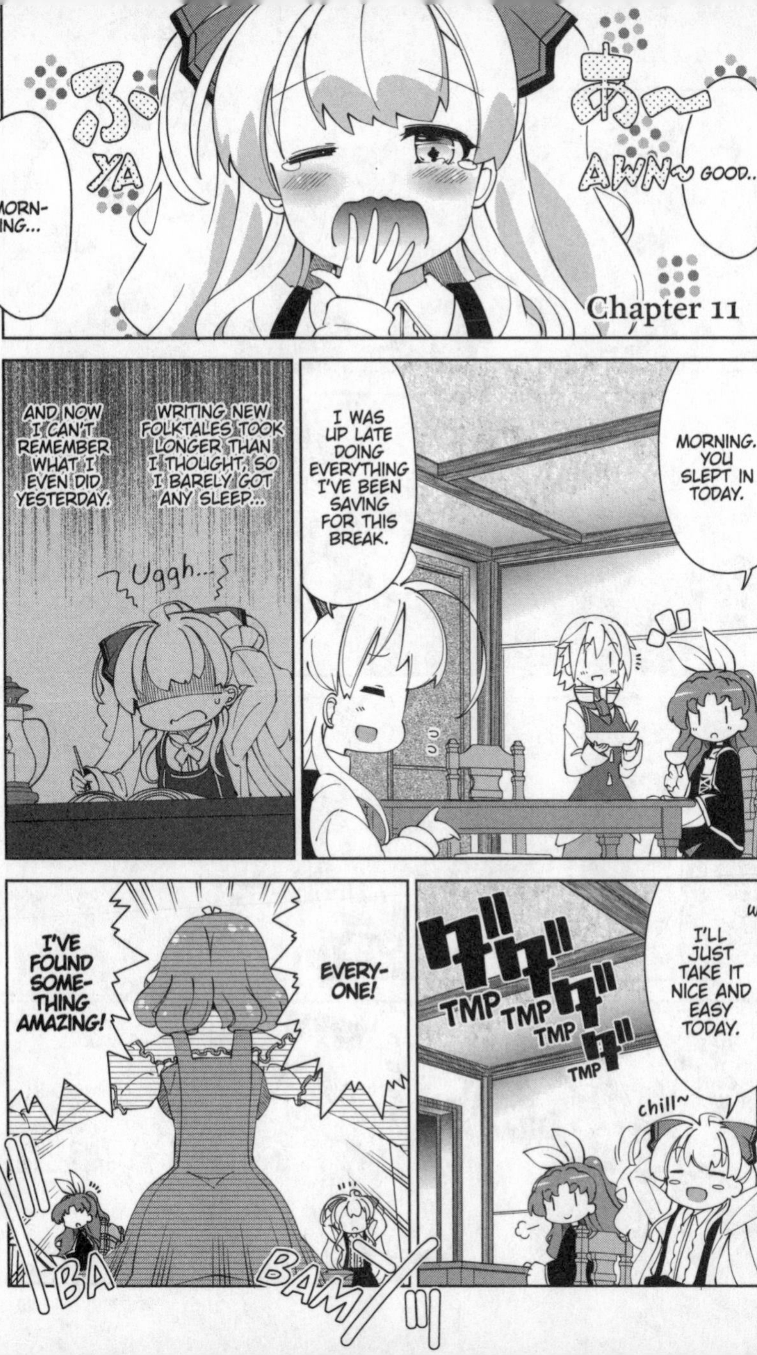
ふ YA
あ~ AWN~
GOOD...
MORN-ING...
Chapter 11
MORNING. YOU SLEPT IN TODAY.
I WAS UP LATE DOING EVERYTHING I'VE BEEN SAVING FOR THIS BREAK.
WRITING NEW FOLKTALES TOOK LONGER THAN I THOUGHT, SO I BARELY GOT ANY SLEEP...
AND NOW I CAN'T REMEMBER WHAT I EVEN DID YESTERDAY.
Uggh...
WELP.
I'LL JUST TAKE IT NICE AND EASY TODAY.
ダダダダ
TMP TMP TMP TMP
chill~
EVERY-ONE!
I'VE FOUND SOME-THING AMAZING!
BA
BAM

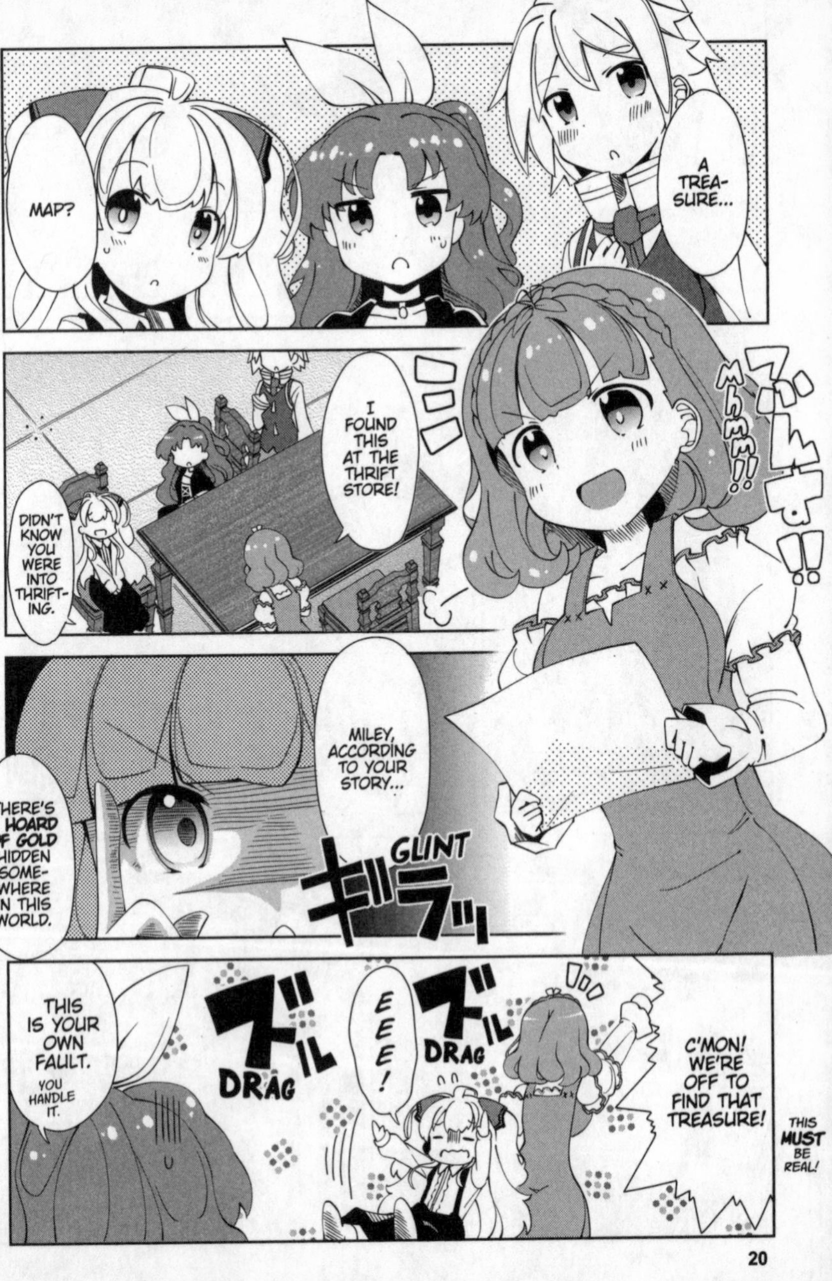
A TREA-SURE...
MAP?
Mhmm!!
I FOUND THIS AT THE THRIFT STORE!
DIDN'T KNOW YOU WERE INTO THRIFT-ING.
MILEY, ACCORDING TO YOUR STORY...
THERE'S A **HOARD OF GOLD** HIDDEN SOME-WHERE IN THIS WORLD.
GLINT
THIS **MUST** BE REAL!
C'MON! WE'RE OFF TO FIND THAT TREASURE!
DRAG
EEE!
DRAG
THIS IS YOUR OWN FAULT.
YOU HANDLE IT.

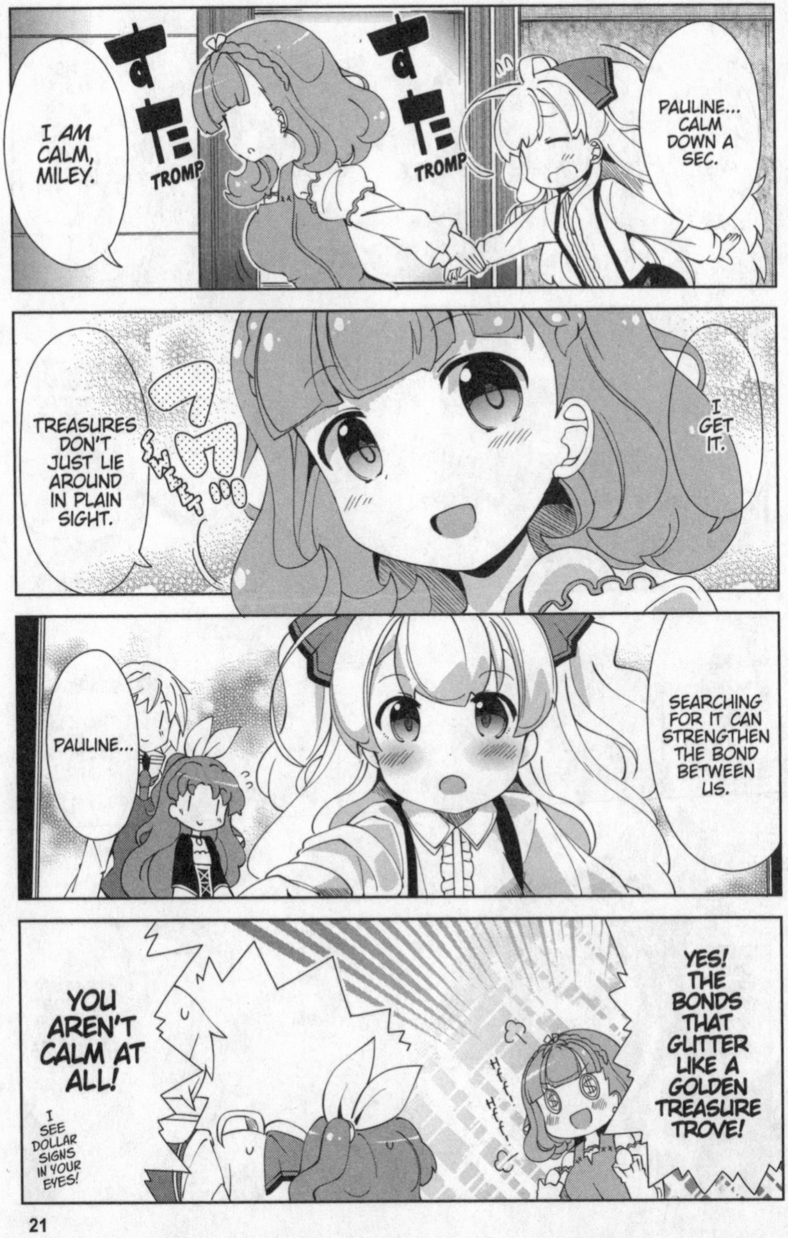
PAULINE... CALM DOWN A SEC.
TROMP
TROMP
I *AM* CALM, MILEY.
I GET IT.
TREASURES DON'T JUST LIE AROUND IN PLAIN SIGHT.
SEARCHING FOR IT CAN STRENGTHEN THE BOND BETWEEN US.
PAULINE...
YES! THE BONDS THAT GLITTER LIKE A GOLDEN TREASURE TROVE!
Hff! Hff!
YOU AREN'T CALM AT ALL!
I SEE DOLLAR SIGNS IN YOUR EYES!

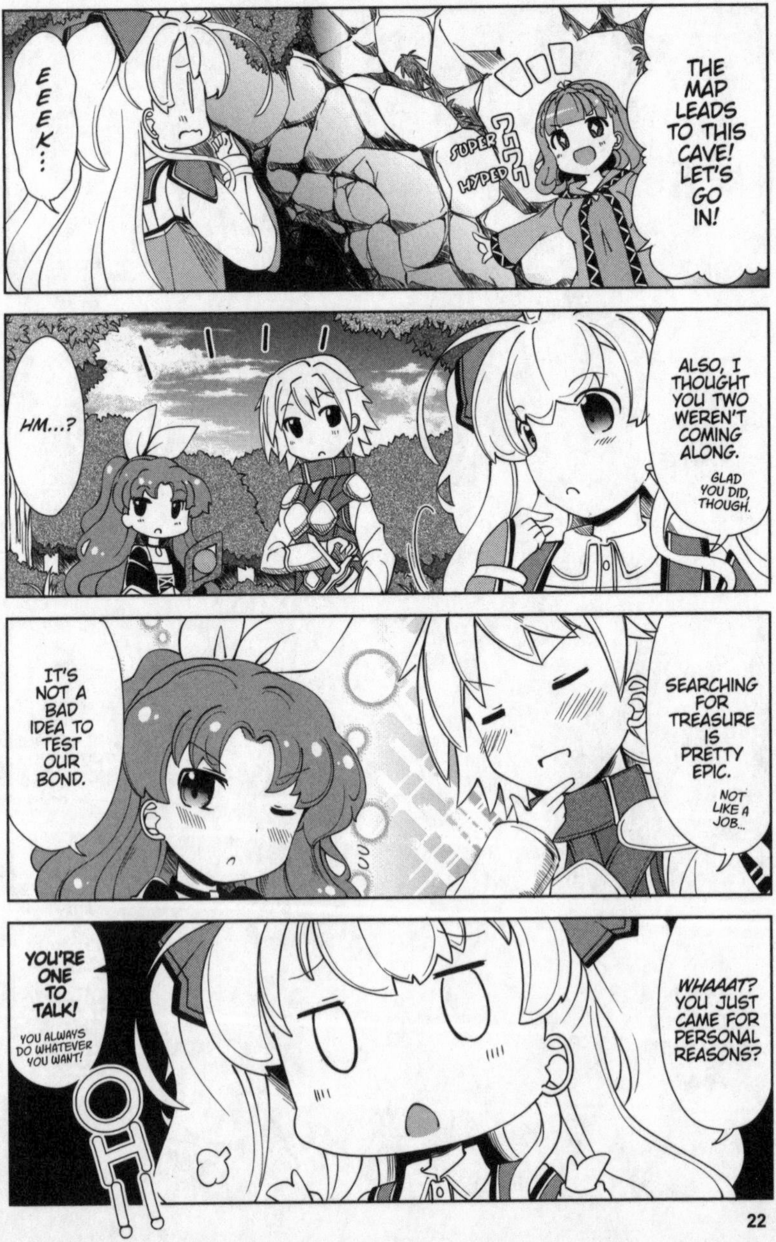
THE MAP LEADS TO THIS CAVE! LET'S GO IN!
SUPER HYPED
EEEK...
ALSO, I THOUGHT YOU TWO WEREN'T COMING ALONG.
GLAD YOU DID, THOUGH.
HM...?
SEARCHING FOR TREASURE IS PRETTY EPIC.
NOT LIKE A JOB...
IT'S NOT A BAD IDEA TO TEST OUR BOND.
WHAAAT? YOU JUST CAME FOR PERSONAL REASONS?
YOU'RE ONE TO TALK!
YOU ALWAYS DO WHATEVER YOU WANT!
OH

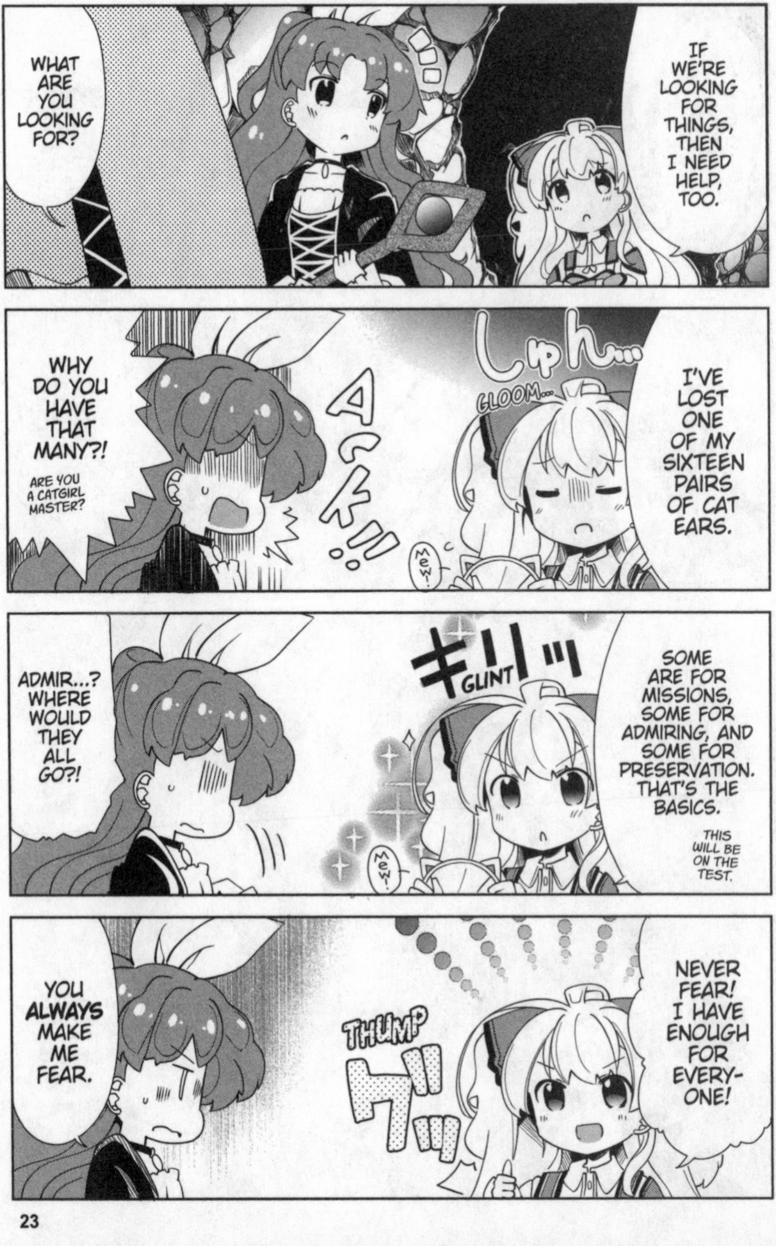
IF WE'RE LOOKING FOR THINGS, THEN I NEED HELP, TOO.
WHAT ARE YOU LOOKING FOR?
しゅん…
GLOOM…
I'VE LOST ONE OF MY SIXTEEN PAIRS OF CAT EARS.
ACK!!
MEW!
WHY DO YOU HAVE THAT MANY?!
ARE YOU A CATGIRL MASTER?
SOME ARE FOR MISSIONS, SOME FOR ADMIRING, AND SOME FOR PRESERVATION. THAT'S THE BASICS.
THIS WILL BE ON THE TEST.
キリッ
GLINT
MEW!
ADMIR...? WHERE WOULD THEY ALL GO?!
NEVER FEAR! I HAVE ENOUGH FOR EVERY-ONE!
THUMP
グッ
YOU ALWAYS MAKE ME FEAR.

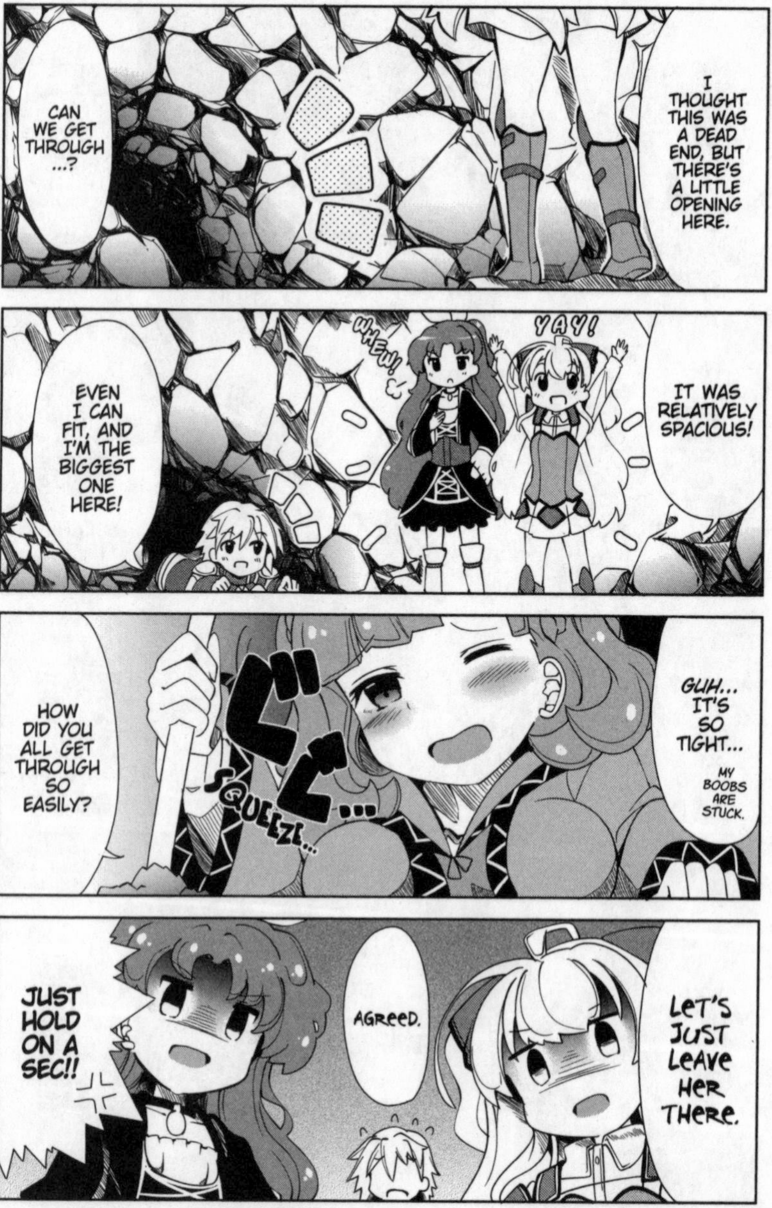

I THOUGHT THIS WAS A DEAD END, BUT THERE'S A LITTLE OPENING HERE.
CAN WE GET THROUGH ...?
IT WAS RELATIVELY SPACIOUS!
YAY!
WHEW!
EVEN I CAN FIT, AND I'M THE BIGGEST ONE HERE!
GUH... IT'S SO TIGHT...
MY BOOBS ARE STUCK.
SQUEEZE...
HOW DID YOU ALL GET THROUGH SO EASILY?
LET'S JUST LEAVE HER THERE.
AGREED.
JUST HOLD ON A SEC!!

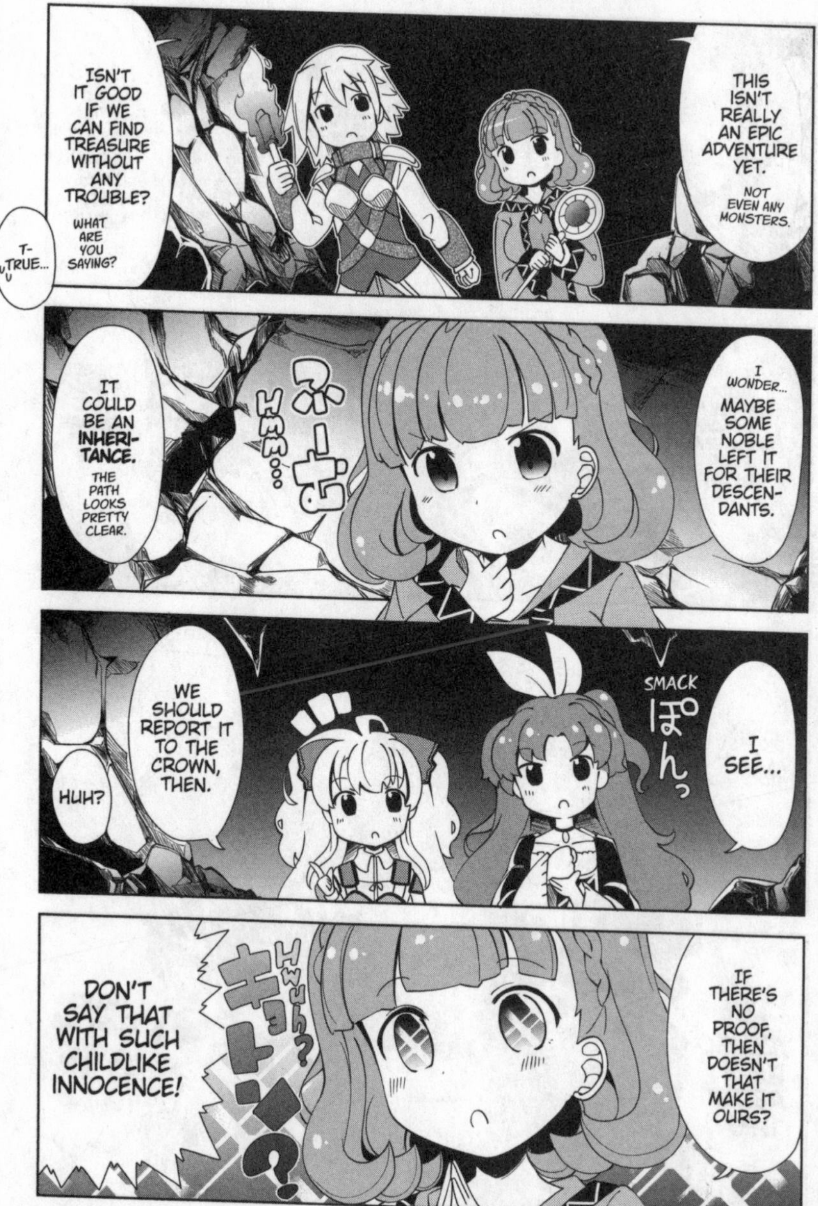
THIS ISN'T REALLY AN EPIC ADVENTURE YET.
NOT EVEN ANY MONSTERS.
ISN'T IT GOOD IF WE CAN FIND TREASURE WITHOUT ANY TROUBLE?
WHAT ARE YOU SAYING?
T-TRUE...
I WONDER... MAYBE SOME NOBLE LEFT IT FOR THEIR DESCENDANTS.
ふーむ
HMM...
IT COULD BE AN **INHERITANCE.**
THE PATH LOOKS PRETTY CLEAR.
I SEE...
SMACK
ぽんっ
WE SHOULD REPORT IT TO THE CROWN, THEN.
HUH?
IF THERE'S NO PROOF, THEN DOESN'T THAT MAKE IT OURS?
キョトン？
HWUH?
DON'T SAY THAT WITH SUCH CHILDLIKE INNOCENCE!

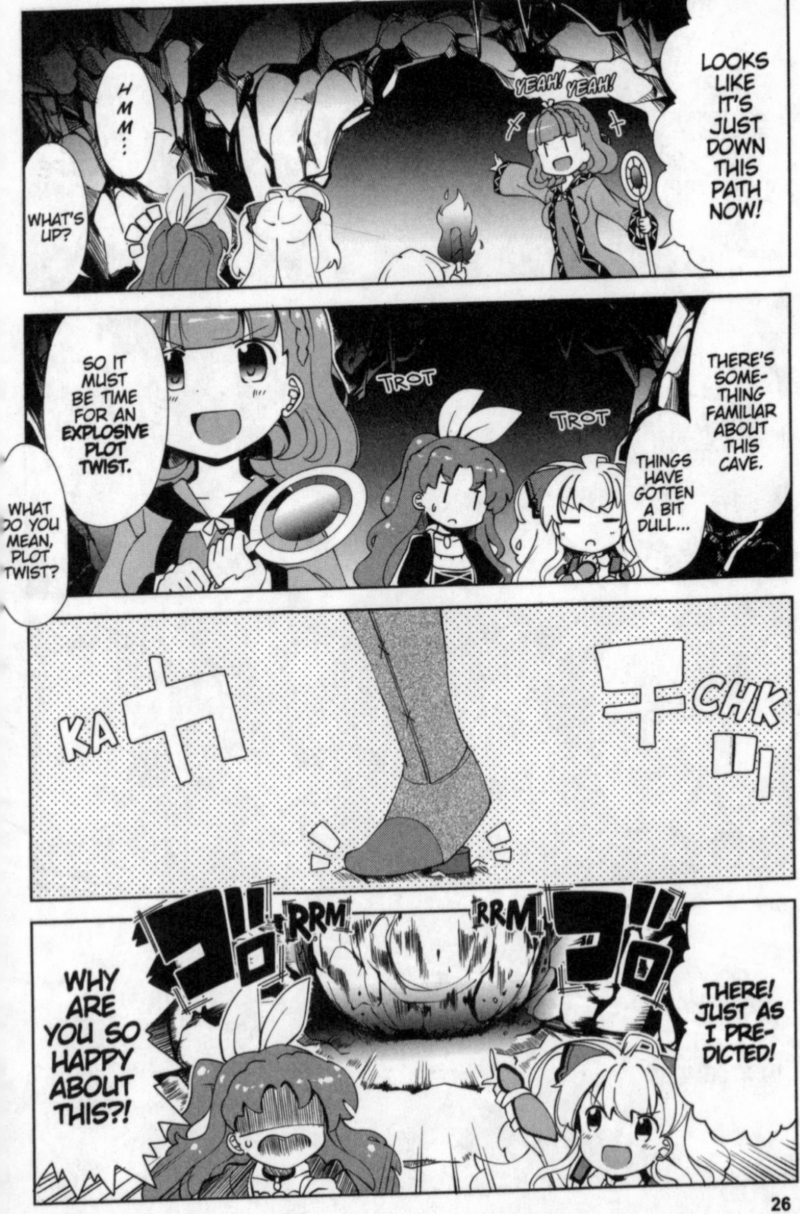
LOOKS LIKE IT'S JUST DOWN THIS PATH NOW!
YEAH! YEAH!
HMM...
WHAT'S UP?
THERE'S SOME-THING FAMILIAR ABOUT THIS CAVE.
THINGS HAVE GOTTEN A BIT DULL...
TROT
TROT
SO IT MUST BE TIME FOR AN EXPLOSIVE PLOT TWIST.
WHAT DO YOU MEAN, PLOT TWIST?
CHK
KA
THERE! JUST AS I PRE-DICTED!
RRM
RRM
WHY ARE YOU SO HAPPY ABOUT THIS?!

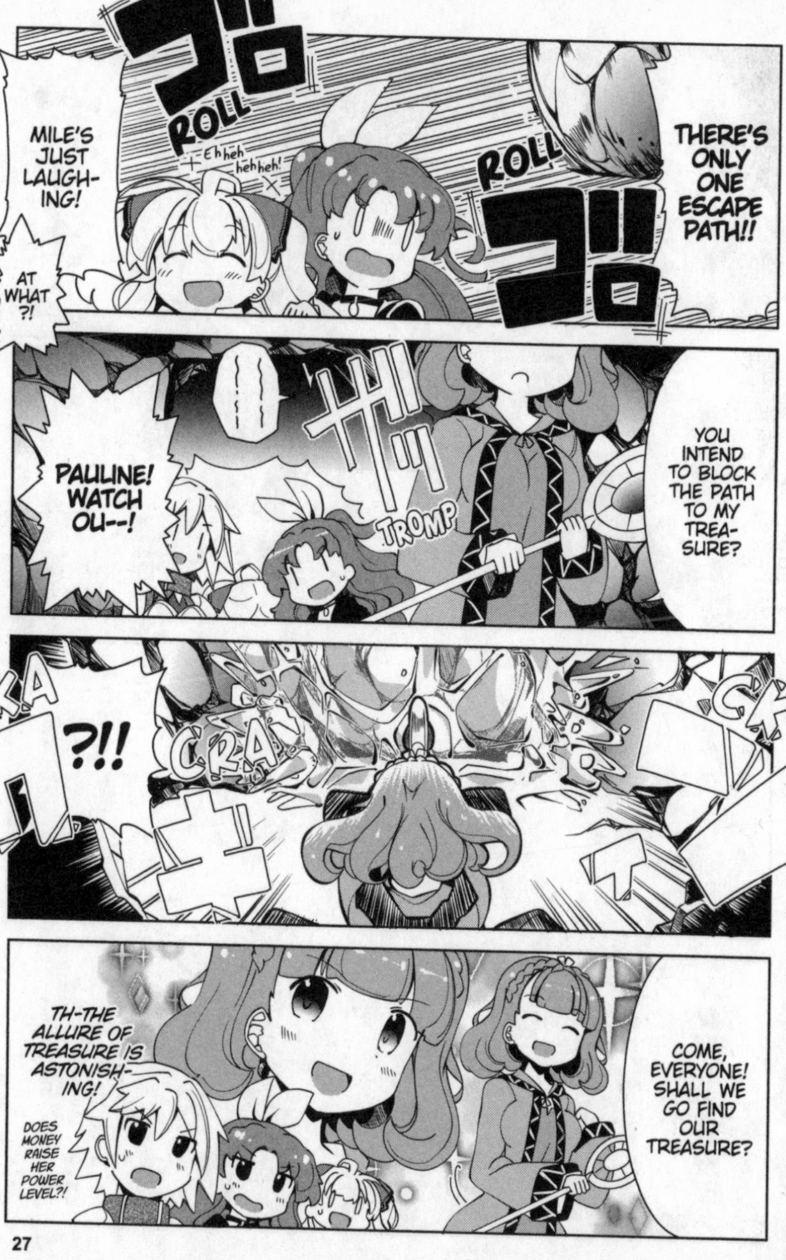

THERE'S ONLY ONE ESCAPE PATH!!
ゴロ
ROLL
ゴロ
ROLL
Ehheh hehheh!
MILE'S JUST LAUGH-ING!
AT WHAT?!
YOU INTEND TO BLOCK THE PATH TO MY TREA-SURE?
TROMP
PAULINE! WATCH OU--!
CK
CRA
KA
?!!
COME, EVERYONE! SHALL WE GO FIND OUR TREASURE?
TH-THE ALLURE OF TREASURE IS ASTONISH-ING!
DOES MONEY RAISE HER POWER LEVEL?!

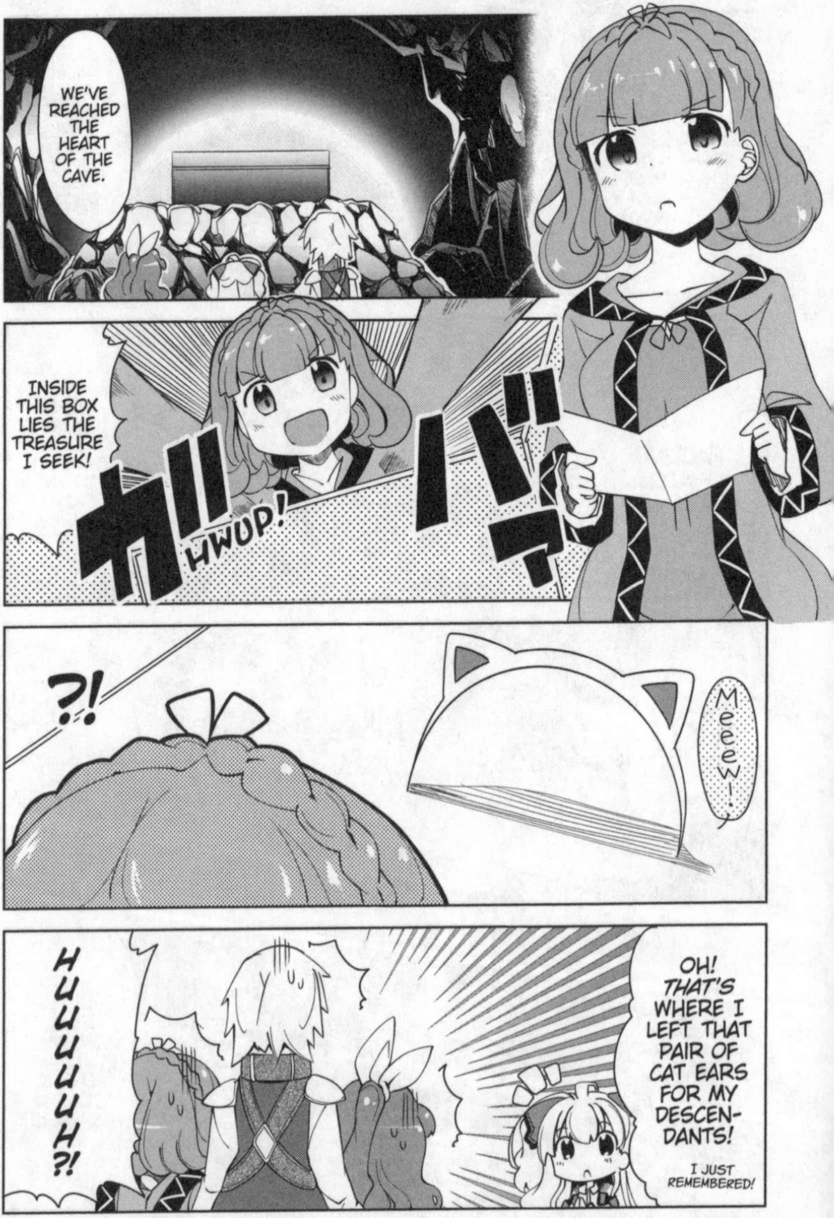
WE'VE REACHED THE HEART OF THE CAVE.
INSIDE THIS BOX LIES THE TREASURE I SEEK!
HWUP!
Meeew!
?!
OH! THAT'S WHERE I LEFT THAT PAIR OF CAT EARS FOR MY DESCEN-DANTS!
I JUST REMEMBERED!
HUUUUUUH?!

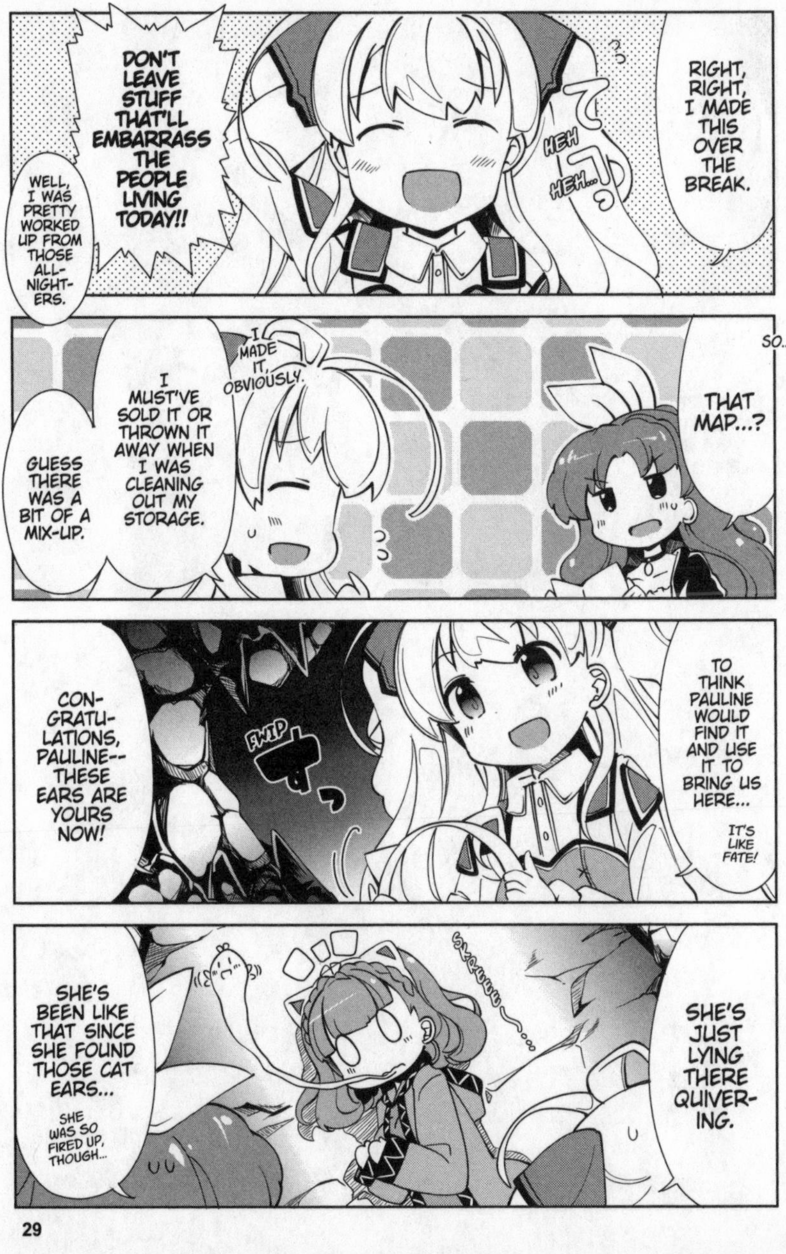
RIGHT, RIGHT, I MADE THIS OVER THE BREAK.
HEH HEH...
DON'T LEAVE STUFF THAT'LL EMBARRASS THE PEOPLE LIVING TODAY!!
WELL, I WAS PRETTY WORKED UP FROM THOSE ALL-NIGHTERS.
SO...
THAT MAP...?
I MADE IT, OBVIOUSLY.
I MUST'VE SOLD IT OR THROWN IT AWAY WHEN I WAS CLEANING OUT MY STORAGE.
GUESS THERE WAS A BIT OF A MIX-UP.
TO THINK PAULINE WOULD FIND IT AND USE IT TO BRING US HERE...
IT'S LIKE FATE!
FWIP
CON-GRATU-LATIONS, PAULINE-- THESE EARS ARE YOURS NOW!
SHE'S JUST LYING THERE QUIVER-ING.
SHE'S BEEN LIKE THAT SINCE SHE FOUND THOSE CAT EARS...
SHE WAS SO FIRED UP, THOUGH...

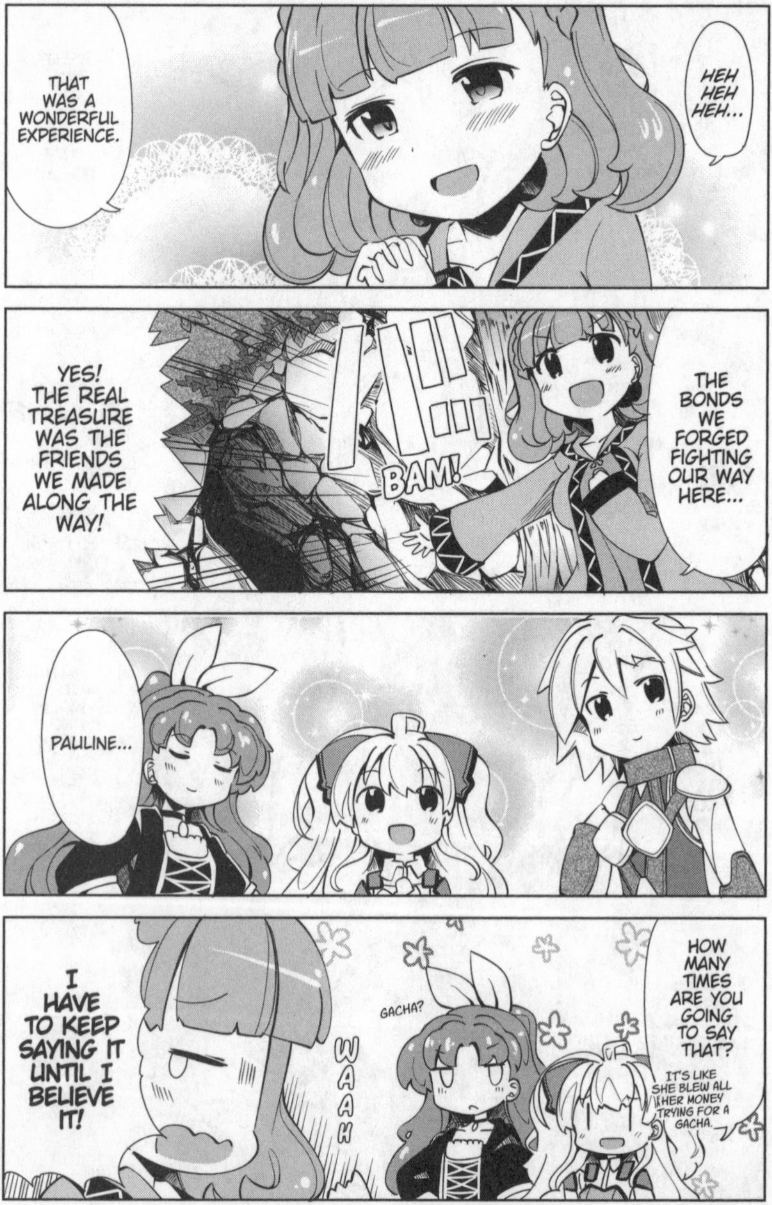
HEH HEH HEH...
THAT WAS A WONDERFUL EXPERIENCE.
THE BONDS WE FORGED FIGHTING OUR WAY HERE...
BAM!
YES! THE REAL TREASURE WAS THE FRIENDS WE MADE ALONG THE WAY!
PAULINE...
HOW MANY TIMES ARE YOU GOING TO SAY THAT?
IT'S LIKE SHE BLEW ALL HER MONEY TRYING FOR A GACHA.
GACHA?
WAAAH
I HAVE TO KEEP SAYING IT UNTIL I BELIEVE IT!

Didn't I Say to Make My Abilities Average in the Next Life?!
EVERYDAY MISADVENTURES!

Meeew!

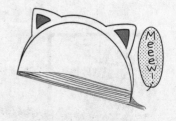

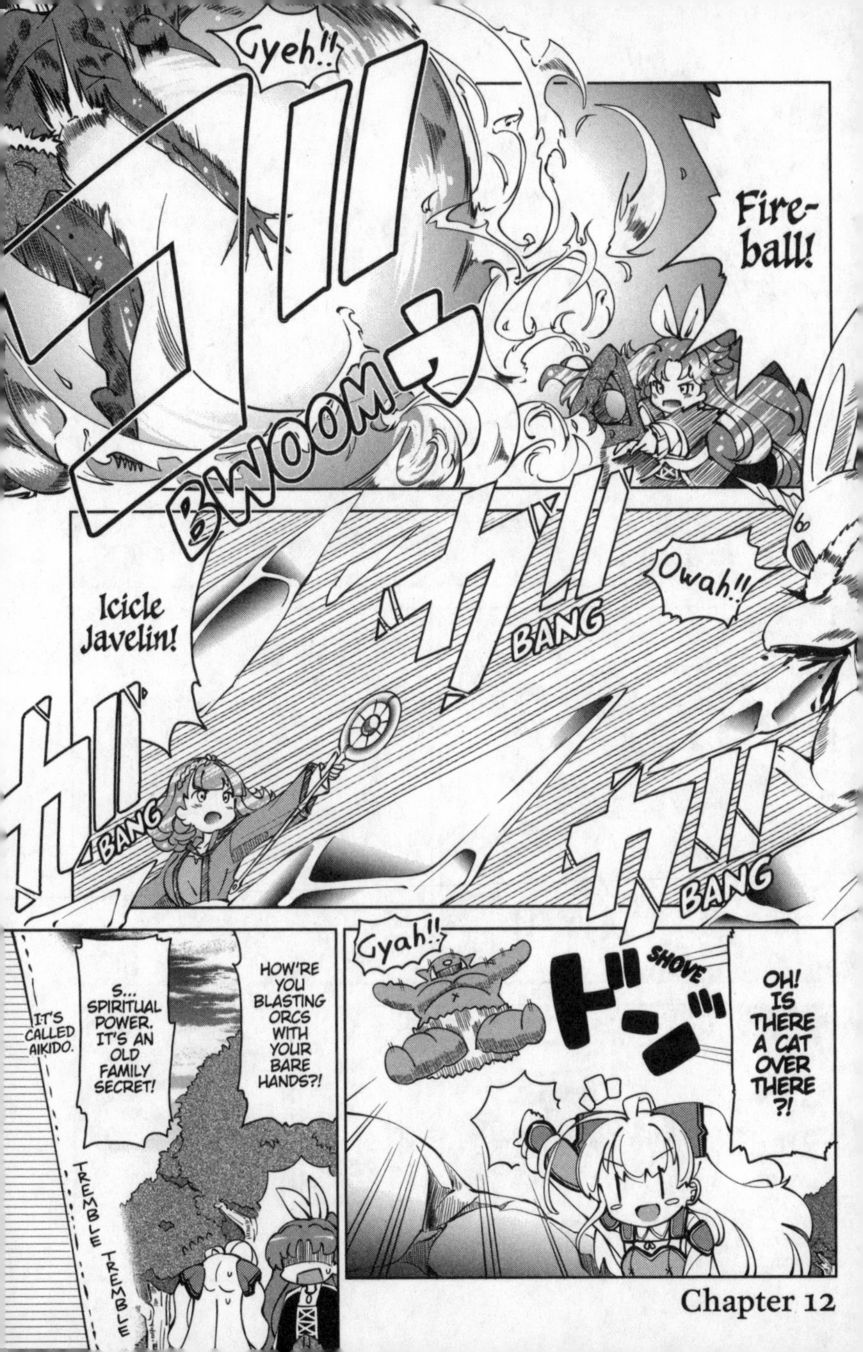

Fire-ball!
Gyeh!!
BWOOM
Owah!!
BANG
Icicle Javelin!
BANG
BANG
OH! IS THERE A CAT OVER THERE?!
SHOVE
Gyah!!
HOW'RE YOU BLASTING ORCS WITH YOUR BARE HANDS?!
S... SPIRITUAL POWER. IT'S AN OLD FAMILY SECRET!
IT'S CALLED AIKIDO.
TREMBLE TREMBLE

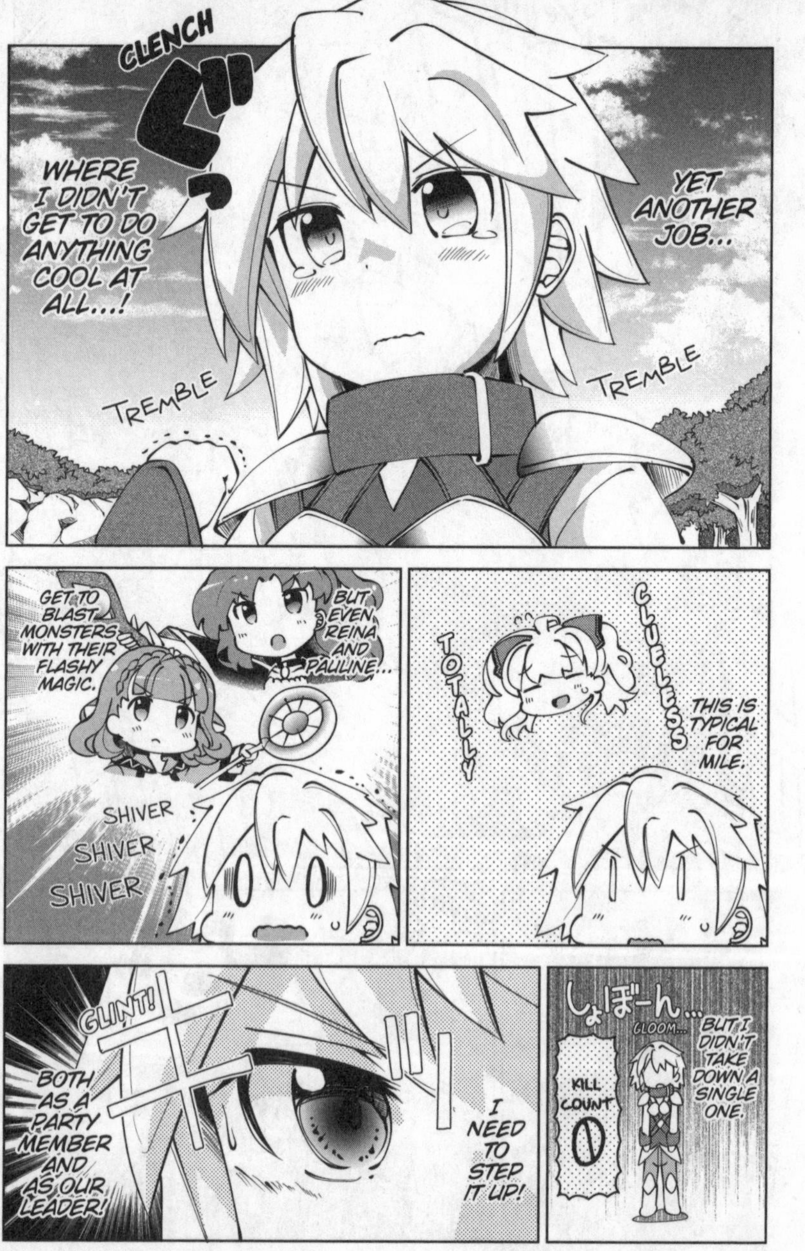
YET ANOTHER JOB...
CLENCH
WHERE I DIDN'T GET TO DO ANYTHING COOL AT ALL...!
TREMBLE
TREMBLE
THIS IS TYPICAL FOR MILE.
CLUELESS
TOTALLY
BUT EVEN REINA AND PAULINE...
GET TO BLAST MONSTERS WITH THEIR FLASHY MAGIC.
SHIVER
SHIVER
SHIVER
しょぼーん...
GLOOM...
BUT I DIDN'T TAKE DOWN A SINGLE ONE.
KILL COUNT
0
I NEED TO STEP IT UP!
GLINT!
BOTH AS A PARTY MEMBER AND AS OUR LEADER!

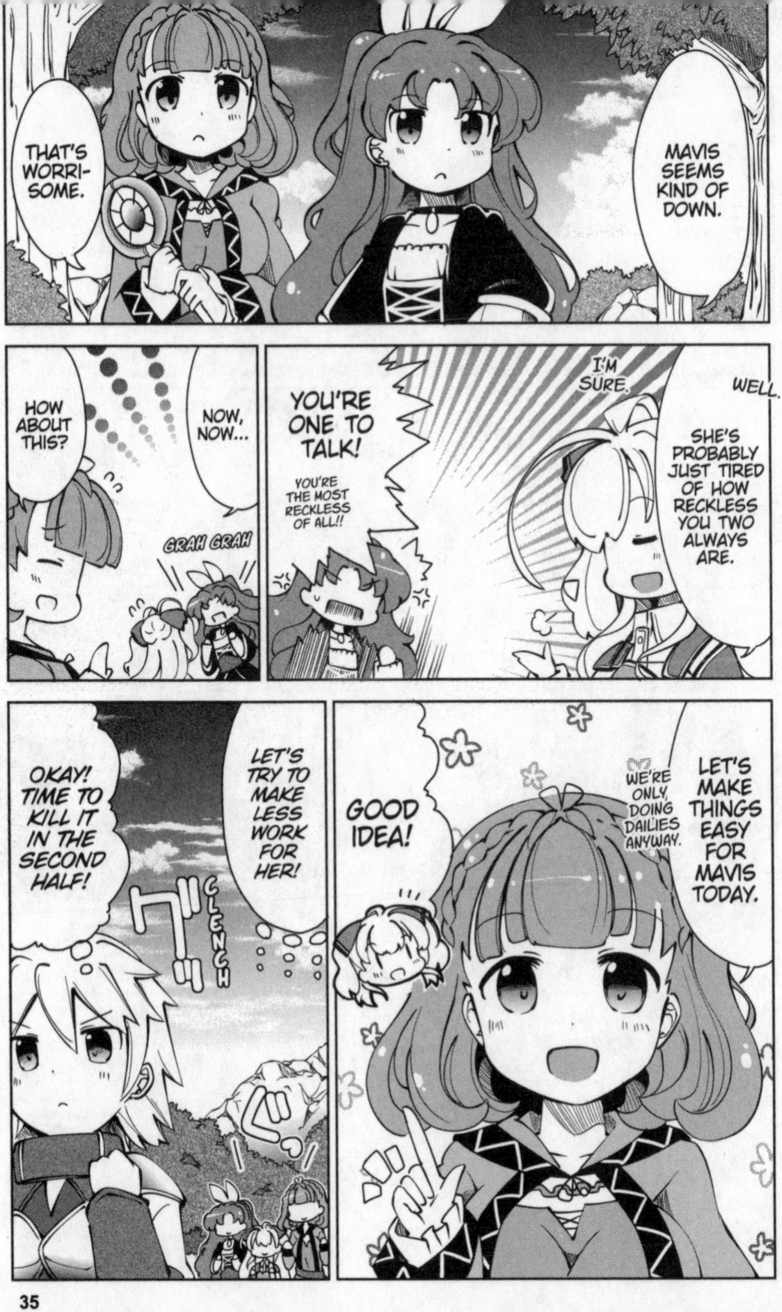
MAVIS SEEMS KIND OF DOWN.
THAT'S WORRI-SOME.
WELL.
I'M SURE.
SHE'S PROBABLY JUST TIRED OF HOW RECKLESS YOU TWO ALWAYS ARE.
YOU'RE ONE TO TALK!
YOU'RE THE MOST RECKLESS OF ALL!!
NOW, NOW...
HOW ABOUT THIS?
GRAH GRAH
LET'S MAKE THINGS EASY FOR MAVIS TODAY.
WE'RE ONLY, DOING DAILIES ANYWAY.
GOOD IDEA!
LET'S TRY TO MAKE LESS WORK FOR HER!
CLENCH
OKAY! TIME TO KILL IT IN THE SECOND HALF!

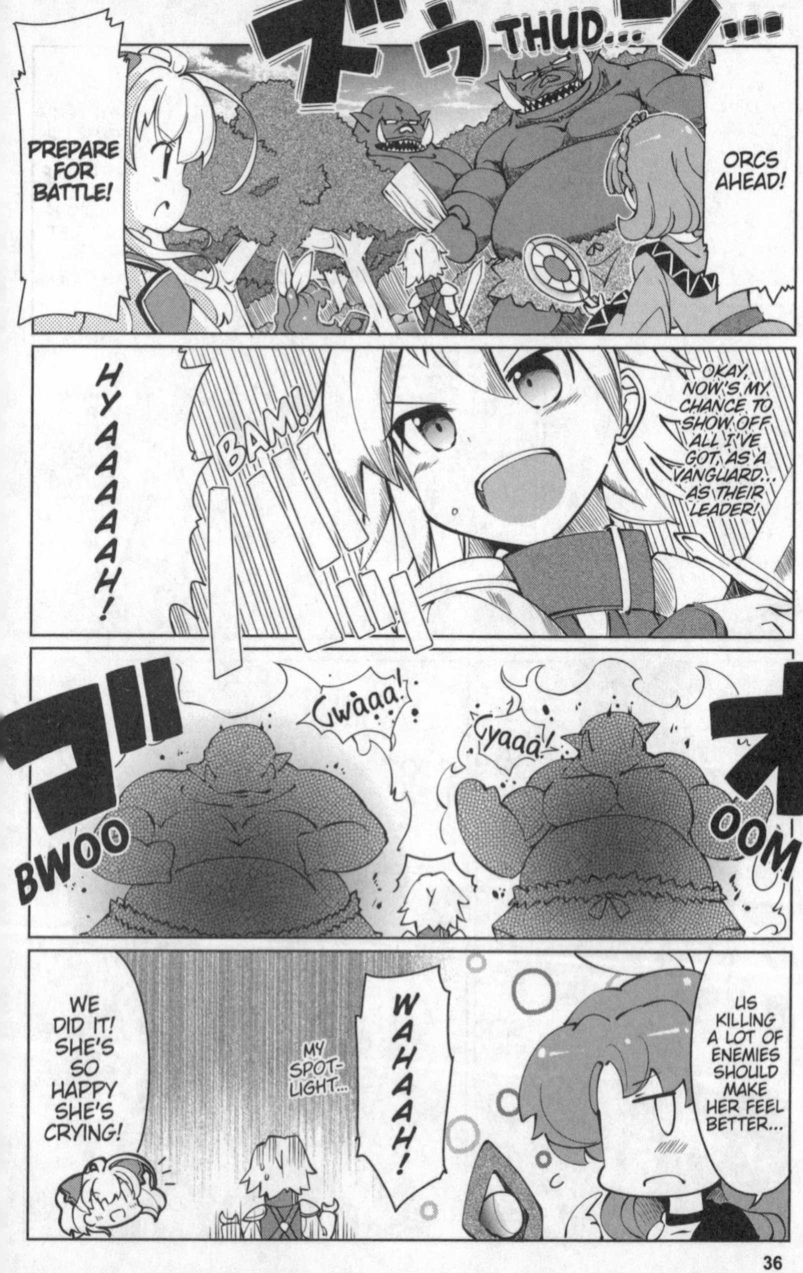
ORCS AHEAD!
THUD...
PREPARE FOR BATTLE!
OKAY, NOW'S MY CHANCE TO SHOW OFF ALL I'VE GOT AS A VANGUARD... AS THEIR LEADER!
BAM!
HYAAAAAAH!
OOM
Gyaaa!
Gwaaa!
BWOO
US KILLING A LOT OF ENEMIES SHOULD MAKE HER FEEL BETTER...
WAHAAAH!
MY SPOT-LIGHT...
WE DID IT! SHE'S SO HAPPY SHE'S CRYING!

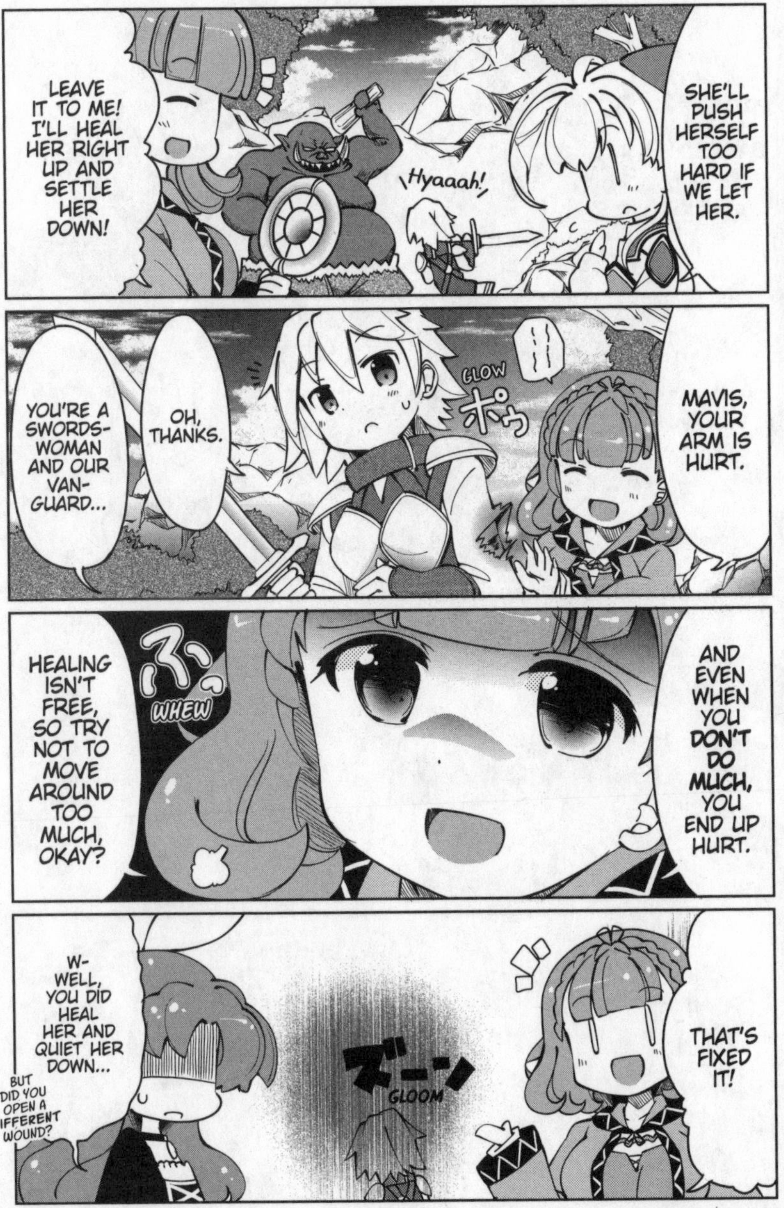
SHE'LL PUSH HERSELF TOO HARD IF WE LET HER.
Hyaaah!
LEAVE IT TO ME! I'LL HEAL HER RIGHT UP AND SETTLE HER DOWN!
MAVIS, YOUR ARM IS HURT.
GLOW ポゥ
OH, THANKS.
YOU'RE A SWORDS-WOMAN AND OUR VAN-GUARD...
AND EVEN WHEN YOU DON'T DO MUCH, YOU END UP HURT.
ふぅ WHEW
HEALING ISN'T FREE, SO TRY NOT TO MOVE AROUND TOO MUCH, OKAY?
THAT'S FIXED IT!
ズーン GLOOM
W-WELL, YOU DID HEAL HER AND QUIET HER DOWN...
BUT DID YOU OPEN A DIFFERENT WOUND?

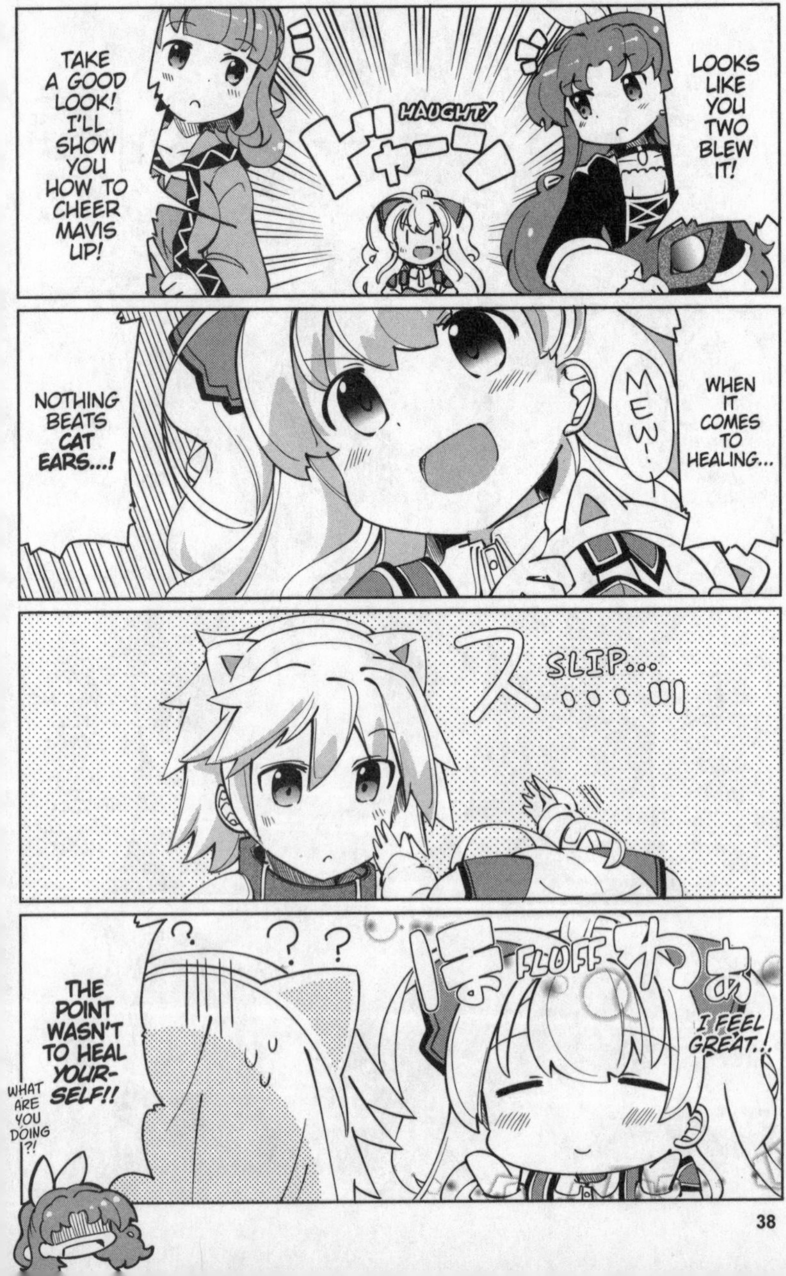
LOOKS LIKE YOU TWO BLEW IT!
HAUGHTY
TAKE A GOOD LOOK! I'LL SHOW YOU HOW TO CHEER MAVIS UP!
WHEN IT COMES TO HEALING...
MEW!
NOTHING BEATS CAT EARS...!
SLIP.......
FLUFF
I FEEL GREAT...
THE POINT WASN'T TO HEAL YOURSELF!!
WHAT ARE YOU DOING ?!

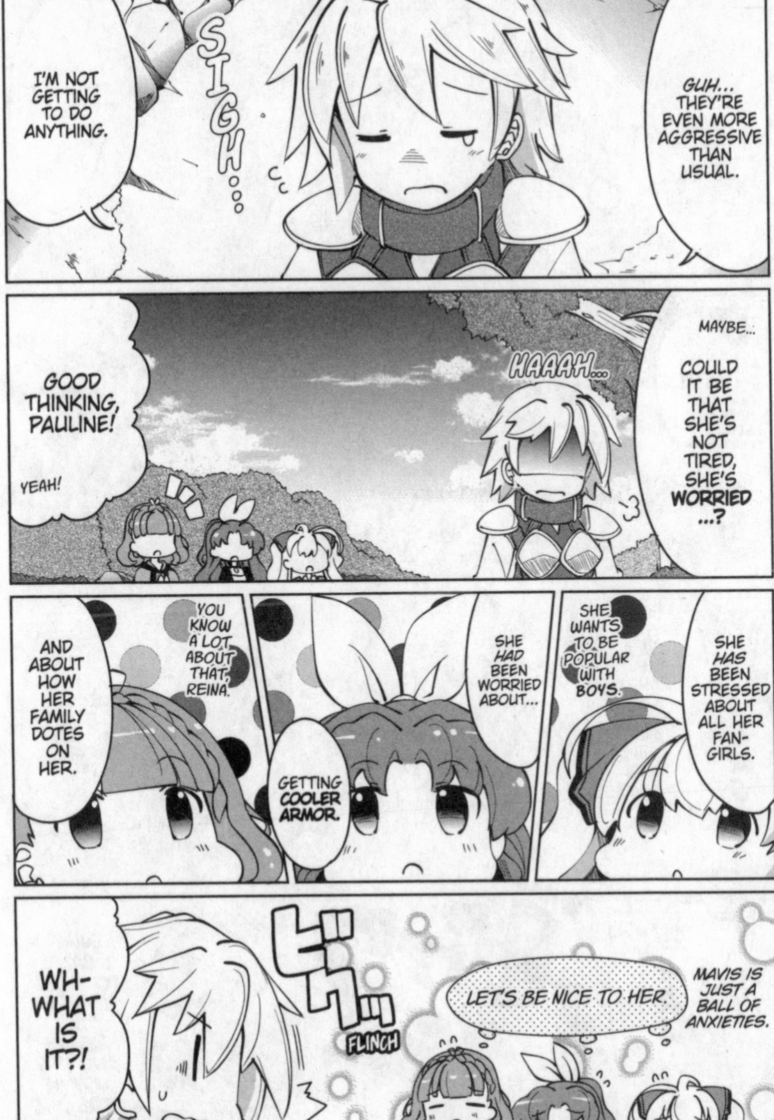
GUH... THEY'RE EVEN MORE AGGRESSIVE THAN USUAL.
SIGH...
I'M NOT GETTING TO DO ANYTHING.
MAYBE...
COULD IT BE THAT SHE'S NOT TIRED, SHE'S **WORRIED**...?
HAAAH...
GOOD THINKING, PAULINE!
YEAH!
SHE HAS BEEN STRESSED ABOUT ALL HER FAN-GIRLS.
SHE WANTS TO BE POPULAR WITH BOYS.
SHE HAD BEEN WORRIED ABOUT...
GETTING **COOLER ARMOR.**
YOU KNOW A LOT ABOUT THAT, REINA.
AND ABOUT HOW HER FAMILY DOTES ON HER.
MAVIS IS JUST A BALL OF ANXIETIES.
LET'S BE NICE TO HER.
ビクッ
FLINCH
WH-WHAT IS IT?!

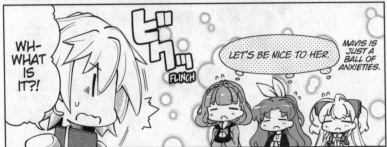

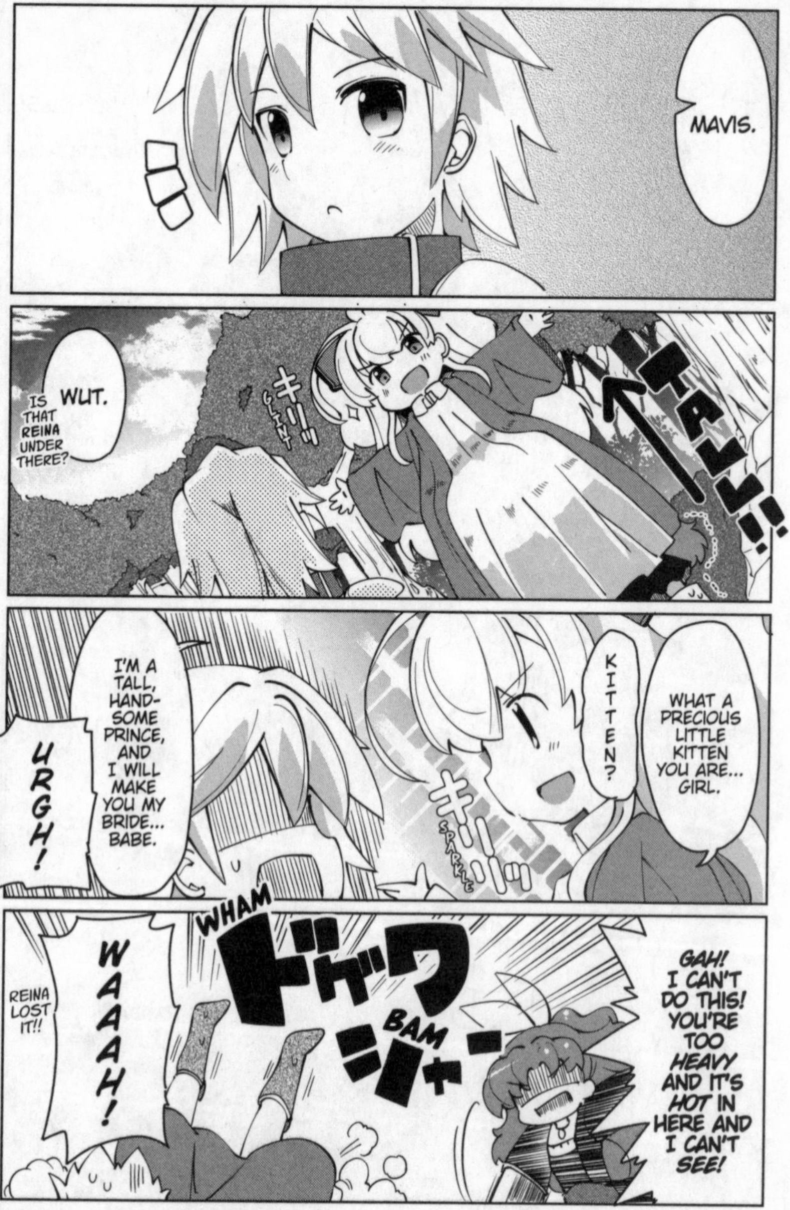
MAVIS.
TALL!!
WUT.
IS THAT REINA UNDER THERE?
GLINT
WHAT A PRECIOUS LITTLE KITTEN YOU ARE... GIRL.
KITTEN?
SPARKLE
I'M A TALL, HANDSOME PRINCE, AND I WILL MAKE YOU MY BRIDE... BABE.
URGH!
GAH! I CAN'T DO THIS! YOU'RE TOO *HEAVY* AND IT'S *HOT* IN HERE AND I CAN'T SEE!
WHAM
BAM
WAAAAH!
REINA LOST IT!!

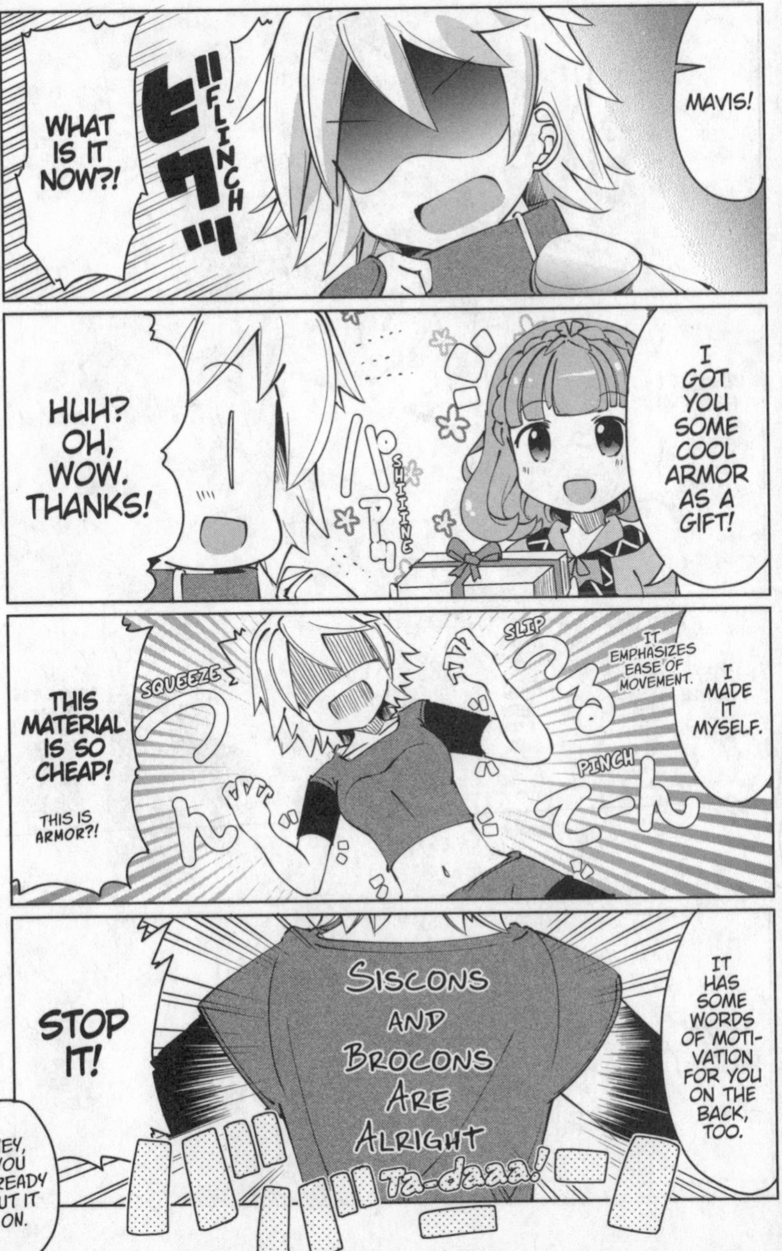
MAVIS!
FLINCH
WHAT IS IT NOW?!
I GOT YOU SOME COOL ARMOR AS A GIFT!
SHIIIINE
HUH? OH, WOW. THANKS!
I MADE IT MYSELF.
IT EMPHASIZES EASE OF MOVEMENT.
SLIP
PINCH
SQUEEZE
THIS MATERIAL IS SO CHEAP!
THIS IS ARMOR?!
IT HAS SOME WORDS OF MOTI-VATION FOR YOU ON THE BACK, TOO.
Siscons and Brocons Are Alright
Ta-daaa!
STOP IT!
HEY, YOU ALREADY PUT IT ON.

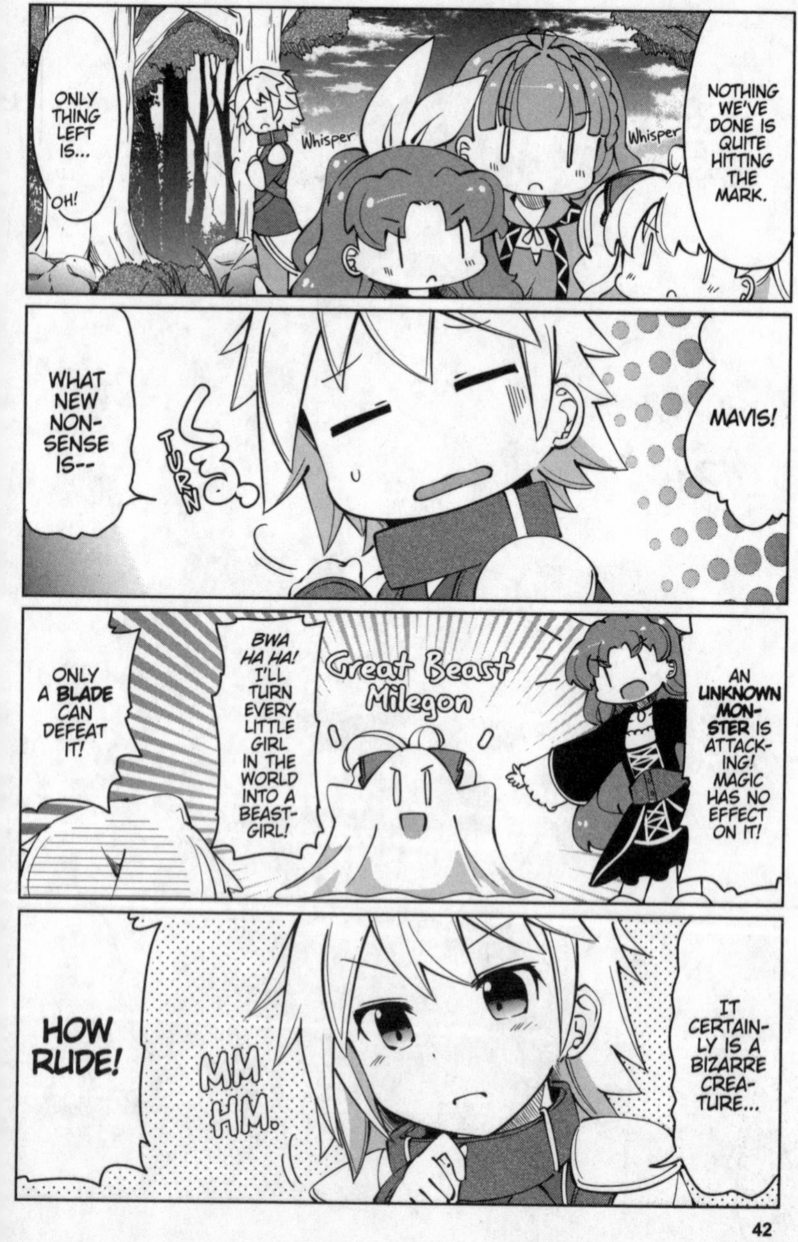
NOTHING WE'VE DONE IS QUITE HITTING THE MARK.
Whisper
Whisper
ONLY THING LEFT IS... OH!
MAVIS!
TURN
WHAT NEW NON-SENSE IS--
AN UNKNOWN MON-STER IS ATTACK-ING! MAGIC HAS NO EFFECT ON IT!
Great Beast Milegon
BWA HA HA! I'LL TURN EVERY LITTLE GIRL IN THE WORLD INTO A BEAST-GIRL!
ONLY A BLADE CAN DEFEAT IT!
IT CERTAIN-LY IS A BIZARRE CREA-TURE...
MM HM.
HOW RUDE!

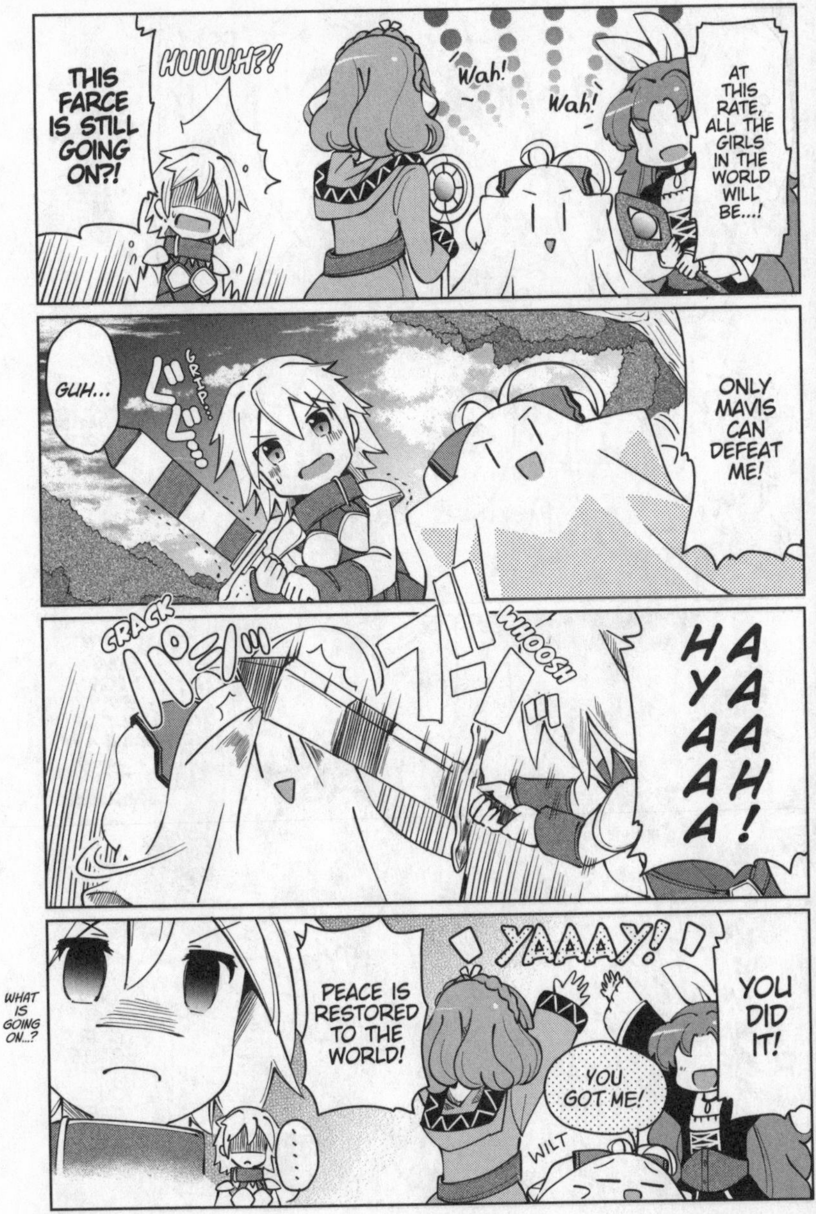
AT THIS RATE, ALL THE GIRLS IN THE WORLD WILL BE...!
Wah!
Wah!
HUUUH?!
THIS FARCE IS STILL GOING ON?!
ONLY MAVIS CAN DEFEAT ME!
GRIP...
GUH...
HAYAAAAAH!
WHOOSH
CRACK
YOU DID IT!
YAAAY!
PEACE IS RESTORED TO THE WORLD!
YOU GOT ME!
WILT
...
WHAT IS GOING ON...?

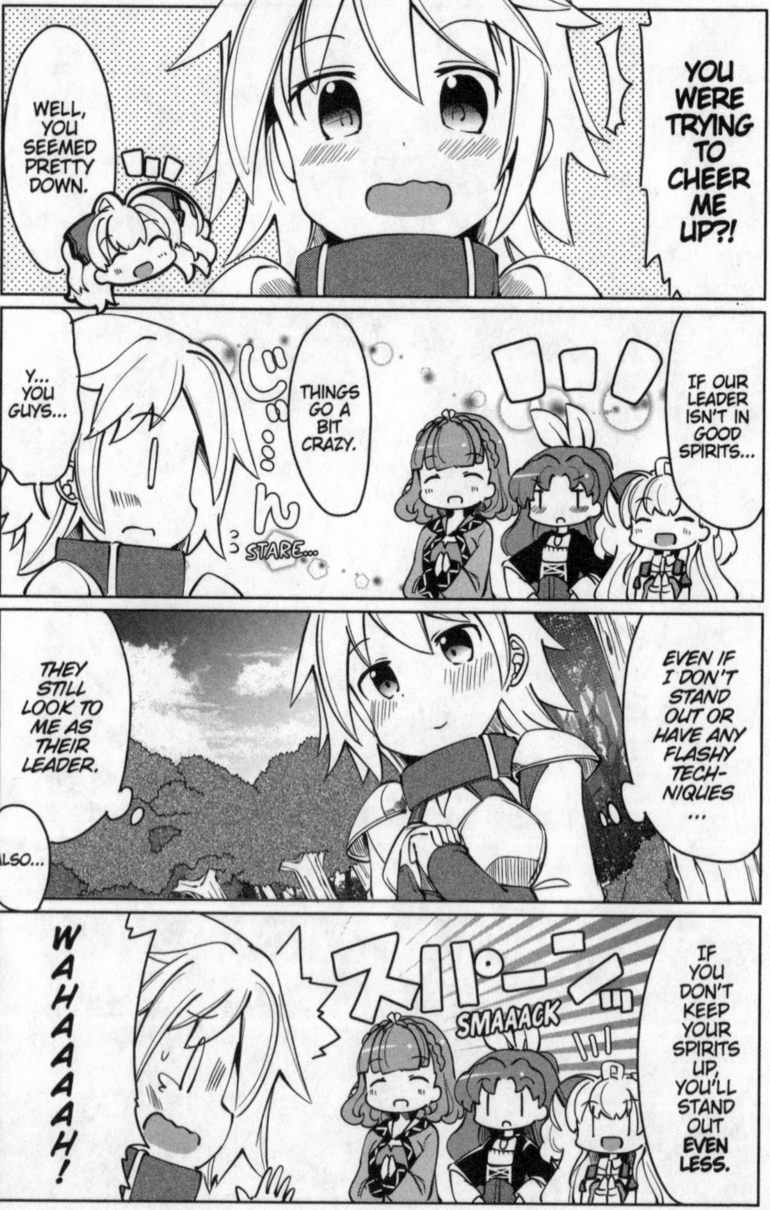
YOU WERE TRYING TO CHEER ME UP?!
WELL, YOU SEEMED PRETTY DOWN.
IF OUR LEADER ISN'T IN GOOD SPIRITS...
THINGS GO A BIT CRAZY.
STARE...
Y... YOU GUYS...
EVEN IF I DON'T STAND OUT OR HAVE ANY FLASHY TECH-NIQUES...
THEY STILL LOOK TO ME AS THEIR LEADER.
ALSO...
IF YOU DON'T KEEP YOUR SPIRITS UP, YOU'LL STAND OUT EVEN LESS.
SMAAACK
WAHAAAAH!

Didn't I Say
to Make My
Abilities
Average in the
Next Life?!
EVERYDAY MISADVENTURES!

Great Beast
Milegon

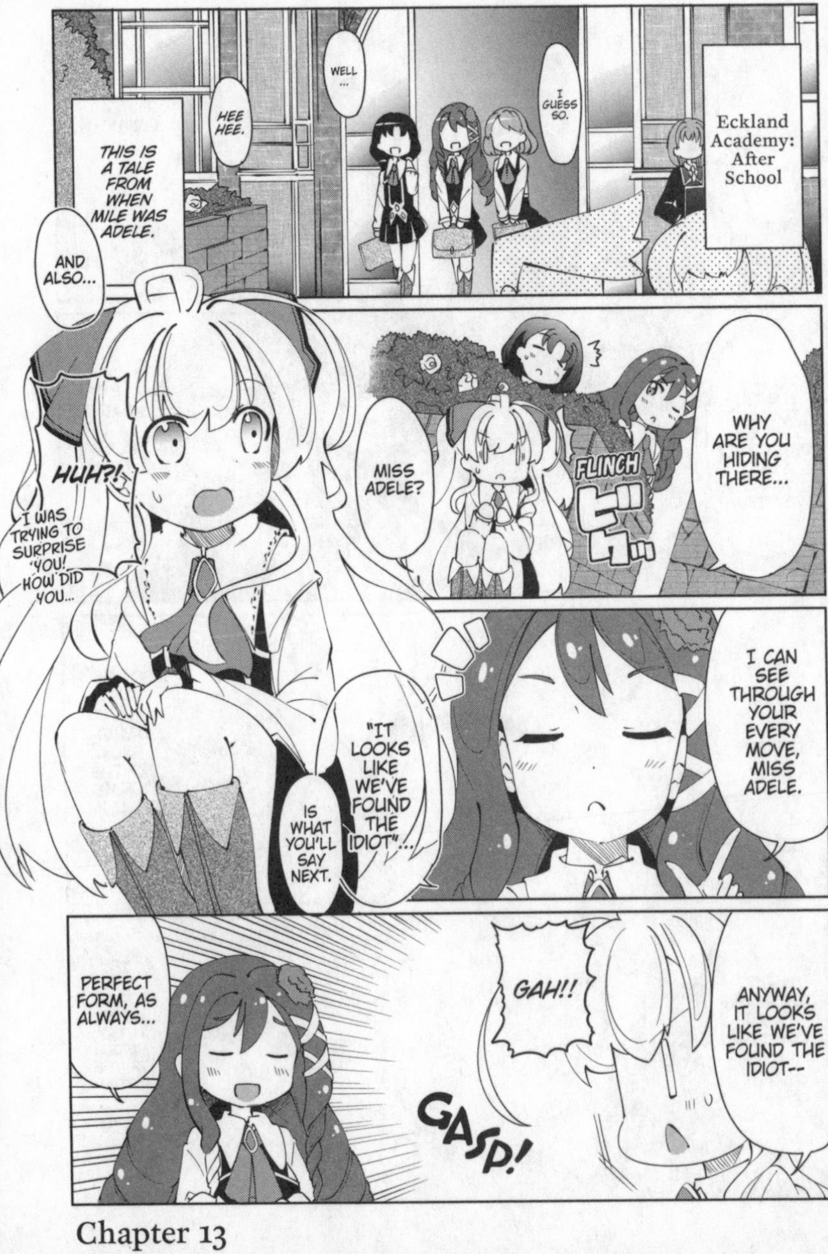
Eckland Academy: After School
I GUESS SO.
WELL...
HEE HEE.
THIS IS A TALE FROM WHEN MILE WAS ADELE.
AND ALSO...
WHY ARE YOU HIDING THERE...
FLINCH
MISS ADELE?
HUH?!
I WAS TRYING TO SURPRISE YOU! HOW DID YOU...
I CAN SEE THROUGH YOUR EVERY MOVE, MISS ADELE.
"IT LOOKS LIKE WE'VE FOUND THE IDIOT"...
IS WHAT YOU'LL SAY NEXT.
ANYWAY, IT LOOKS LIKE WE'VE FOUND THE IDIOT--
GASP!
GAH!!
PERFECT FORM, AS ALWAYS...

Chapter 13

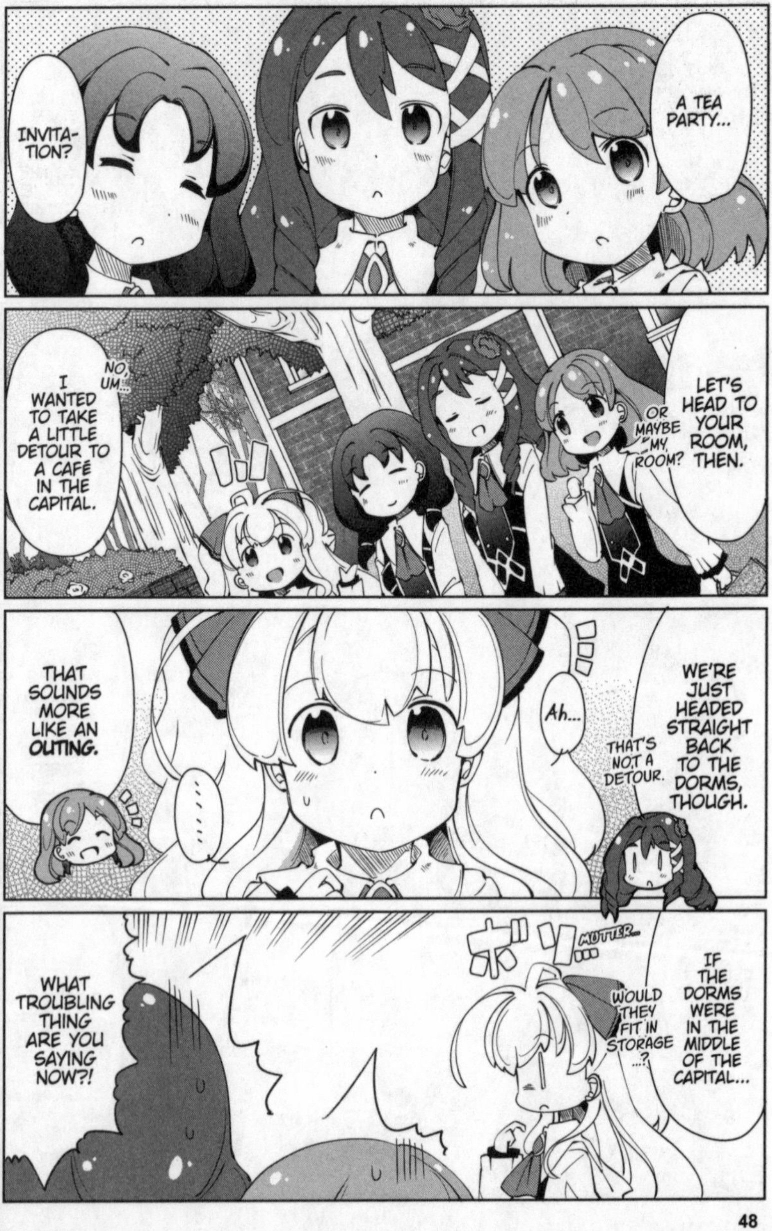
A TEA PARTY...
INVITATION?
LET'S HEAD TO YOUR ROOM, THEN.
OR MAYBE MY ROOM?
NO, UM...
I WANTED TO TAKE A LITTLE DETOUR TO A CAFÉ IN THE CAPITAL.
WE'RE JUST HEADED STRAIGHT BACK TO THE DORMS, THOUGH.
THAT'S NOT A DETOUR.
Ah...
......
THAT SOUNDS MORE LIKE AN **OUTING.**
IF THE DORMS WERE IN THE MIDDLE OF THE CAPITAL...
WOULD THEY FIT IN STORAGE ...?
MUTTER...
WHAT TROUBLING THING ARE YOU SAYING NOW?!

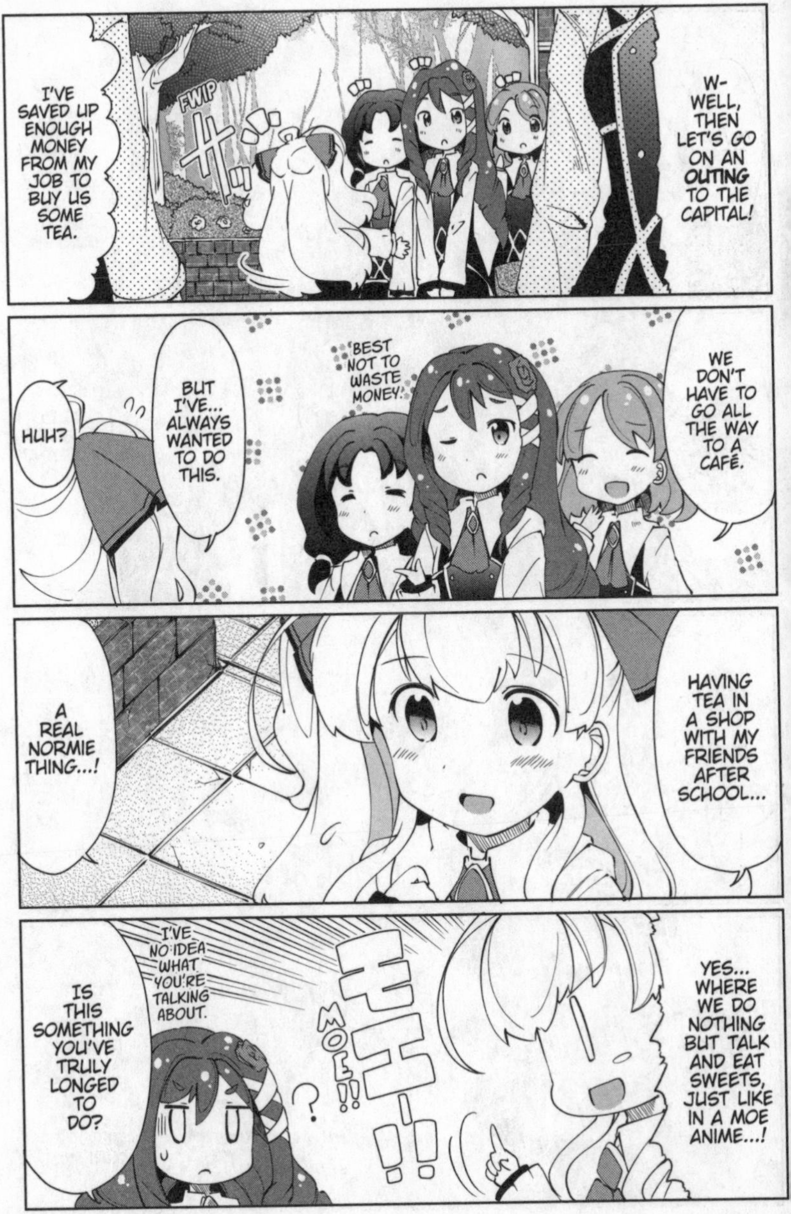
W-WELL, THEN LET'S GO ON AN **OUTING** TO THE CAPITAL!
FWIP
I'VE SAVED UP ENOUGH MONEY FROM MY JOB TO BUY US SOME TEA.
WE DON'T HAVE TO GO ALL THE WAY TO A CAFÉ.
'BEST NOT TO WASTE MONEY.'
BUT I'VE... ALWAYS WANTED TO DO THIS.
HUH?
HAVING TEA IN A SHOP WITH MY FRIENDS AFTER SCHOOL...
A REAL NORMIE THING...!
YES... WHERE WE DO NOTHING BUT TALK AND EAT SWEETS, JUST LIKE IN A MOE ANIME...!
MOE!!
I'VE NO IDEA WHAT YOU'RE TALKING ABOUT.
IS THIS SOMETHING YOU'VE TRULY LONGED TO DO?

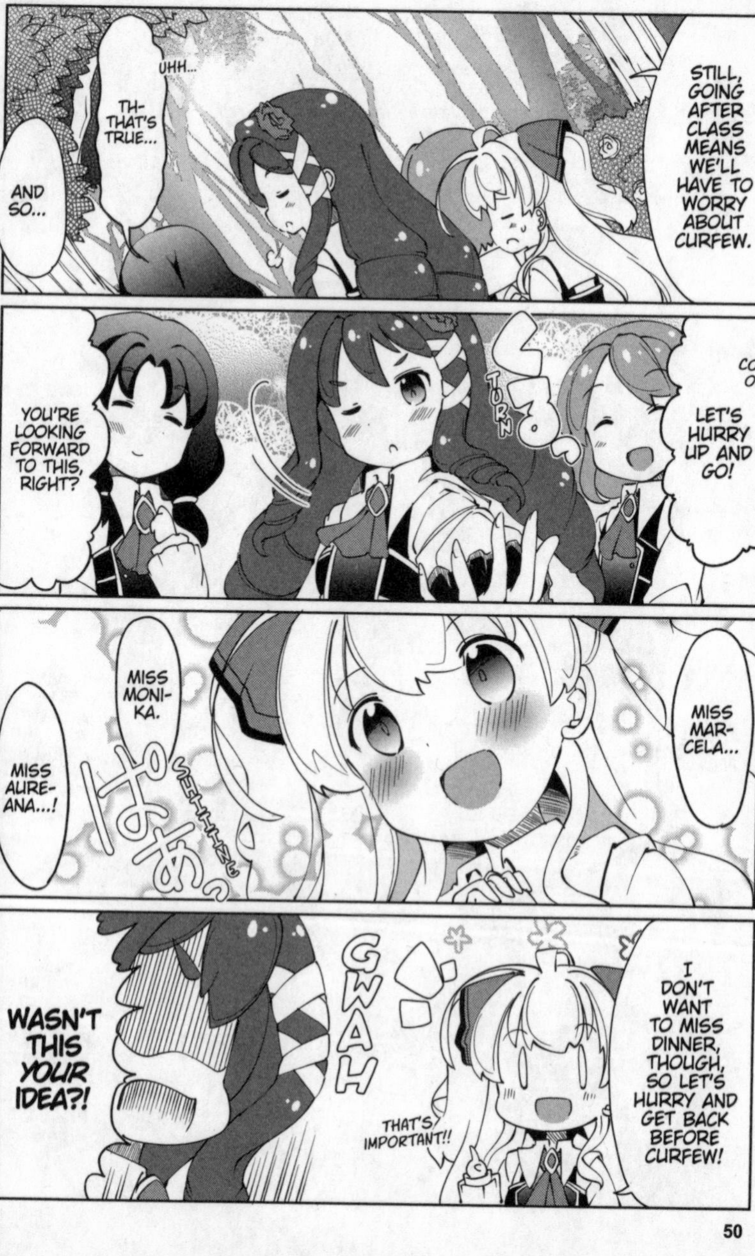

STILL, GOING AFTER CLASS MEANS WE'LL HAVE TO WORRY ABOUT CURFEW.
UHH...
TH-THAT'S TRUE...
AND SO...
COME ON!
LET'S HURRY UP AND GO!
TORN
YOU'RE LOOKING FORWARD TO THIS, RIGHT?
MISS MAR-CELA...
MISS MONI-KA.
SHIIIINE
MISS AURE-ANA...!
I DON'T WANT TO MISS DINNER, THOUGH, SO LET'S HURRY AND GET BACK BEFORE CURFEW!
THAT'S IMPORTANT!!
GWAH
WASN'T THIS *YOUR* IDEA?!

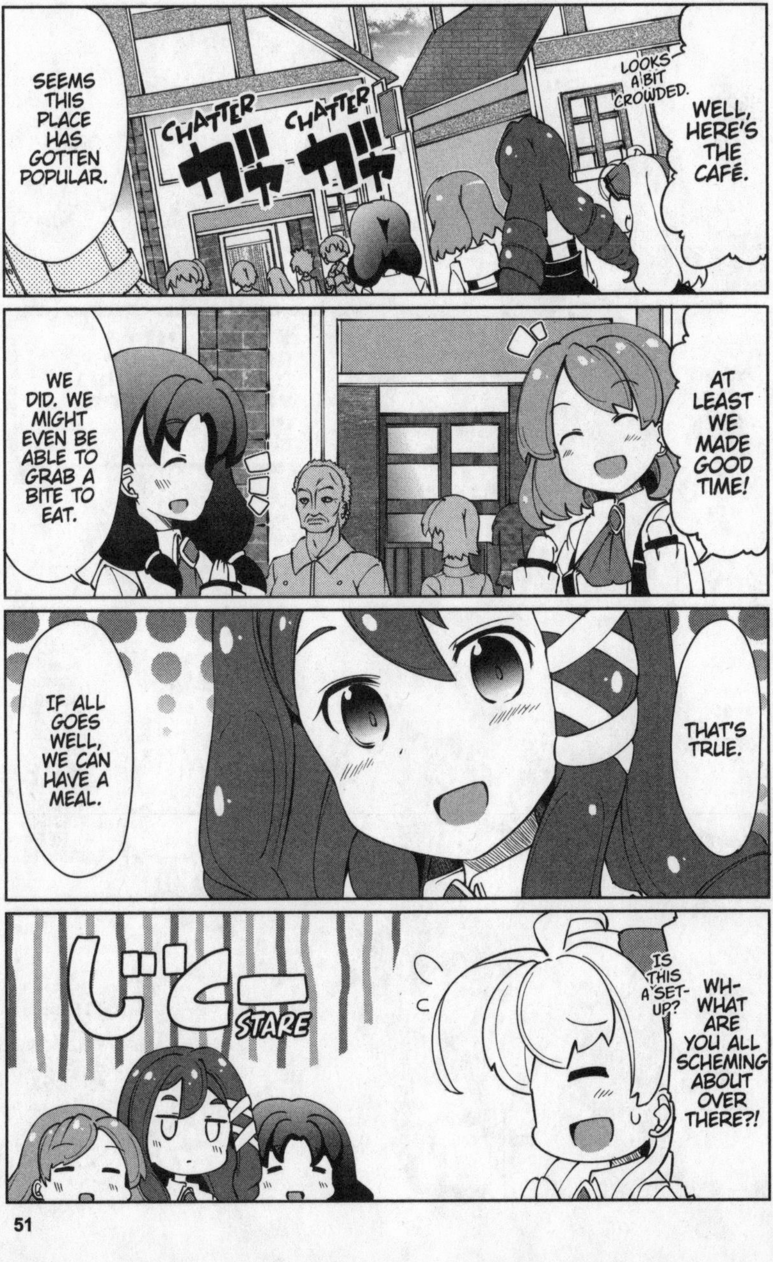
WELL, HERE'S THE CAFÉ.
LOOKS A BIT CROWDED.
ガヤ ガヤ CHATTER CHATTER
SEEMS THIS PLACE HAS GOTTEN POPULAR.
AT LEAST WE MADE GOOD TIME!
WE DID. WE MIGHT EVEN BE ABLE TO GRAB A BITE TO EAT.
THAT'S TRUE.
IF ALL GOES WELL, WE CAN HAVE A MEAL.
WH-WHAT ARE YOU ALL SCHEMING ABOUT OVER THERE?!
IS THIS A SET-UP?
じーー STARE

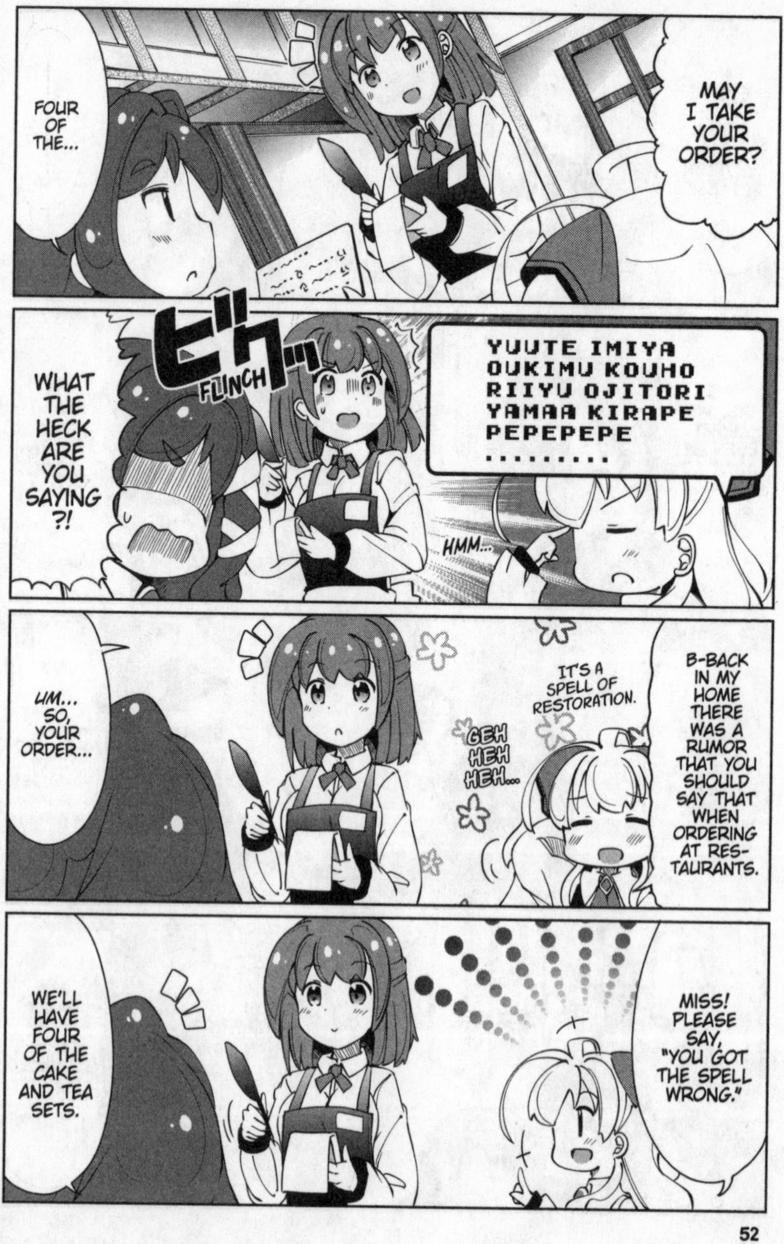
MAY I TAKE YOUR ORDER?
FOUR OF THE...
YUUTE IMIYA OUKIMU KOUHO RIIYU OJITORI YAMAA KIRAPE PEPEPEPE ....
ビクッ
FLINCH
WHAT THE HECK ARE YOU SAYING?!
HMM...
IT'S A SPELL OF RESTORATION.
B-BACK IN MY HOME THERE WAS A RUMOR THAT YOU SHOULD SAY THAT WHEN ORDERING AT RESTAURANTS.
GEH HEH HEH...
UM... SO, YOUR ORDER...
MISS! PLEASE SAY, "YOU GOT THE SPELL WRONG."
WE'LL HAVE FOUR OF THE CAKE AND TEA SETS.

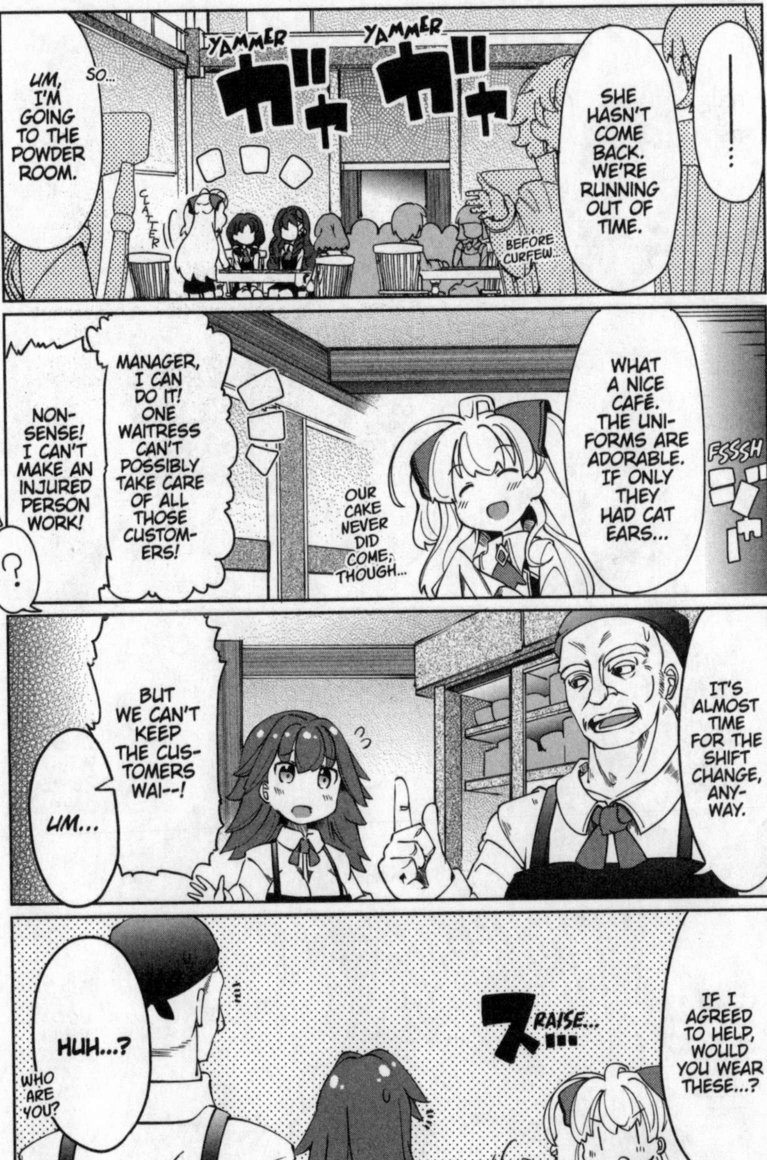
......
SHE HASN'T COME BACK. WE'RE RUNNING OUT OF TIME.
BEFORE CURFEW.
YAMMER YAMMER
CLATTER
SO...
UM, I'M GOING TO THE POWDER ROOM.
FSSSH
WHAT A NICE CAFÉ. THE UNIFORMS ARE ADORABLE. IF ONLY THEY HAD CAT EARS...
OUR CAKE NEVER DID COME, THOUGH...
MANAGER, I CAN DO IT! ONE WAITRESS CAN'T POSSIBLY TAKE CARE OF ALL THOSE CUSTOMERS!
NONSENSE! I CAN'T MAKE AN INJURED PERSON WORK!
?
IT'S ALMOST TIME FOR THE SHIFT CHANGE, ANYWAY.
BUT WE CAN'T KEEP THE CUSTOMERS WAI--!
UM...
IF I AGREED TO HELP, WOULD YOU WEAR THESE...?
RAISE...
HUH...?
WHO ARE YOU?

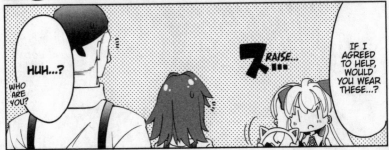

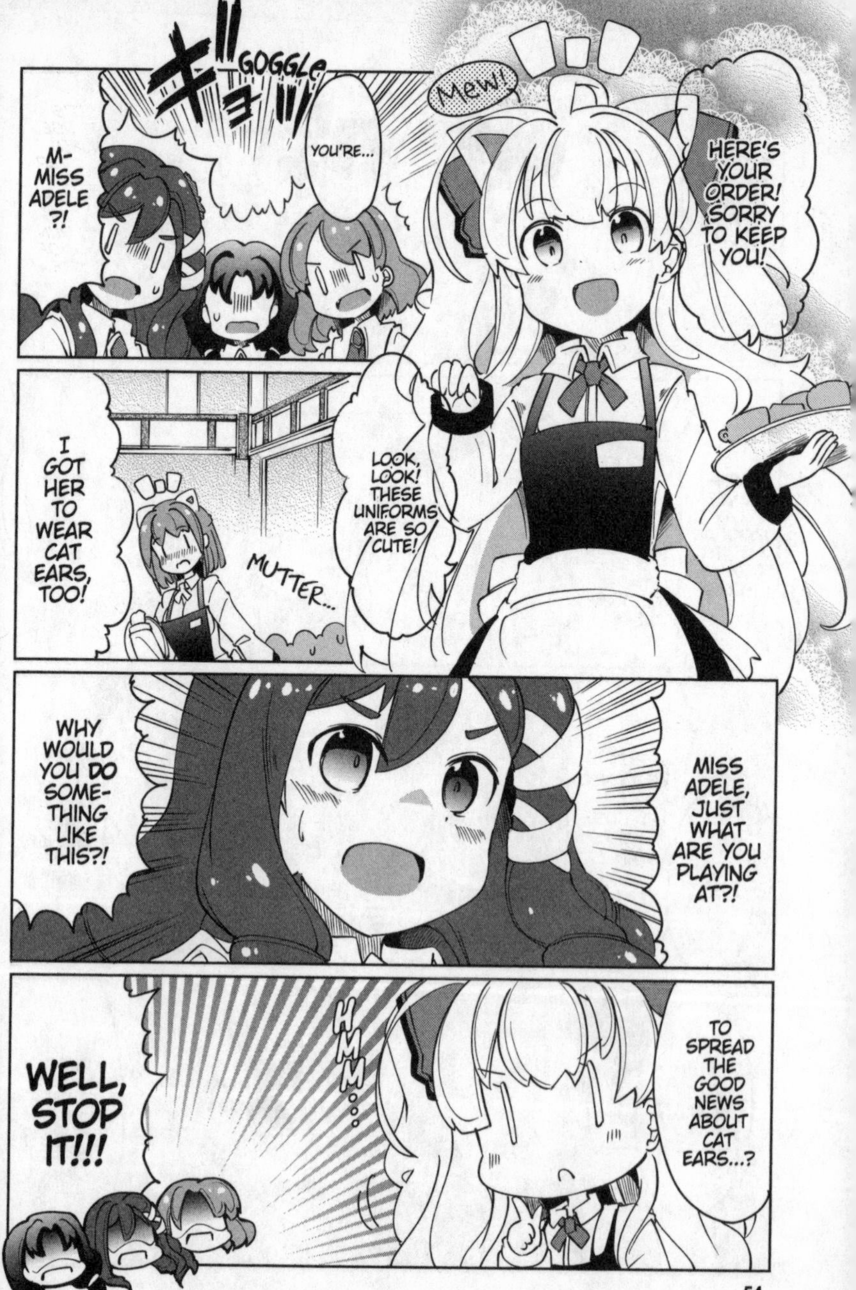
Mew!
HERE'S YOUR ORDER! SORRY TO KEEP YOU!
LOOK, LOOK! THESE UNIFORMS ARE SO CUTE!
ギョ
GOGGLE
YOU'RE...
M-MISS ADELE?!
I GOT HER TO WEAR CAT EARS, TOO!
MUTTER...
MISS ADELE, JUST WHAT ARE YOU PLAYING AT?!
WHY WOULD YOU DO SOME-THING LIKE THIS?!
TO SPREAD THE GOOD NEWS ABOUT CAT EARS...?
HMM...
WELL, STOP IT!!!

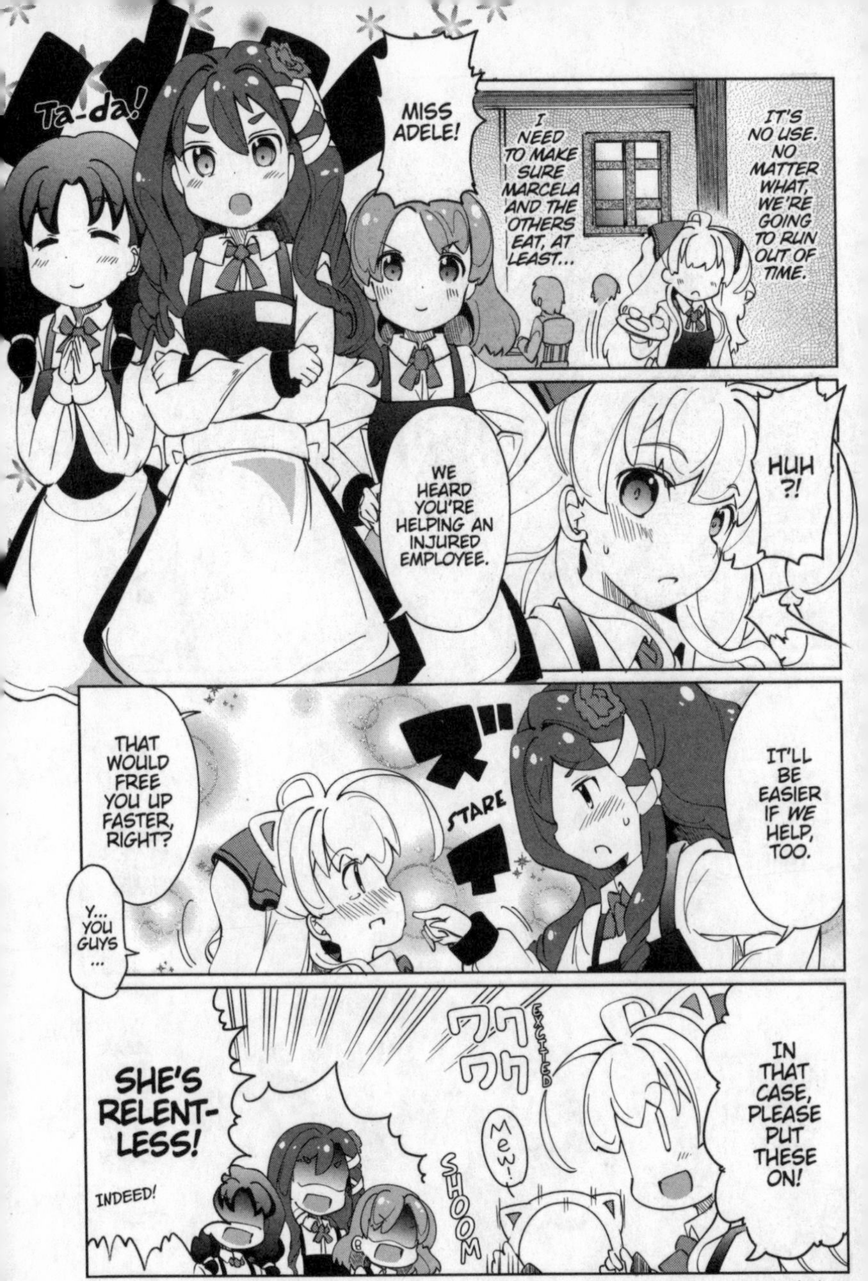
IT'S NO USE. NO MATTER WHAT, WE'RE GOING TO RUN OUT OF TIME.
I NEED TO MAKE SURE MARCELA AND THE OTHERS EAT, AT LEAST...
HUH?!
MISS ADELE!
Ta-da!
WE HEARD YOU'RE HELPING AN INJURED EMPLOYEE.
IT'LL BE EASIER IF WE HELP, TOO.
STARE
THAT WOULD FREE YOU UP FASTER, RIGHT?
Y... YOU GUYS ...
IN THAT CASE, PLEASE PUT THESE ON!
EXCITED
Mew!
SHOOM
SHE'S RELENT-LESS!
INDEED!

These cat ears have become a series regular!

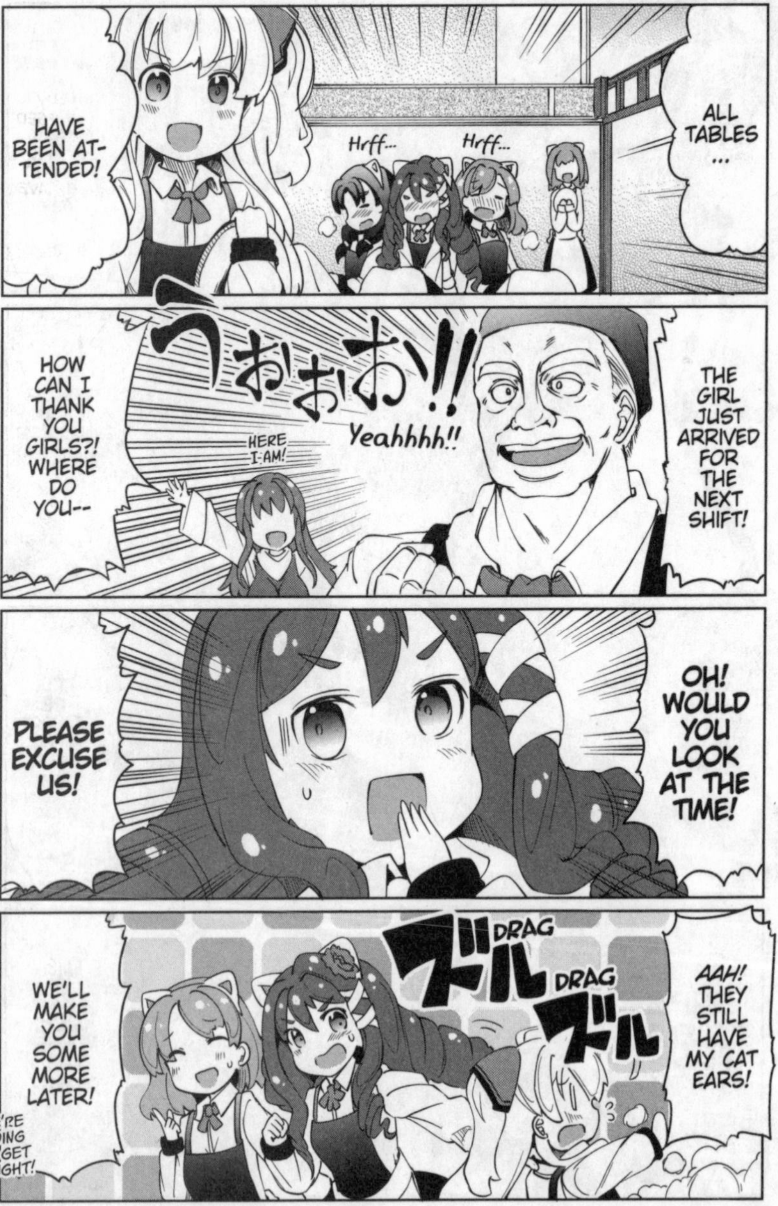
ALL TABLES ...
Hrff...
Hrff...
HAVE BEEN AT-TENDED!
THE GIRL JUST ARRIVED FOR THE NEXT SHIFT!
うおぉお!!
Yeahhhh!!
HERE I AM!
HOW CAN I THANK YOU GIRLS?! WHERE DO YOU--
OH! WOULD YOU LOOK AT THE TIME!
PLEASE EXCUSE US!
ズル
DRAG
ズル
DRAG
AAH! THEY STILL HAVE MY CAT EARS!
WE'LL MAKE YOU SOME MORE LATER!
E'RE OING O GET AUGHT!

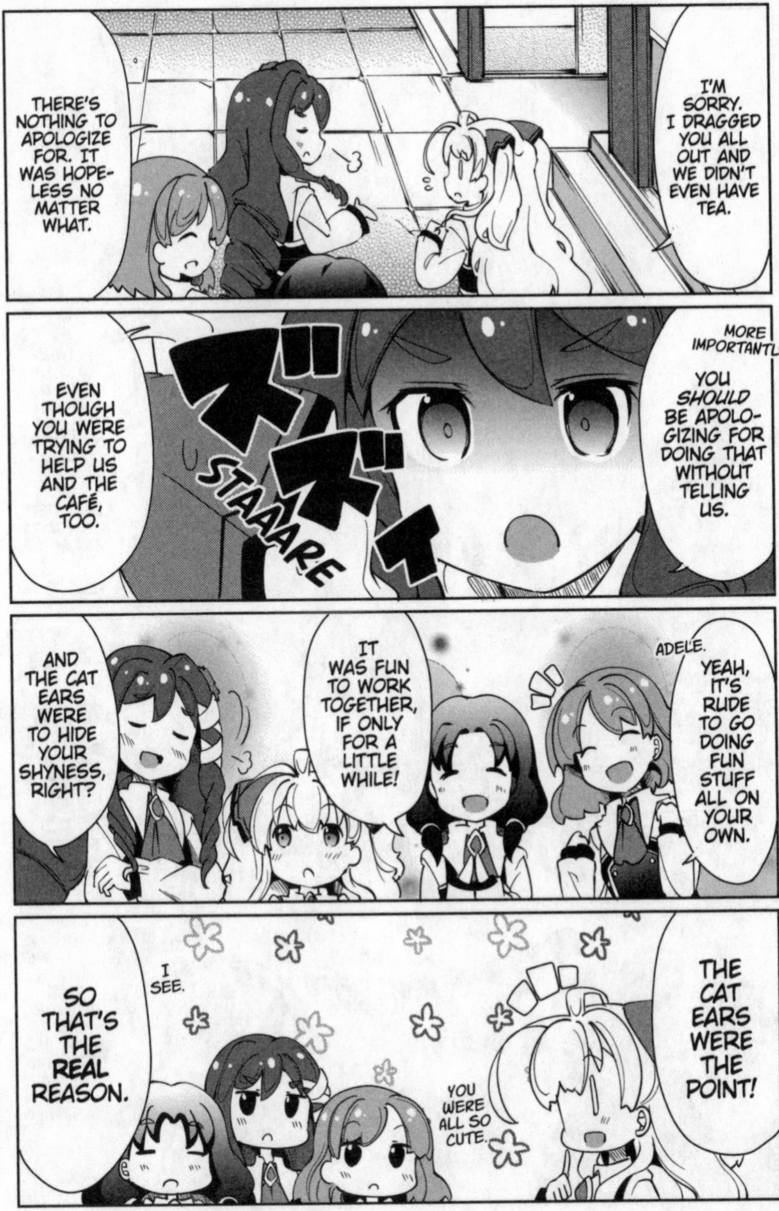
I'M SORRY. I DRAGGED YOU ALL OUT AND WE DIDN'T EVEN HAVE TEA.
THERE'S NOTHING TO APOLOGIZE FOR. IT WAS HOPELESS NO MATTER WHAT.
MORE IMPORTANTLY...
YOU *SHOULD* BE APOLOGIZING FOR DOING THAT WITHOUT TELLING US.
STAAARE
EVEN THOUGH YOU WERE TRYING TO HELP US AND THE CAFÉ, TOO.
ADELE.
YEAH, IT'S RUDE TO GO DOING FUN STUFF ALL ON YOUR OWN.
IT WAS FUN TO WORK TOGETHER, IF ONLY FOR A LITTLE WHILE!
AND THE CAT EARS WERE TO HIDE YOUR SHYNESS, RIGHT?
THE CAT EARS WERE THE POINT!
YOU WERE ALL SO CUTE.
I SEE.
SO THAT'S THE **REAL** REASON.

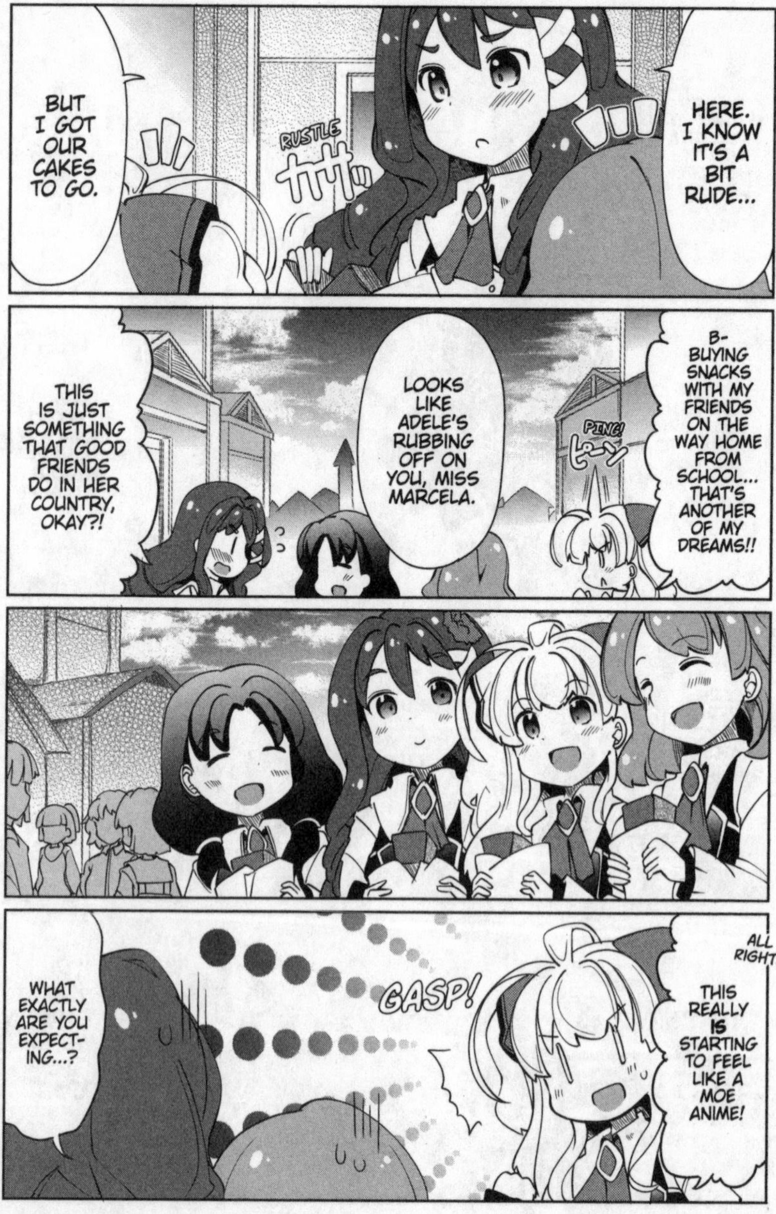
HERE. I KNOW IT'S A BIT RUDE...
RUSTLE
BUT I GOT OUR CAKES TO GO.
B-BUYING SNACKS WITH MY FRIENDS ON THE WAY HOME FROM SCHOOL... THAT'S ANOTHER OF MY DREAMS!!
PING!
LOOKS LIKE ADELE'S RUBBING OFF ON YOU, MISS MARCELA.
THIS IS JUST SOMETHING THAT GOOD FRIENDS DO IN HER COUNTRY, OKAY?!
ALL RIGHT!
THIS REALLY **IS** STARTING TO FEEL LIKE A MOE ANIME!
GASP!
WHAT EXACTLY ARE YOU EXPECTING...?

Didn't I Say to Make My Abilities Average in the Next Life?!
EVERYDAY MISADVENTURES!

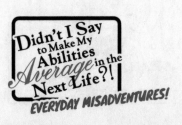

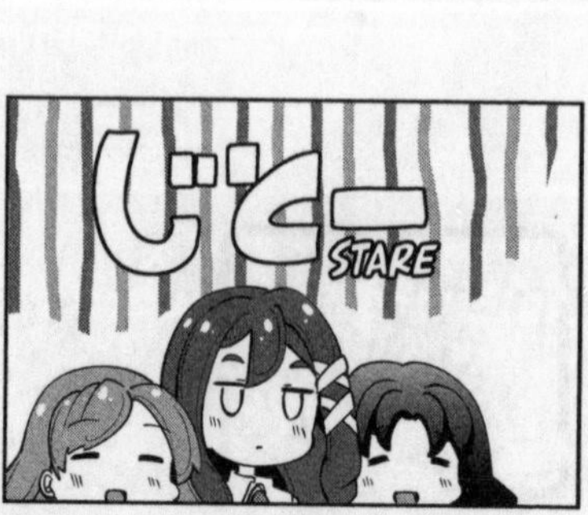
じ～
STARE

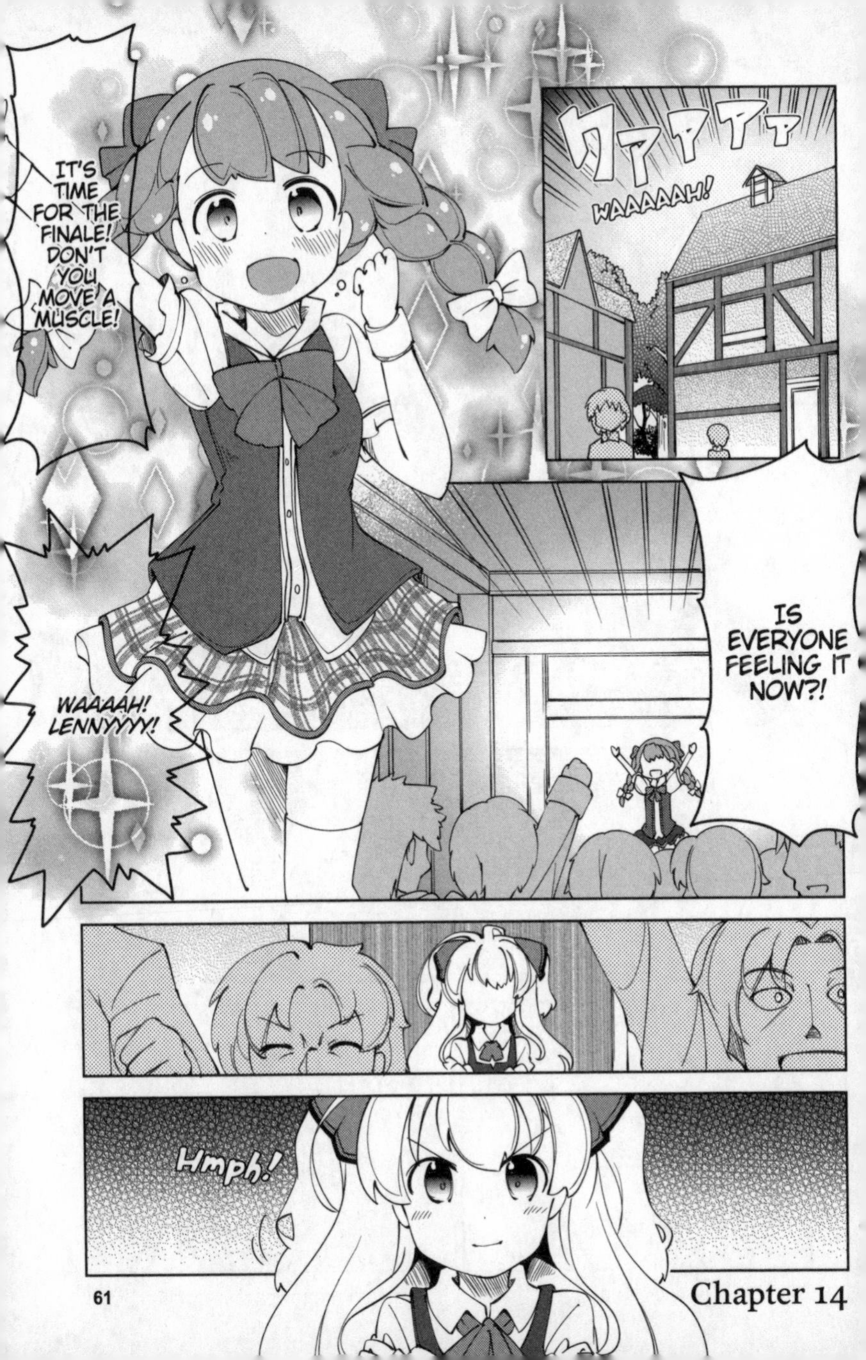
ワァァァァ
WAAAAAH!
IS EVERYONE FEELING IT NOW?!
IT'S TIME FOR THE FINALE! DON'T YOU MOVE A MUSCLE!
WAAAAH! LENNYYYY!
Hmph!
Chapter 14

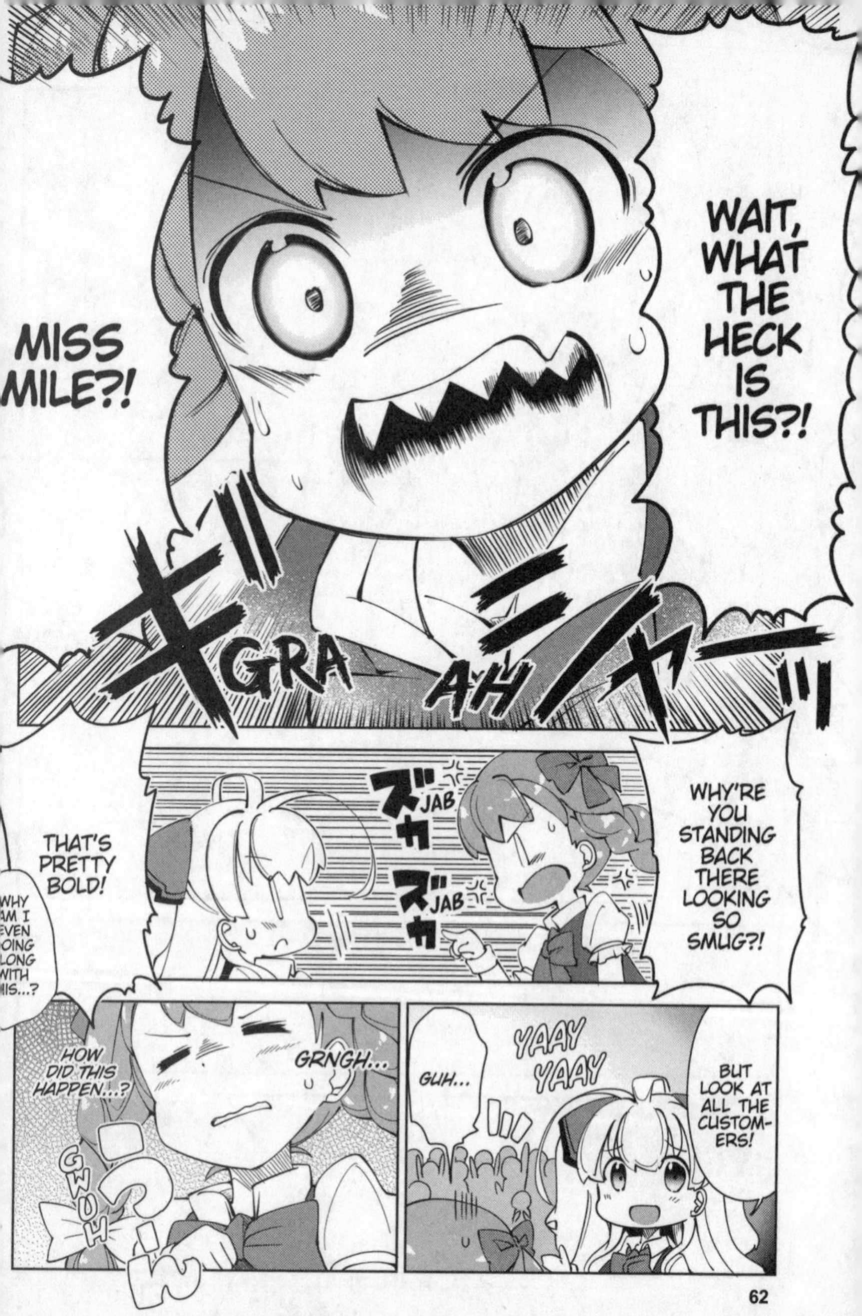
WAIT, WHAT THE HECK IS THIS?!
MISS MILE?!
GRA AH
WHY'RE YOU STANDING BACK THERE LOOKING SO SMUG?!
JAB
JAB
THAT'S PRETTY BOLD!
WHY AM I EVEN OING LONG WITH IS...?
BUT LOOK AT ALL THE CUSTOM-ERS!
YAAY YAAY
GUH...
GRNGH...
HOW DID THIS HAPPEN...?
GWUH

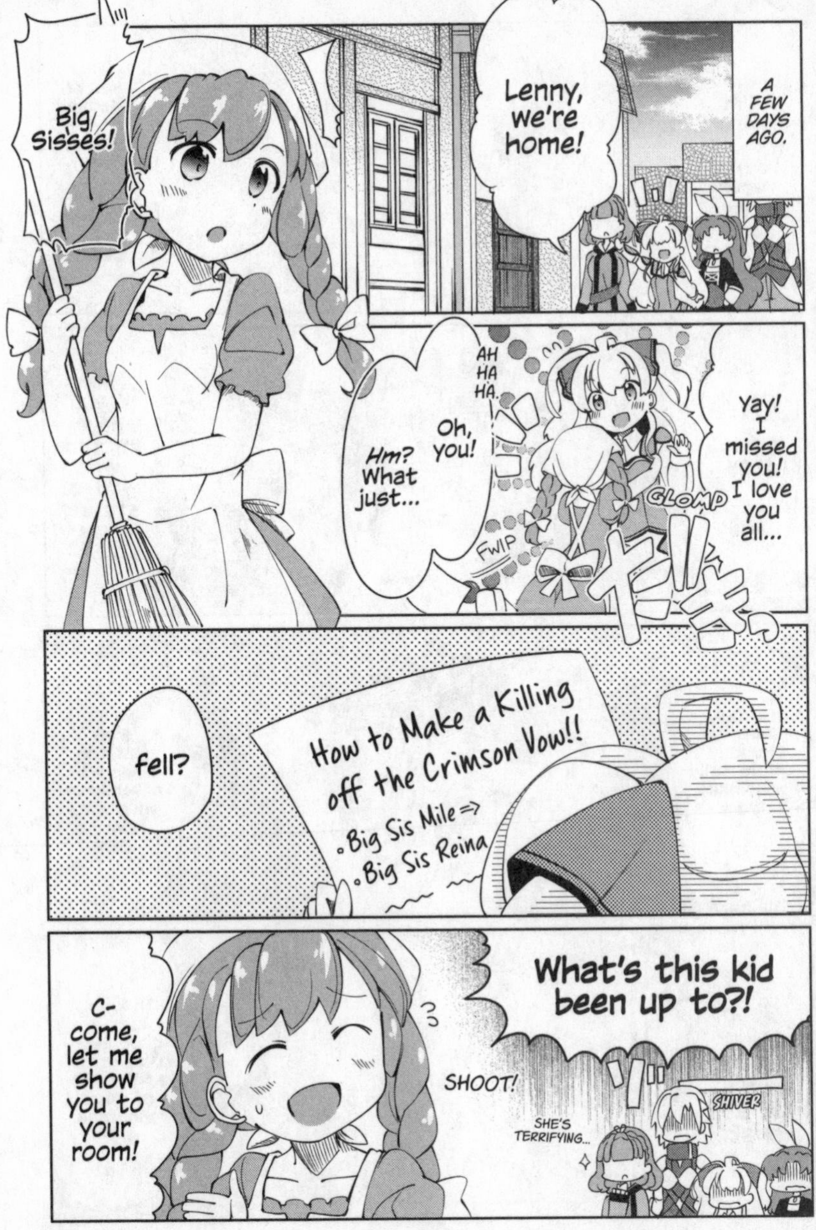
A FEW DAYS AGO.
Lenny, we're home!
Yay! I missed you! I love you all...
GLOMP
AH HA HA.
Oh, you!
Hm? What just...
FWIP
Big Sisses!
How to Make a Killing off the Crimson Vow!!
Big Sis Mile ⇒
Big Sis Reina
fell?
What's this kid been up to?!
SHIVER
SHOOT!
SHE'S TERRIFYING...
C-come, let me show you to your room!

Once you've sampled the sweetest honey, you never forget the taste.

I'm saying I want to borrow your power again.

So, if you have any time while you're staying here...!

HELP ME OUT!

Look, Lenny...

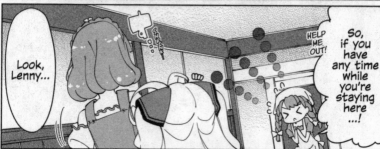

We never stay for long, and we never know when we'll have to leave.

ズイッ
SERIOUS

You need to think up a more solid business plan!

Though, it *is* a good idea to take full advantage of your resources, yes?

チラッ
GLANCE...

EEP!

I SEE!

Stop looking at me when you say that!

64

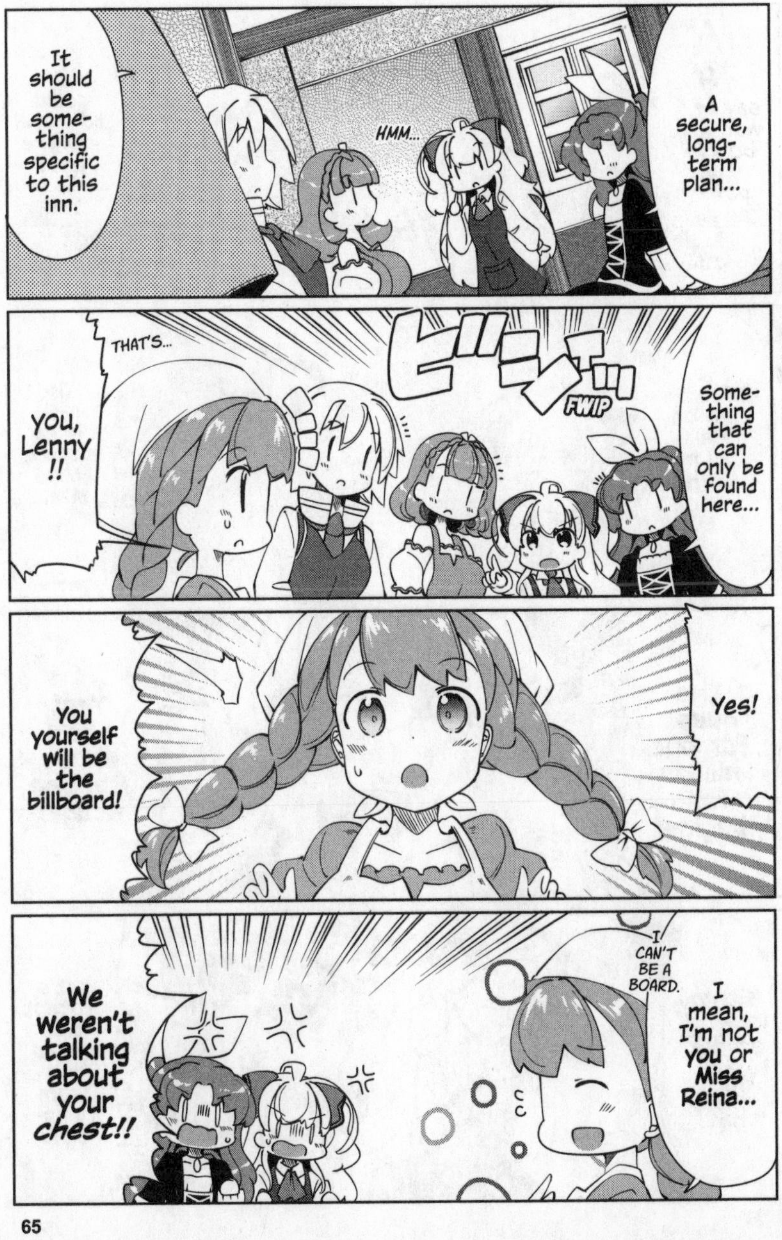
A secure, long-term plan...
HMM...
It should be some-thing specific to this inn.
Some-thing that can only be found here...
FWIP
THAT'S...
YOU, Lenny !!
Yes!
You yourself will be the billboard!
I mean, I'm not you or Miss Reina...
I CAN'T BE A BOARD.
We weren't talking about your chest!!

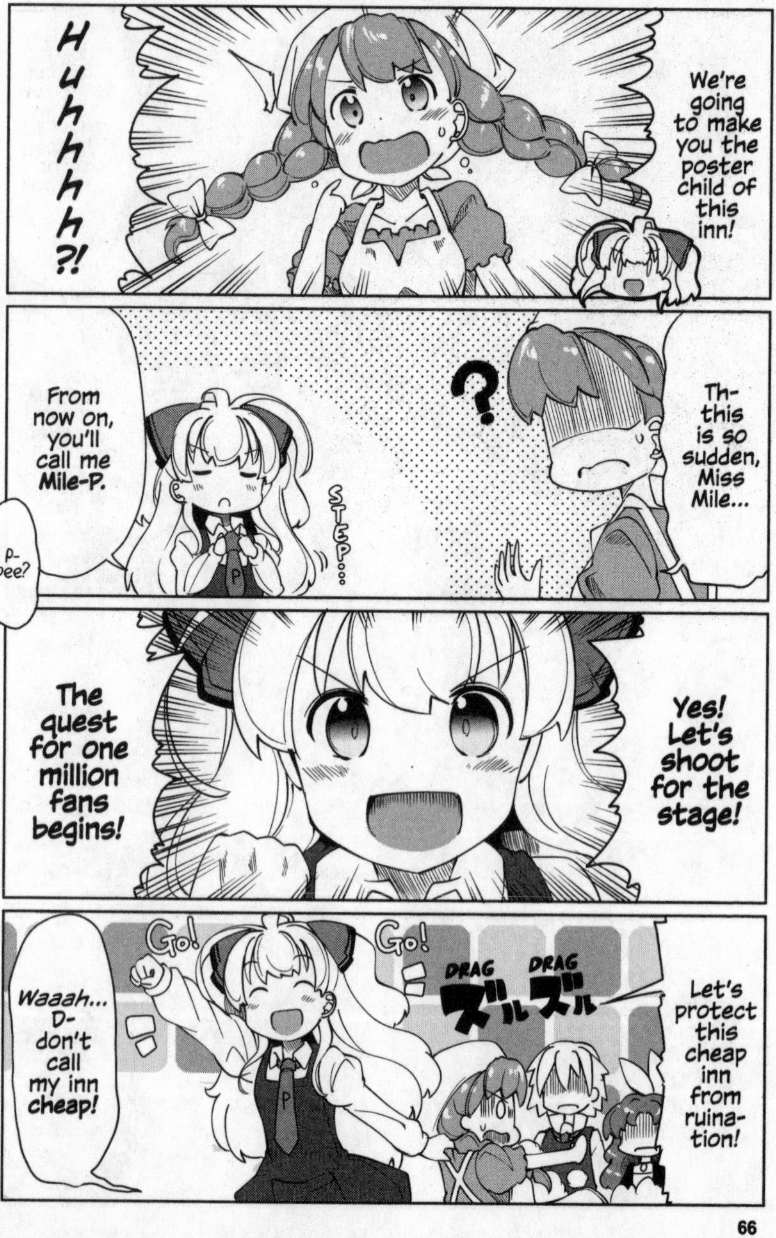
We're going to make you the poster child of this inn!
Huhhhhh?!
Th-this is so sudden, Miss Mile...
?
From now on, you'll call me Mile-P.
STEP...
P-pee?
Yes! Let's shoot for the stage!
The quest for one million fans begins!
Let's protect this cheap inn from ruination!
DRAG DRAG
ズルズル
Go! Go!
Waaah... D-don't call my inn cheap!

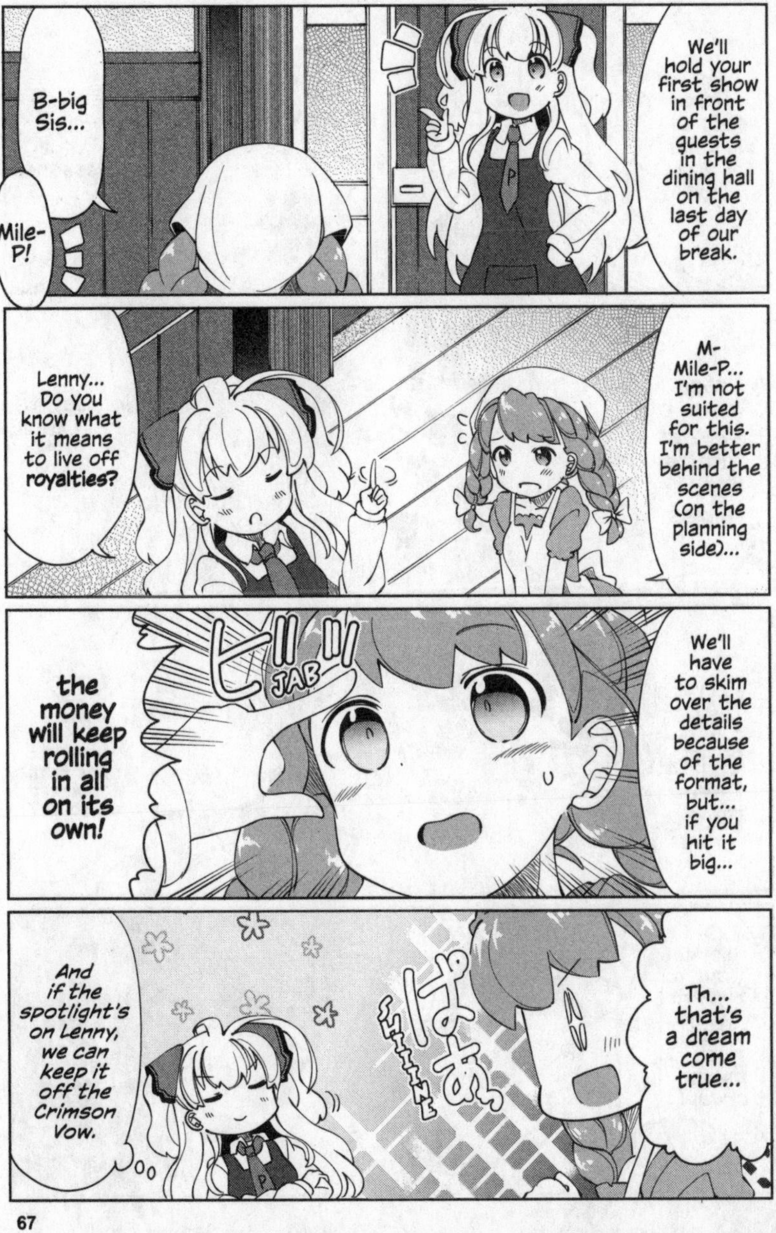
We'll hold your first show in front of the guests in the dining hall on the last day of our break.
B-big Sis...
Mile-P!
M-Mile-P... I'm not suited for this. I'm better behind the scenes (on the planning side)...
Lenny... Do you know what it means to live off **royalties?**
We'll have to skim over the details because of the format, but... if you hit it big...
ビシッ
JAB
the money will keep rolling in all on its own!
Th... that's a dream come true...
ぱぁ
SHIIIINE
And if the spotlight's on Lenny, we can keep it off the Crimson Vow.

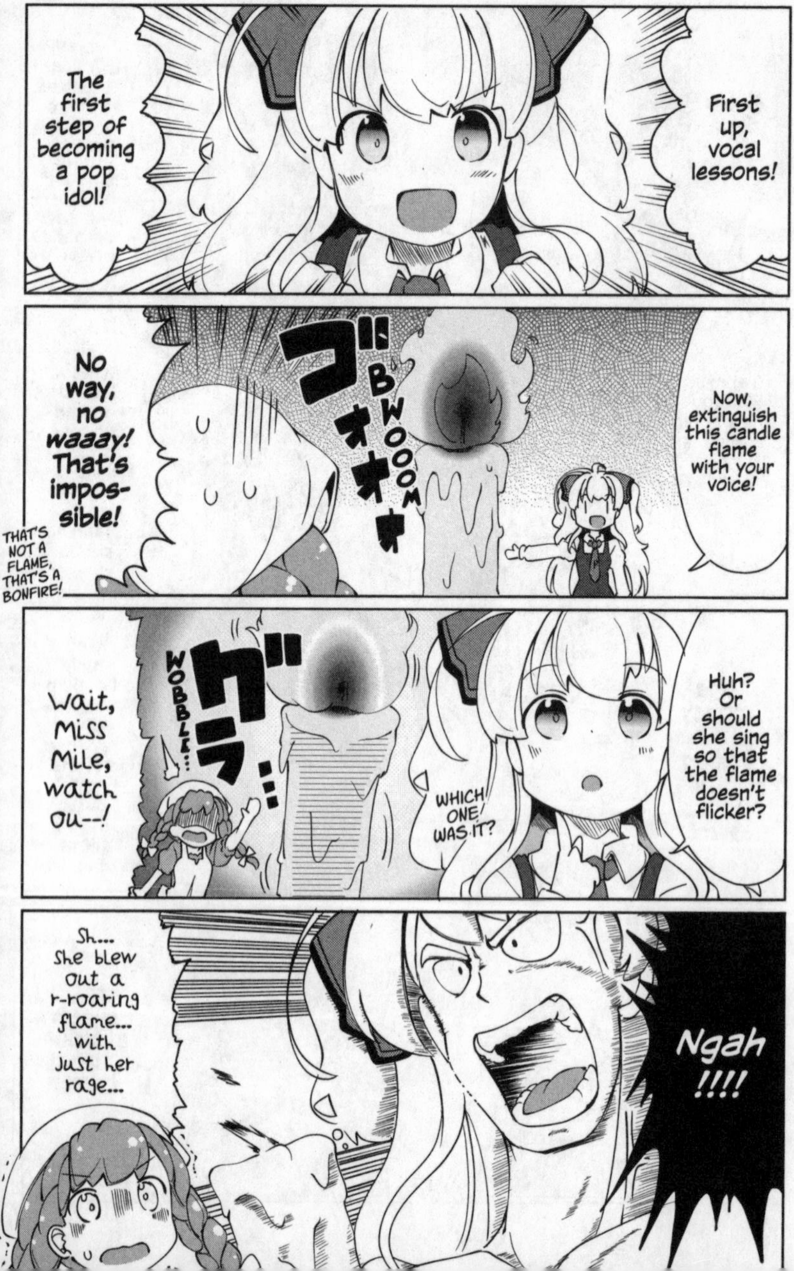
First up, vocal lessons!
The first step of becoming a pop idol!
Now, extinguish this candle flame with your voice!
BWOOOM
No way, no waaay! That's impossible!
THAT'S NOT A FLAME, THAT'S A BONFIRE!
Huh? Or should she sing so that the flame doesn't flicker?
WHICH ONE WAS IT?
WOBBLE...
Wait, Miss Mile, watch ou--!
Ngah!!!!
Sh... She blew out a r-roaring flame... with just her rage...

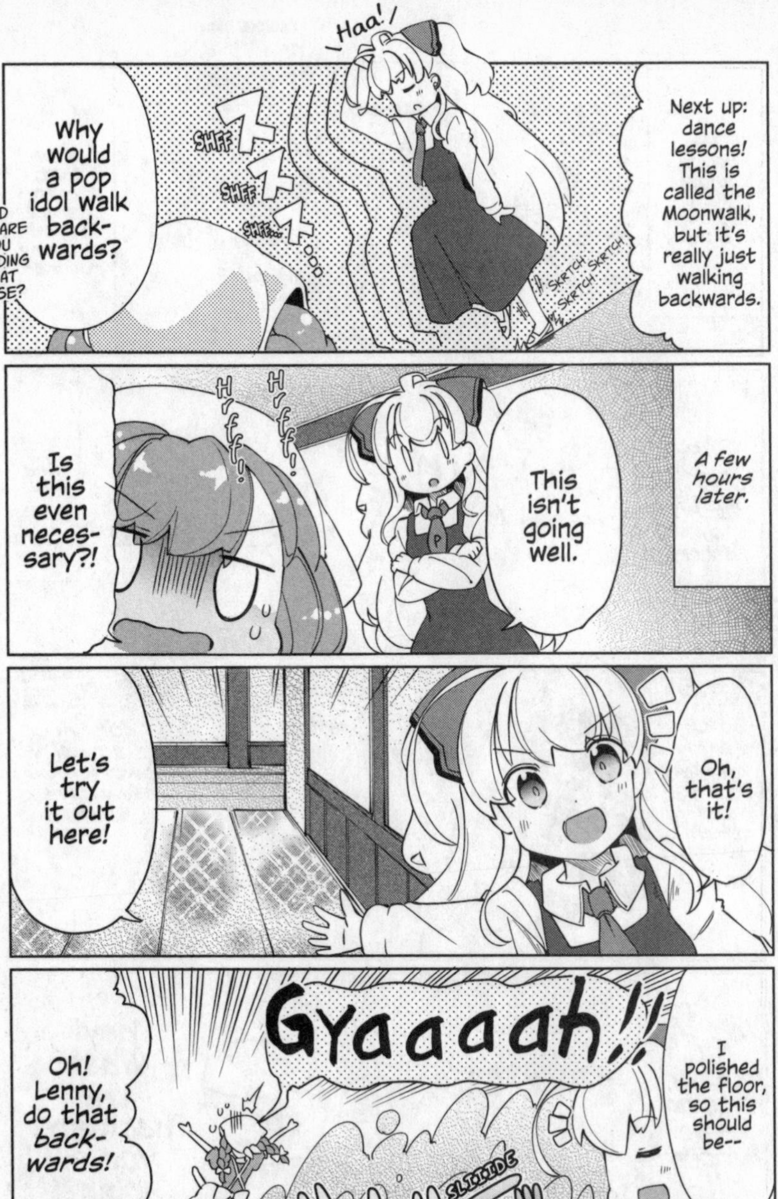
Haa!
Next up: dance lessons! This is called the Moonwalk, but it's really just walking backwards.
SKRTCH SKRTCH SKRTCH
SHFF SHFF SHFF...
Why would a pop idol walk backwards?
AND WHY ARE YOU HOLDING THAT POSE?
A few hours later.
This isn't going well.
Hiff! Hiff!
Is this even neces-sary?!
Oh, that's it!
Let's try it out here!
I polished the floor, so this should be--
Gyaaaah!!
SLIIIDE
Oh! Lenny, do that back-wards!

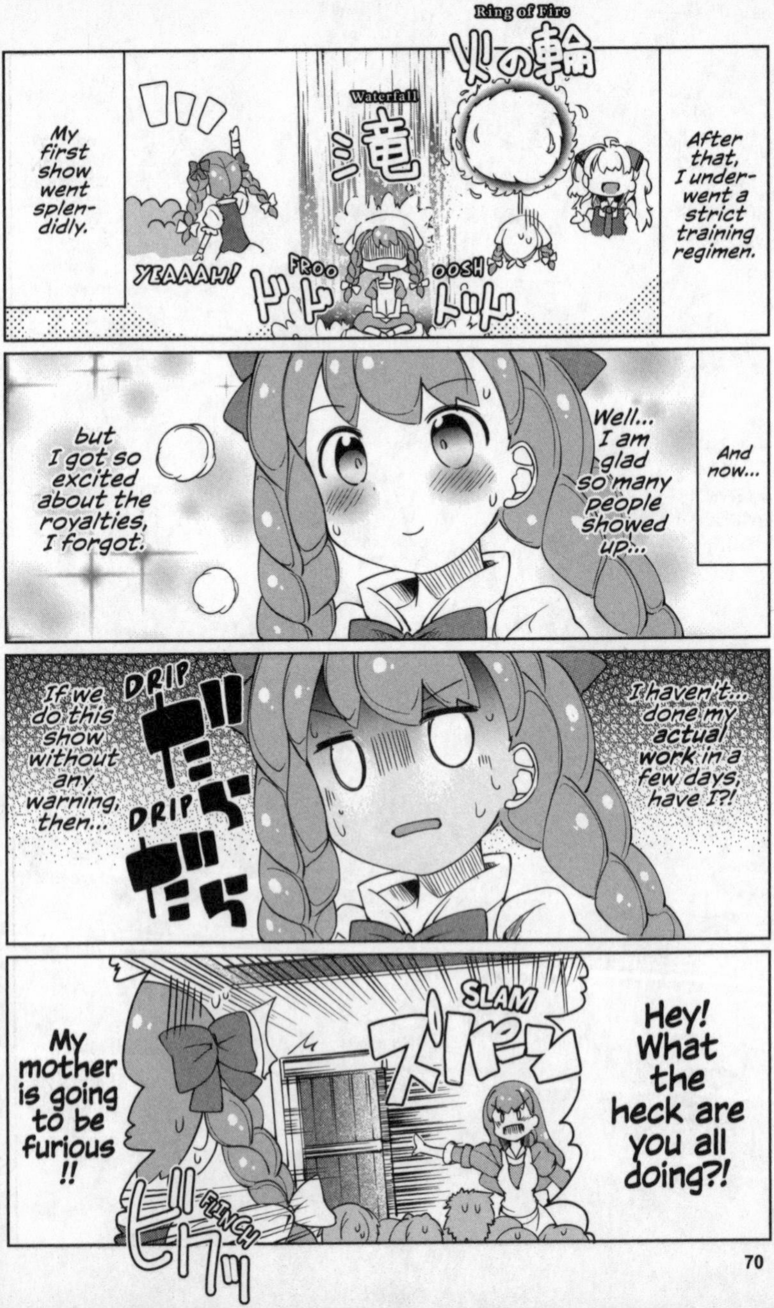
After that, I underwent a strict training regimen.
Ring of Fire
火の輪
Waterfall
OOSH
FROO
YEAAAH!
My first show went splendidly.
And now...
Well... I am glad so many people showed up...
but I got so excited about the royalties, I forgot.
I haven't... done my actual work in a few days, have I?!
DRIP
DRIP
If we do this show without any warning, then...
Hey! What the heck are you all doing?!
SLAM
My mother is going to be furious!!
FLINCH

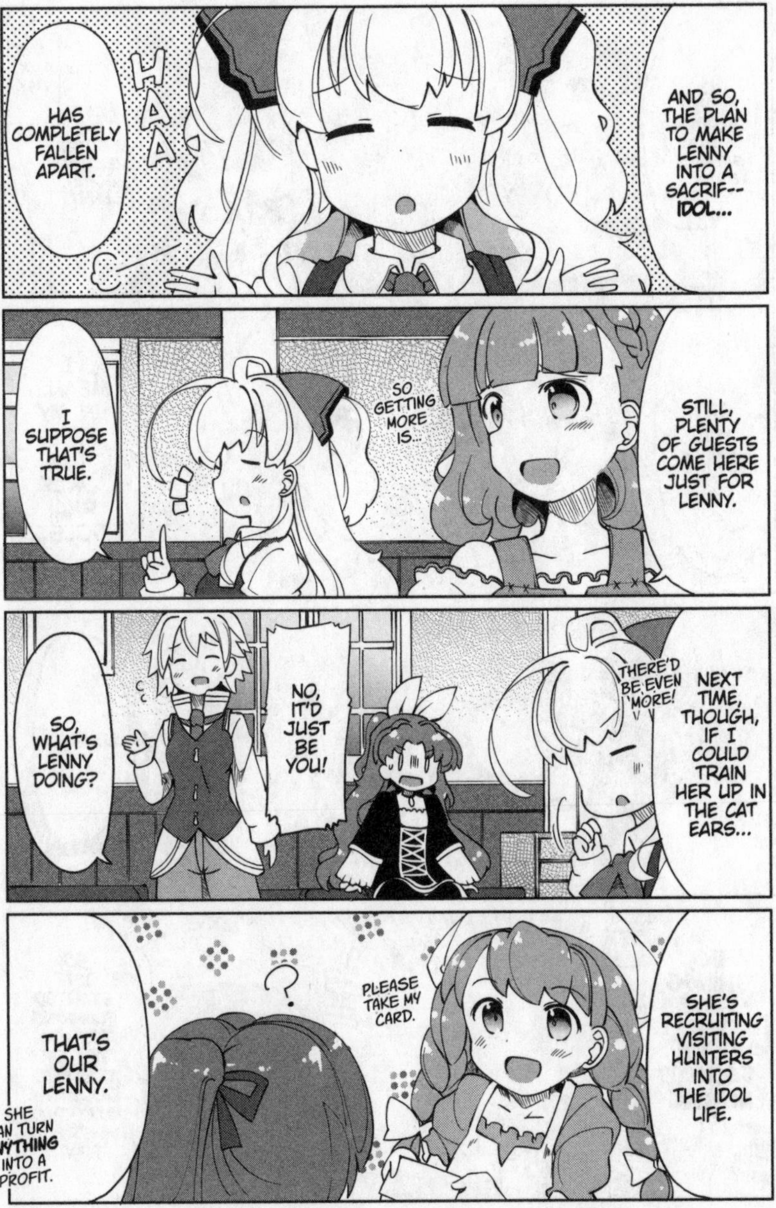
AND SO, THE PLAN TO MAKE LENNY INTO A SACRIF-- IDOL...
HAA
HAS COMPLETELY FALLEN APART.
STILL, PLENTY OF GUESTS COME HERE JUST FOR LENNY.
SO GETTING MORE IS...
I SUPPOSE THAT'S TRUE.
NEXT TIME, THOUGH, IF I COULD TRAIN HER UP IN THE CAT EARS...
THERE'D BE EVEN MORE!
NO, IT'D JUST BE YOU!
SO, WHAT'S LENNY DOING?
SHE'S RECRUITING VISITING HUNTERS INTO THE IDOL LIFE.
PLEASE TAKE MY CARD.
?
THAT'S OUR LENNY.
SHE CAN TURN ANYTHING INTO A PROFIT.

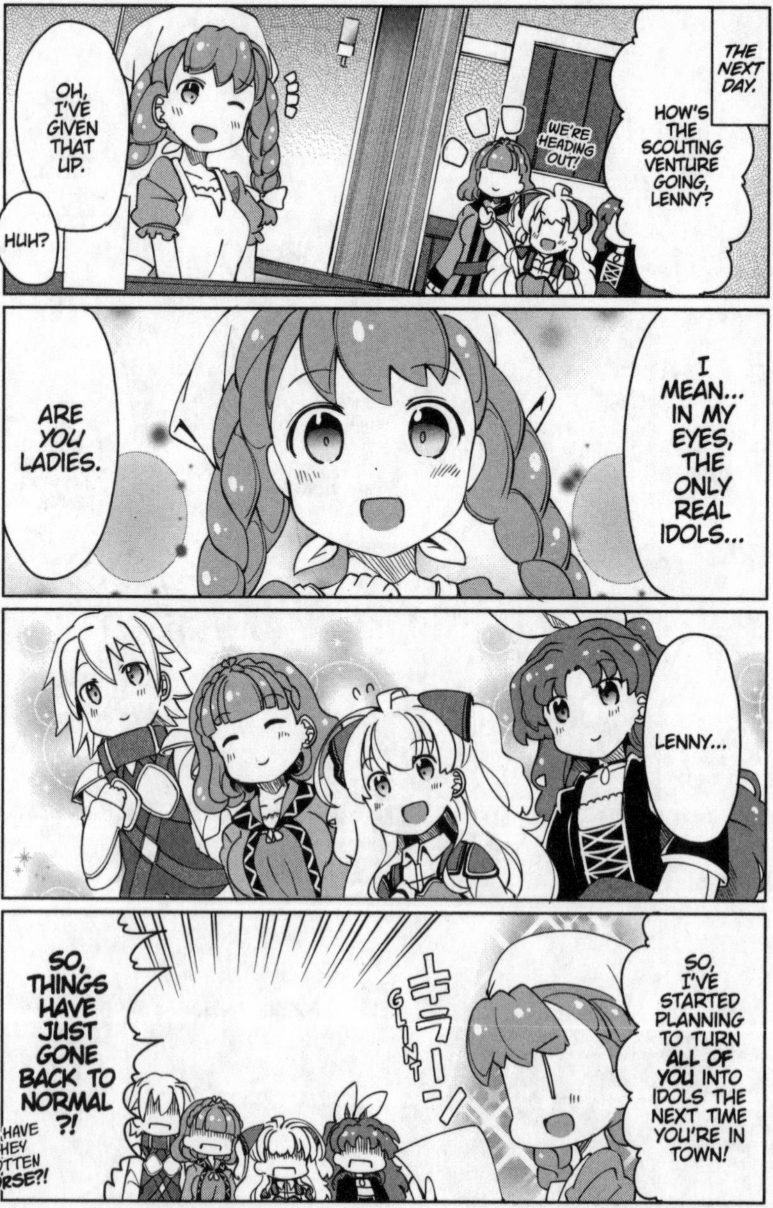
THE NEXT DAY.
HOW'S THE SCOUTING VENTURE GOING, LENNY?
WE'RE HEADING OUT!
OH, I'VE GIVEN THAT UP.
HUH?
I MEAN... IN MY EYES, THE ONLY REAL IDOLS...
ARE YOU LADIES.
LENNY...
SO, I'VE STARTED PLANNING TO TURN ALL OF YOU INTO IDOLS THE NEXT TIME YOU'RE IN TOWN!
キラーン
GLINT
SO, THINGS HAVE JUST GONE BACK TO NORMAL?!
OR, HAVE THEY GOTTEN WORSE?!

Didn't I Say to Make My Abilities Average in the Next Life?!

EVERYDAY MISADVENTURES!

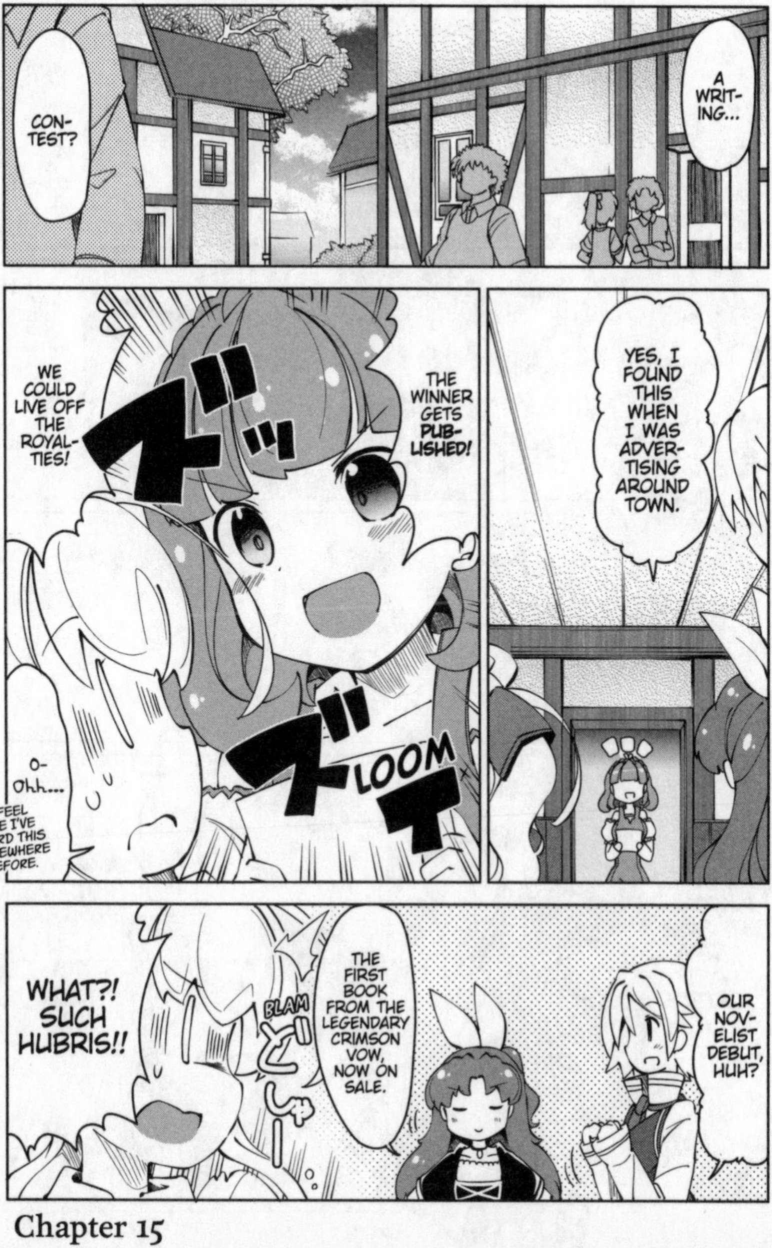
A WRIT-ING...
CON-TEST?
YES, I FOUND THIS WHEN I WAS ADVER-TISING AROUND TOWN.
THE WINNER GETS PUB-LISHED!
WE COULD LIVE OFF THE ROYAL-TIES!
LOOM
O-Ohh...
I FEEL LIKE I'VE HEARD THIS SOMEWHERE BEFORE.
OUR NOV-ELIST DEBUT, HUH?
THE FIRST BOOK FROM THE LEGENDARY CRIMSON VOW, NOW ON SALE.
BLAM
WHAT?! SUCH HUBRIS!!

Chapter 15

※Mile's penname. No one knows this is her.

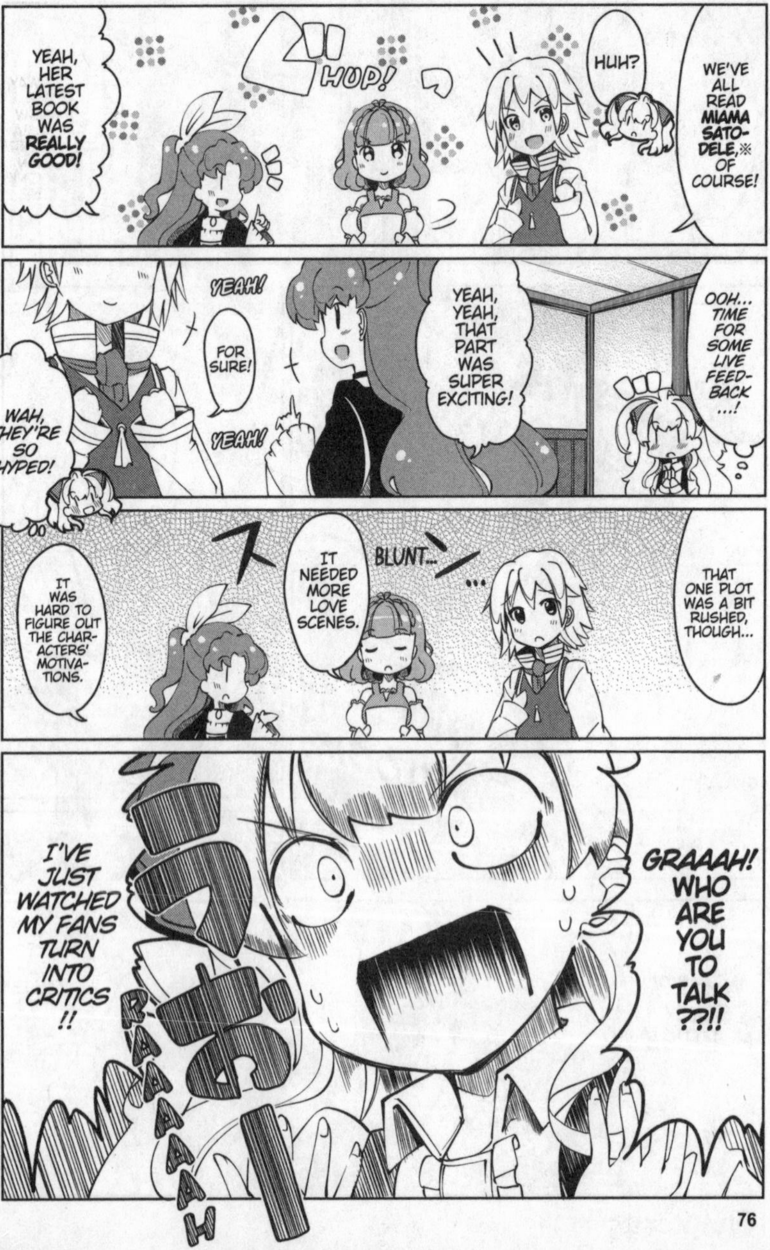
WE'VE ALL READ MIAMA SATODELE,※ OF COURSE!
HUH?
HUP!
YEAH, HER LATEST BOOK WAS REALLY GOOD!
OOH... TIME FOR SOME LIVE FEEDBACK...!
YEAH, YEAH, THAT PART WAS SUPER EXCITING!
YEAH!
FOR SURE!
YEAH!
WAH, THEY'RE SO HYPED!
THAT ONE PLOT WAS A BIT RUSHED, THOUGH...
...
BLUNT...
IT NEEDED MORE LOVE SCENES.
IT WAS HARD TO FIGURE OUT THE CHARACTERS' MOTIVATIONS.
GRAAAH! WHO ARE YOU TO TALK??!!
I'VE JUST WATCHED MY FANS TURN INTO CRITICS!!
RAAAAAAAH

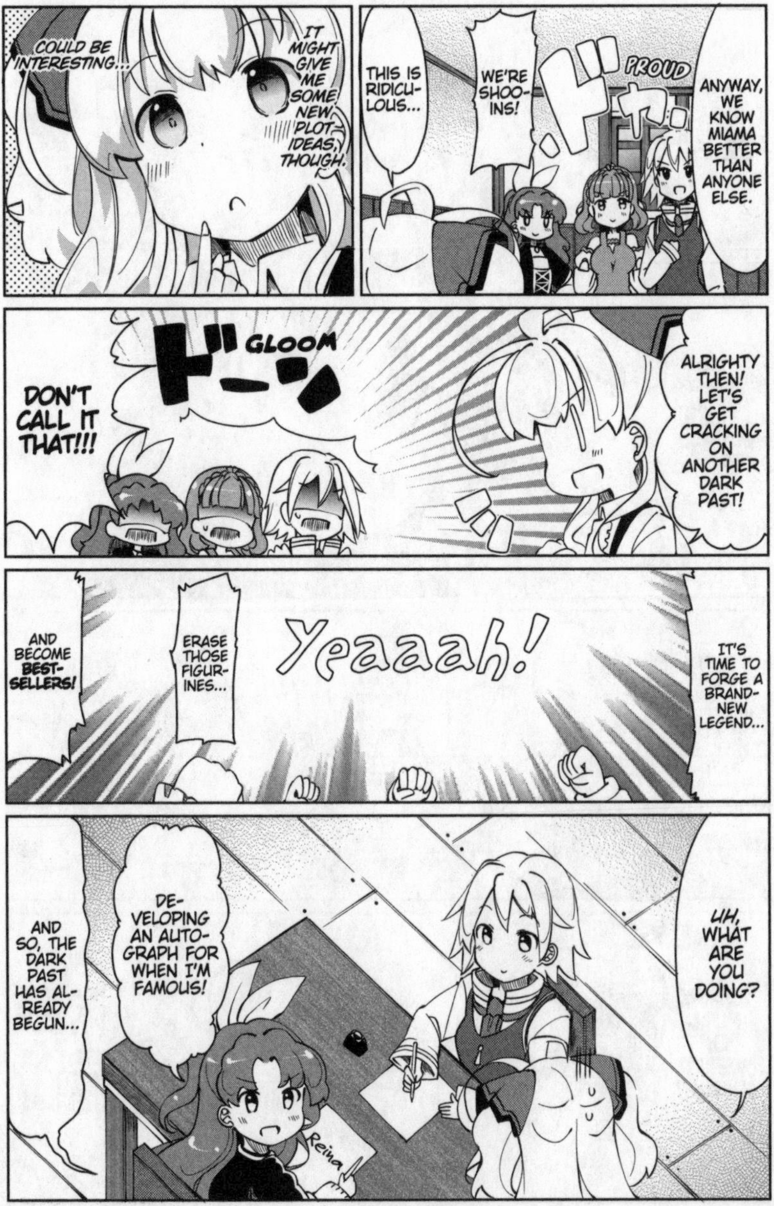
ANYWAY, WE KNOW MIAMA BETTER THAN ANYONE ELSE.
ドヤッ
PROUD
WE'RE SHOOO-INS!
THIS IS RIDICULOUS...
IT MIGHT GIVE ME SOME NEW PLOT IDEAS, THOUGH.
COULD BE INTERESTING...
ALRIGHTY THEN! LET'S GET CRACKING ON ANOTHER DARK PAST!
ドーン
GLOOM
DON'T CALL IT THAT!!!
IT'S TIME TO FORGE A BRAND-NEW LEGEND...
Yeaaah!
ERASE THOSE FIGURINES...
AND BECOME BEST-SELLERS!
UH, WHAT ARE YOU DOING?
DEVELOPING AN AUTOGRAPH FOR WHEN I'M FAMOUS!
Reina
AND SO, THE DARK PAST HAS ALREADY BEGUN...

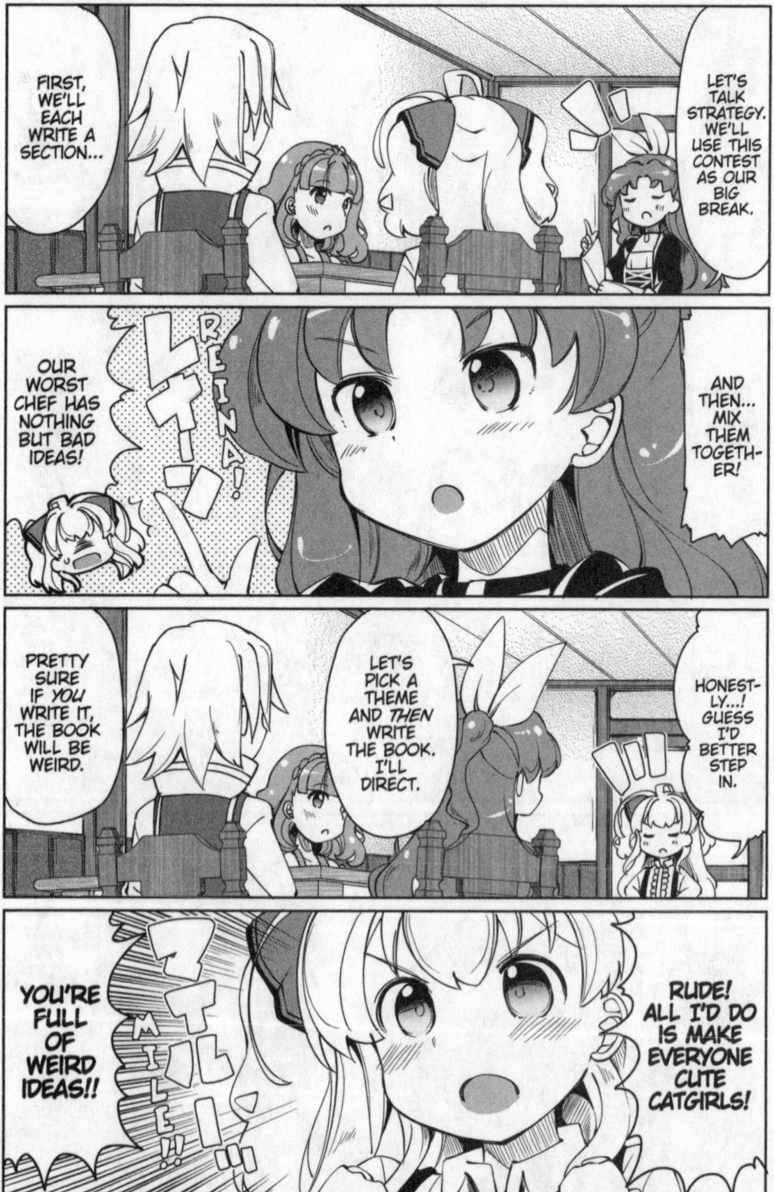
LET'S TALK STRATEGY. WE'LL USE THIS CONTEST AS OUR BIG BREAK.
FIRST, WE'LL EACH WRITE A SECTION...
AND THEN... MIX THEM TOGETH-ER!
REINA!
OUR WORST CHEF HAS NOTHING BUT BAD IDEAS!
HONEST-LY...! GUESS I'D BETTER STEP IN.
LET'S PICK A THEME AND *THEN* WRITE THE BOOK. I'LL DIRECT.
PRETTY SURE IF *YOU* WRITE IT, THE BOOK WILL BE WEIRD.
RUDE! ALL I'D DO IS MAKE EVERYONE CUTE CATGIRLS!
MILE!!
YOU'RE FULL OF WEIRD IDEAS!!

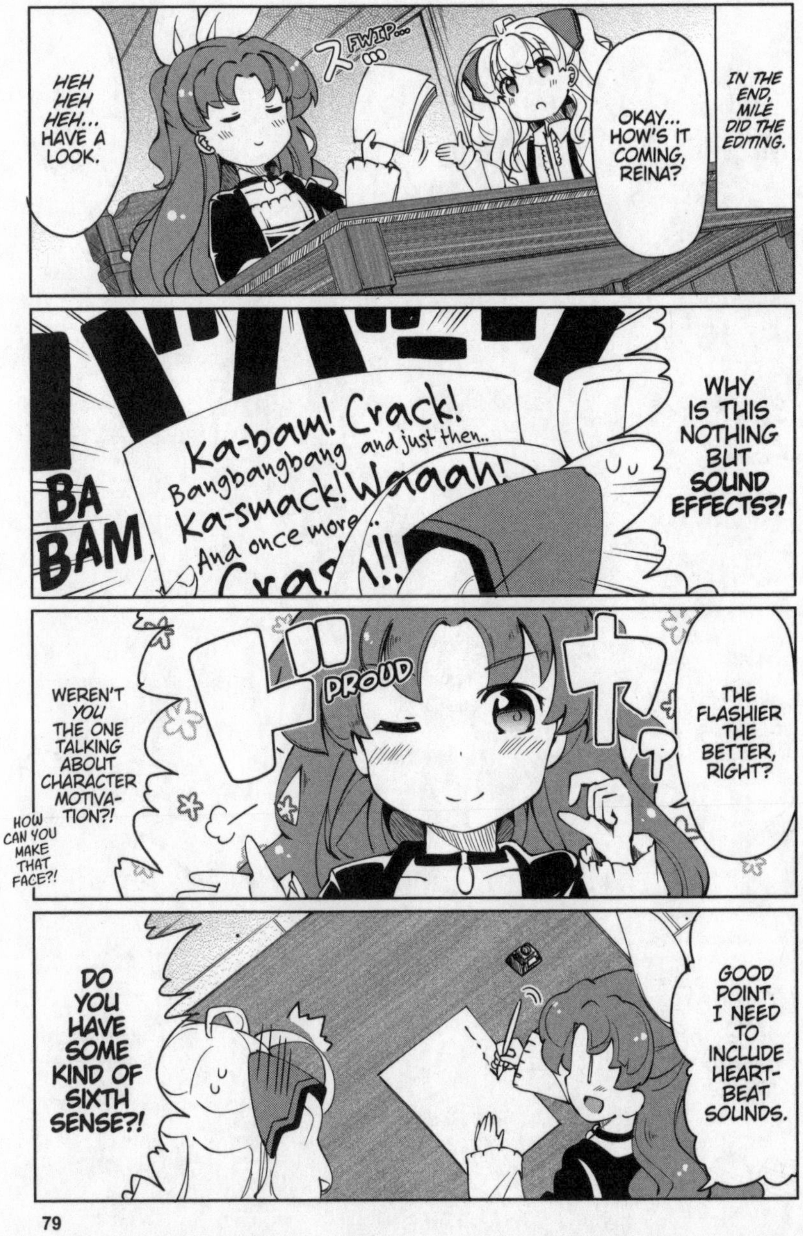
IN THE END, MILE DID THE EDITING.
OKAY... HOW'S IT COMING, REINA?
FWIP...
HEH HEH HEH... HAVE A LOOK.
WHY IS THIS NOTHING BUT SOUND EFFECTS?!
Ka-bam! Crack! Bangbangbang and just then.. Ka-smack! Waaah! And once more..
BA BAM
THE FLASHIER THE BETTER, RIGHT?
PROUD
WEREN'T YOU THE ONE TALKING ABOUT CHARACTER MOTIVATION?!
HOW CAN YOU MAKE THAT FACE?!
GOOD POINT. I NEED TO INCLUDE HEART-BEAT SOUNDS.
DO YOU HAVE SOME KIND OF SIXTH SENSE?!

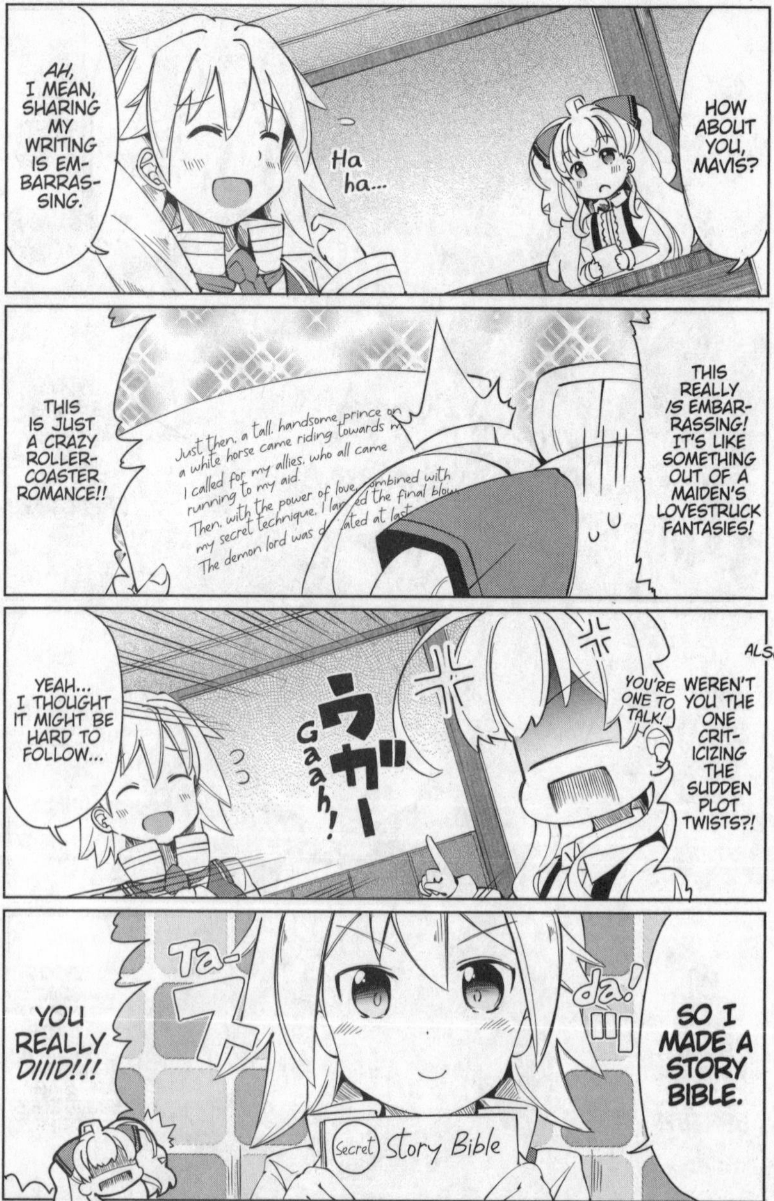
HOW ABOUT YOU, MAVIS?
Ha ha...
AH, I MEAN, SHARING MY WRITING IS EMBARRASSING.
THIS REALLY IS EMBARRASSING! IT'S LIKE SOMETHING OUT OF A MAIDEN'S LOVESTRUCK FANTASIES!
Just then, a tall, handsome prince on
a white horse came riding towards m
I called for my allies, who all came
running to my aid.
Then, with the power of love, combined with
my secret technique, I la ed the final blow
The demon lord was d ated at last
THIS IS JUST A CRAZY ROLLERCOASTER ROMANCE!!
ALSO!
WEREN'T YOU THE ONE CRITICIZING THE SUDDEN PLOT TWISTS?!
YOU'RE ONE TO TALK!
ウガー
Gaah!
YEAH... I THOUGHT IT MIGHT BE HARD TO FOLLOW...
SO I MADE A STORY BIBLE.
Ta-
ス
da!
Secret Story Bible
YOU REALLY DIIIID!!!

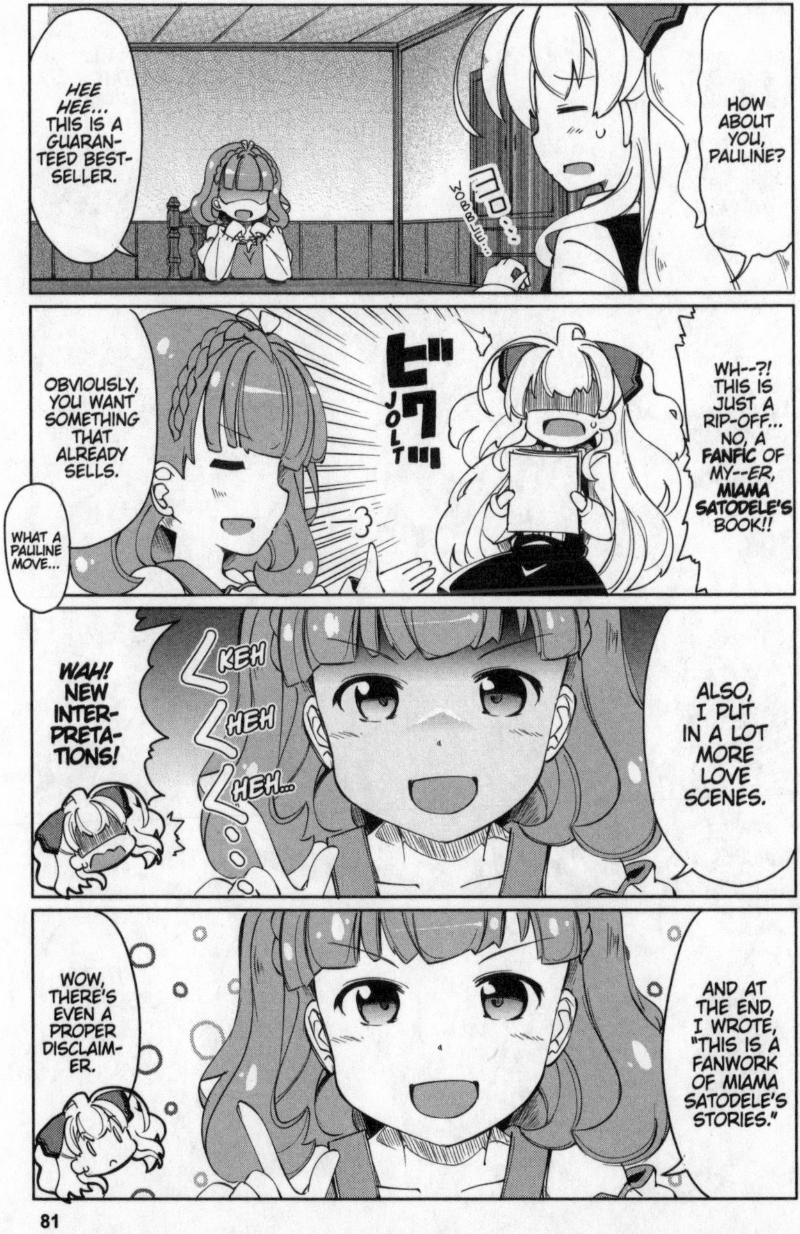

HOW ABOUT YOU, PAULINE?
WOBBLE...
HEE HEE... THIS IS A GUARAN-TEED BEST-SELLER.
WH--?! THIS IS JUST A RIP-OFF... NO, A FANFIC OF MY--ER, MIAMA SATODELE'S BOOK!!
ビク JOLT
OBVIOUSLY, YOU WANT SOMETHING THAT ALREADY SELLS.
WHAT A PAULINE MOVE...
ALSO, I PUT IN A LOT MORE LOVE SCENES.
KEH HEH HEH...
WAH! NEW INTER-PRETA-TIONS!
AND AT THE END, I WROTE, "THIS IS A FANWORK OF MIAMA SATODELE'S STORIES."
WOW, THERE'S EVEN A PROPER DISCLAIM-ER.

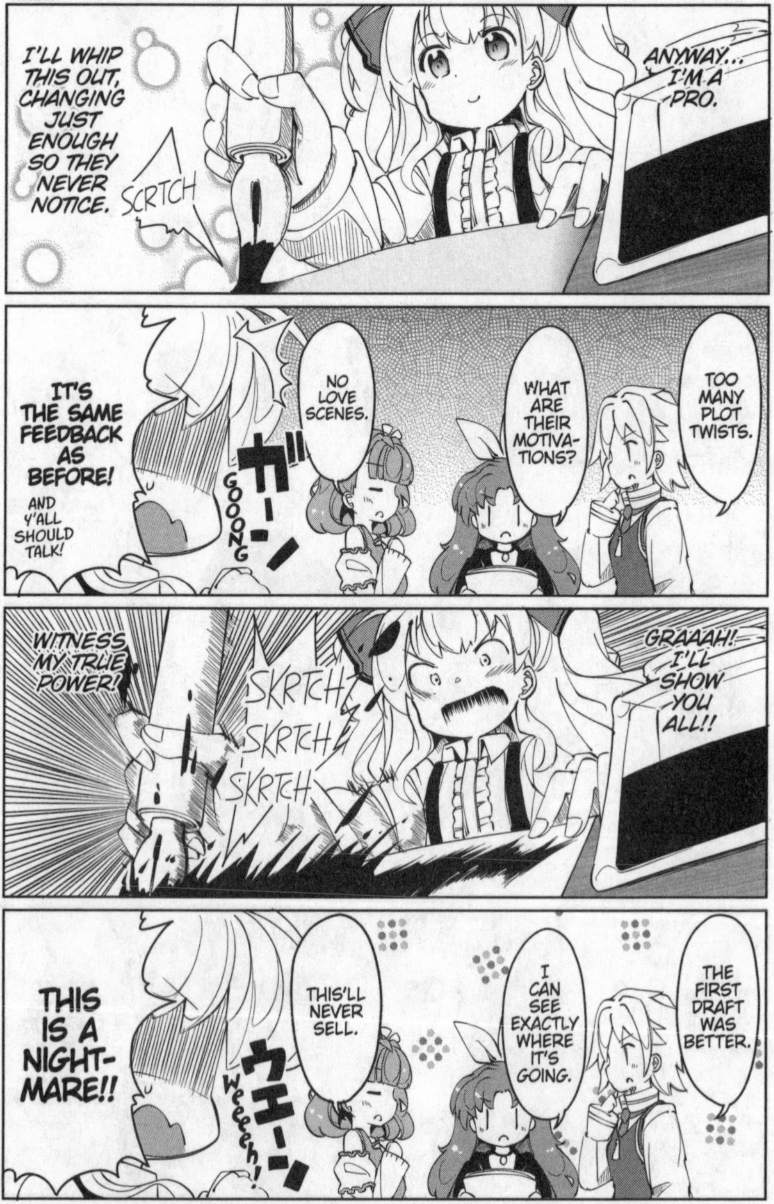
ANYWAY... I'M A PRO.
I'LL WHIP THIS OUT, CHANGING JUST ENOUGH SO THEY NEVER NOTICE.
SCRTCH
TOO MANY PLOT TWISTS.
WHAT ARE THEIR MOTIVA-TIONS?
NO LOVE SCENES.
ガーン
GOOONG
IT'S THE SAME FEEDBACK AS BEFORE!
AND Y'ALL SHOULD TALK!
GRAAAH! I'LL SHOW YOU ALL!!
SKRTCH
SKRTCH
SKRTCH
WITNESS MY TRUE POWER!
THE FIRST DRAFT WAS BETTER.
I CAN SEE EXACTLY WHERE IT'S GOING.
THIS'LL NEVER SELL.
ウエーン
Weeeh!
THIS IS A NIGHT-MARE!!

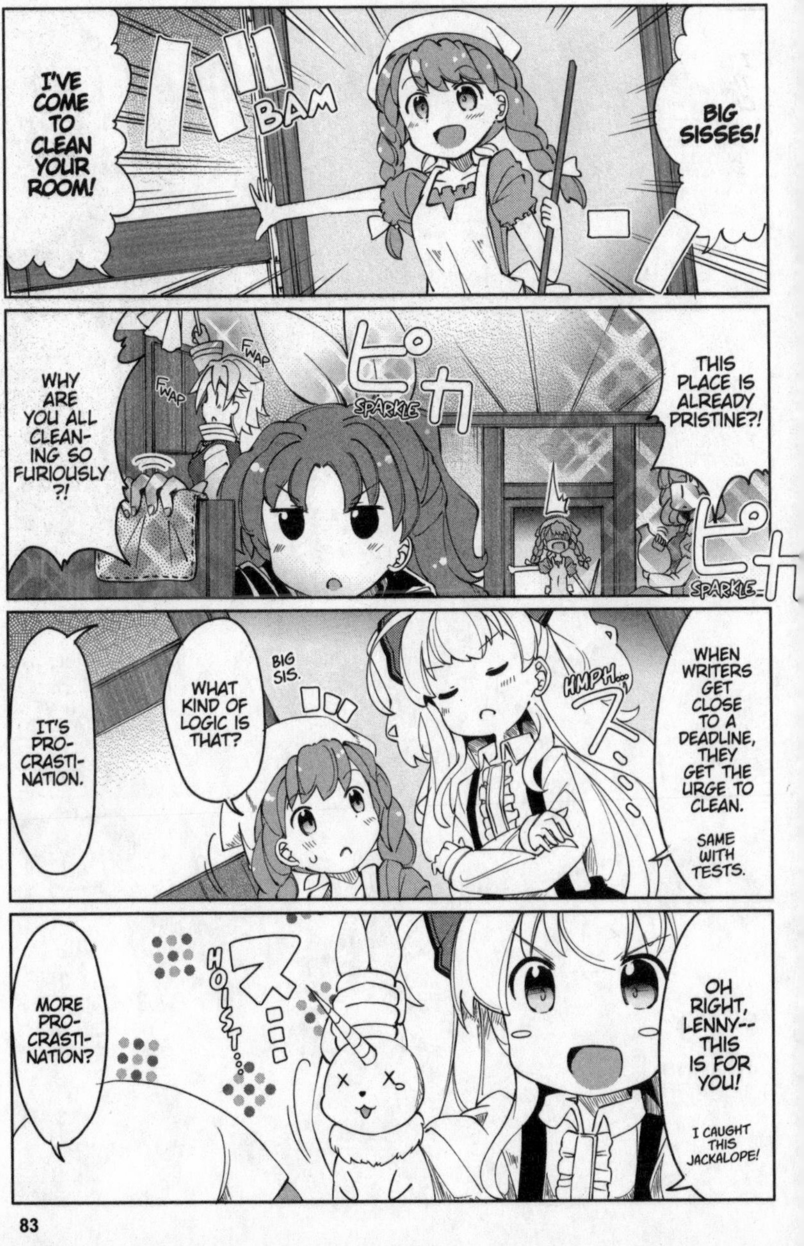
BIG SISSES!
BAM
I'VE COME TO CLEAN YOUR ROOM!
THIS PLACE IS ALREADY PRISTINE?!
SPARKLE
SPARKLE
FWAP
FWAP
WHY ARE YOU ALL CLEANING SO FURIOUSLY?!
WHEN WRITERS GET CLOSE TO A DEADLINE, THEY GET THE URGE TO CLEAN.
SAME WITH TESTS.
HMPH...
BIG SIS.
WHAT KIND OF LOGIC IS THAT?
IT'S PROCRASTINATION.
OH RIGHT, LENNY-- THIS IS FOR YOU!
I CAUGHT THIS JACKALOPE!
HOIST...
MORE PROCRASTINATION?

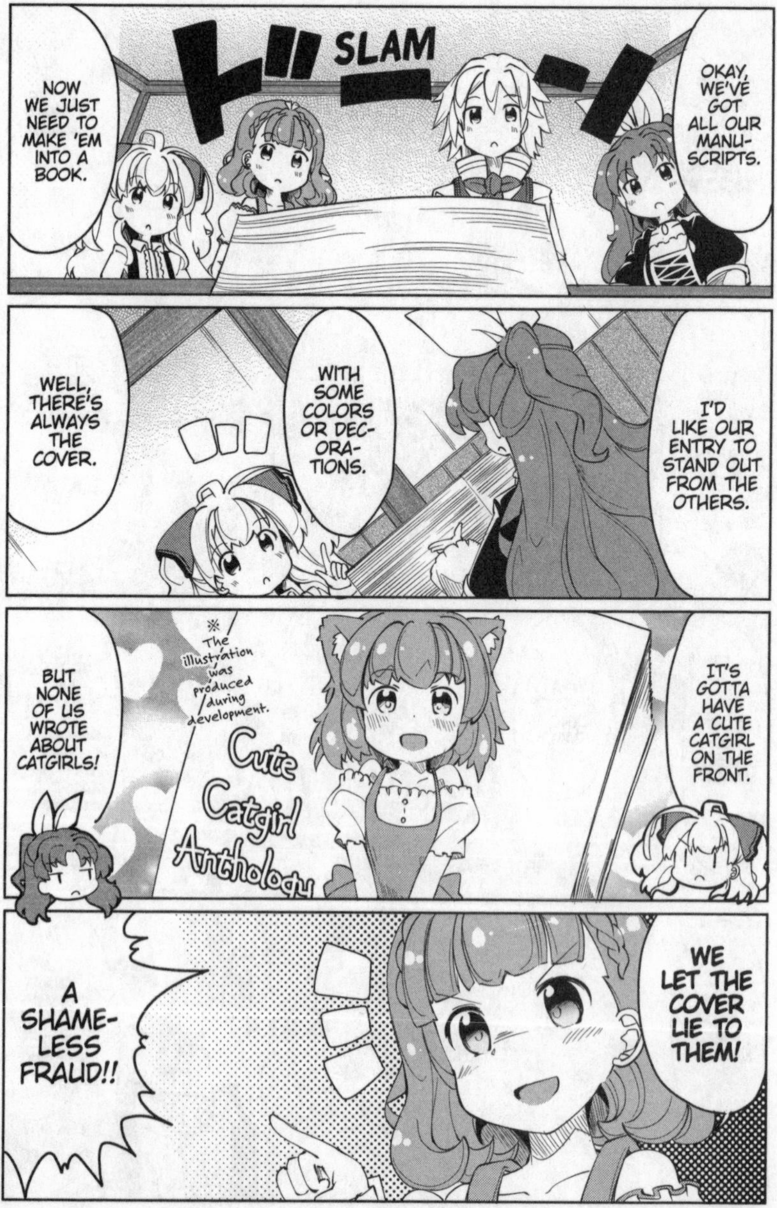
OKAY, WE'VE GOT ALL OUR MANUSCRIPTS.
SLAM
NOW WE JUST NEED TO MAKE 'EM INTO A BOOK.
I'D LIKE OUR ENTRY TO STAND OUT FROM THE OTHERS.
WITH SOME COLORS OR DECORATIONS.
WELL, THERE'S ALWAYS THE COVER.
IT'S GOTTA HAVE A CUTE CATGIRL ON THE FRONT.
※ The illustration was produced during development.
Cute Catgirl Anthology
BUT NONE OF US WROTE ABOUT CATGIRLS!
WE LET THE COVER LIE TO THEM!
A SHAMELESS FRAUD!!

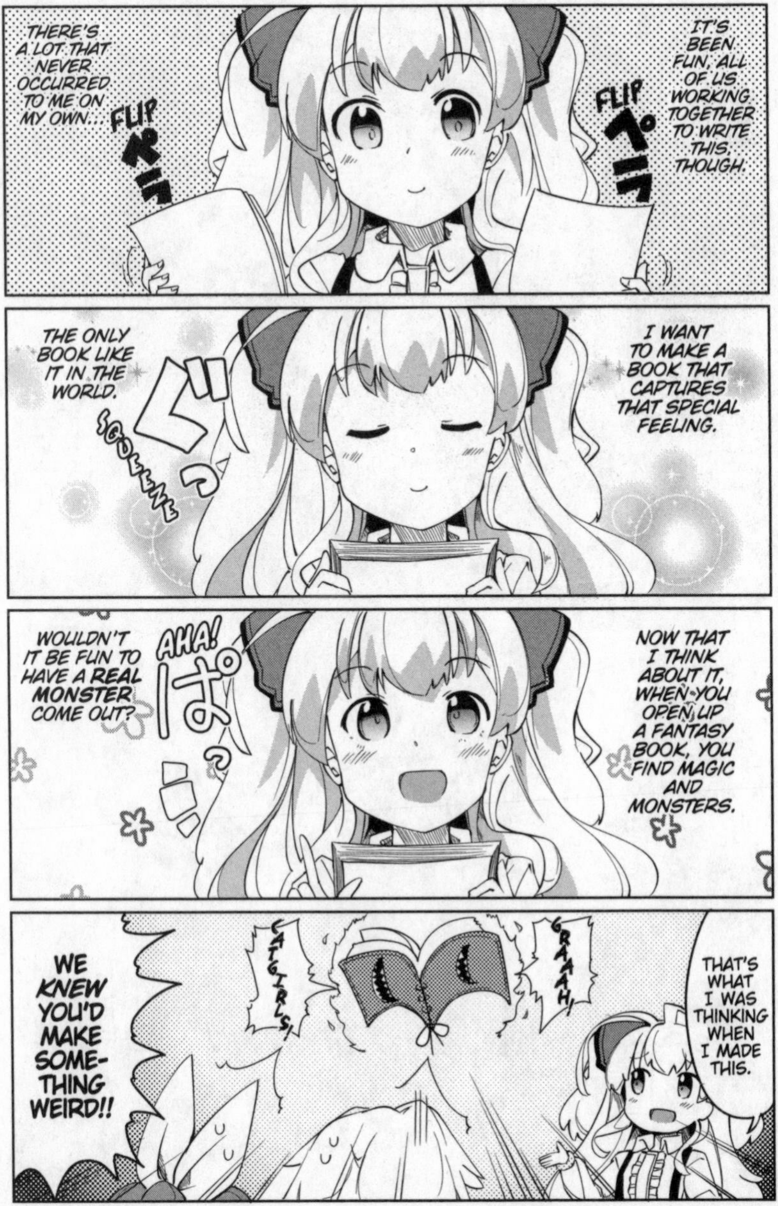
IT'S BEEN FUN, ALL OF US WORKING TOGETHER TO WRITE THIS, THOUGH.
FLIP ペラ
FLIP ペラ
THERE'S A LOT THAT NEVER OCCURRED TO ME ON MY OWN...
I WANT TO MAKE A BOOK THAT CAPTURES THAT SPECIAL FEELING.
ぐっ SQUEEEZE
THE ONLY BOOK LIKE IT IN THE WORLD.
NOW THAT I THINK ABOUT IT, WHEN YOU OPEN UP A FANTASY BOOK, YOU FIND MAGIC AND MONSTERS.
AHA! ぱっ
WOULDN'T IT BE FUN TO HAVE A REAL MONSTER COME OUT?
THAT'S WHAT I WAS THINKING WHEN I MADE THIS.
GRAAAH!
CATGIRLS!
WE KNEW YOU'D MAKE SOME-THING WEIRD!!

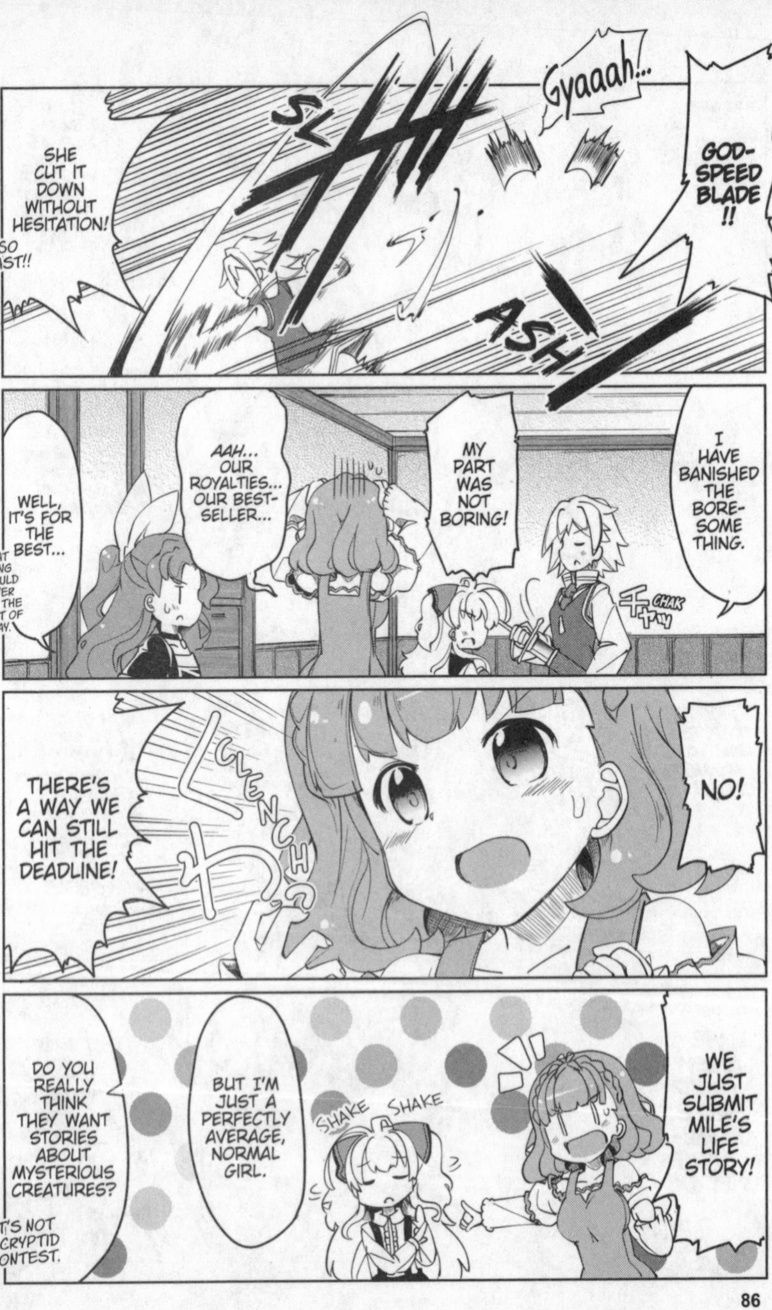
GOD-SPEED BLADE !!
Gyaaah!...
SLASH
SHE CUT IT DOWN WITHOUT HESITATION!
SO FAST!!
I HAVE BANISHED THE BORE-SOME THING.
CHAK
MY PART WAS NOT BORING!
AAH... OUR ROYALTIES... OUR BEST-SELLER...
WELL, IT'S FOR THE BEST...
THAT HING HOULD NEVER EE THE GHT OF DAY.
NO!
THERE'S A WAY WE CAN STILL HIT THE DEADLINE!
CLENCH
WE JUST SUBMIT MILE'S LIFE STORY!
SHAKE SHAKE
BUT I'M JUST A PERFECTLY AVERAGE, NORMAL GIRL.
DO YOU REALLY THINK THEY WANT STORIES ABOUT MYSTERIOUS CREATURES?
IT'S NOT A CRYPTID CONTEST.

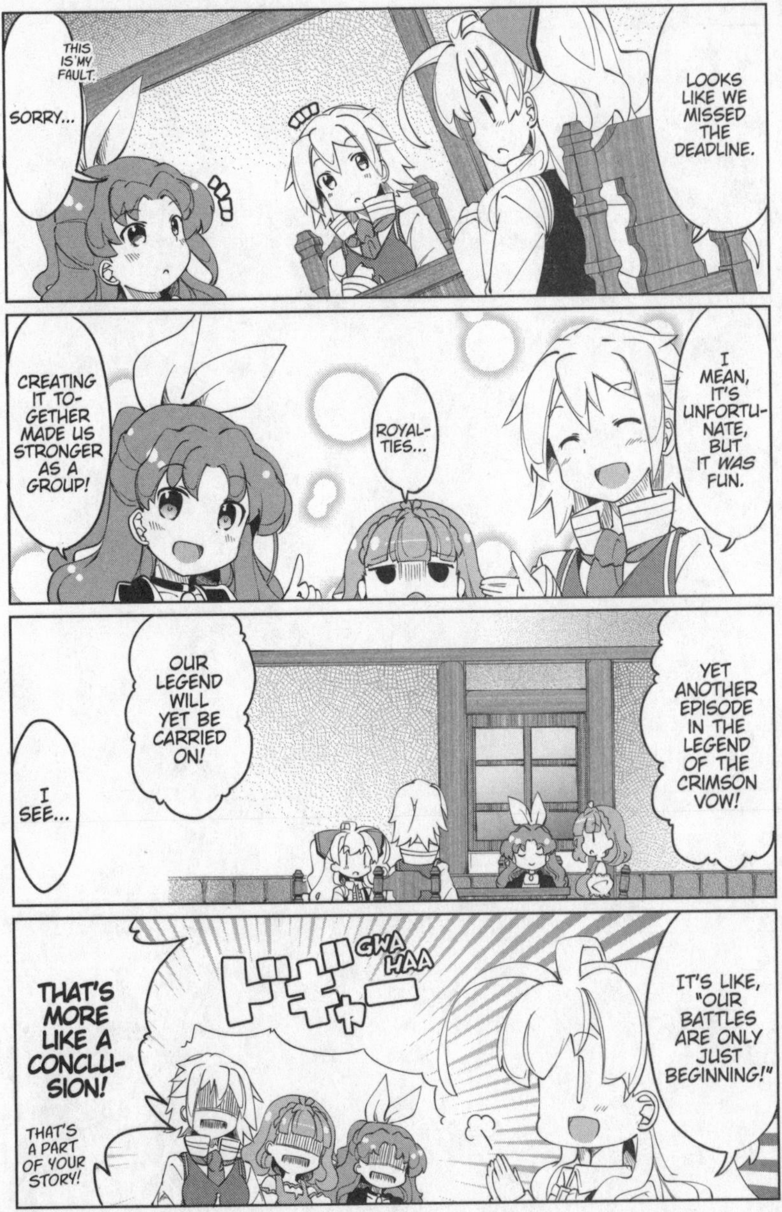
LOOKS LIKE WE MISSED THE DEADLINE.
THIS IS MY FAULT.
SORRY...
I MEAN, IT'S UNFORTUNATE, BUT IT *WAS* FUN.
ROYALTIES...
CREATING IT TOGETHER MADE US STRONGER AS A GROUP!
YET ANOTHER EPISODE IN THE LEGEND OF THE CRIMSON VOW!
OUR LEGEND WILL YET BE CARRIED ON!
I SEE...
IT'S LIKE, "OUR BATTLES ARE ONLY JUST BEGINNING!"
ドギャー
GWA HAA
THAT'S MORE LIKE A CONCLUSION!
THAT'S A PART OF YOUR STORY!

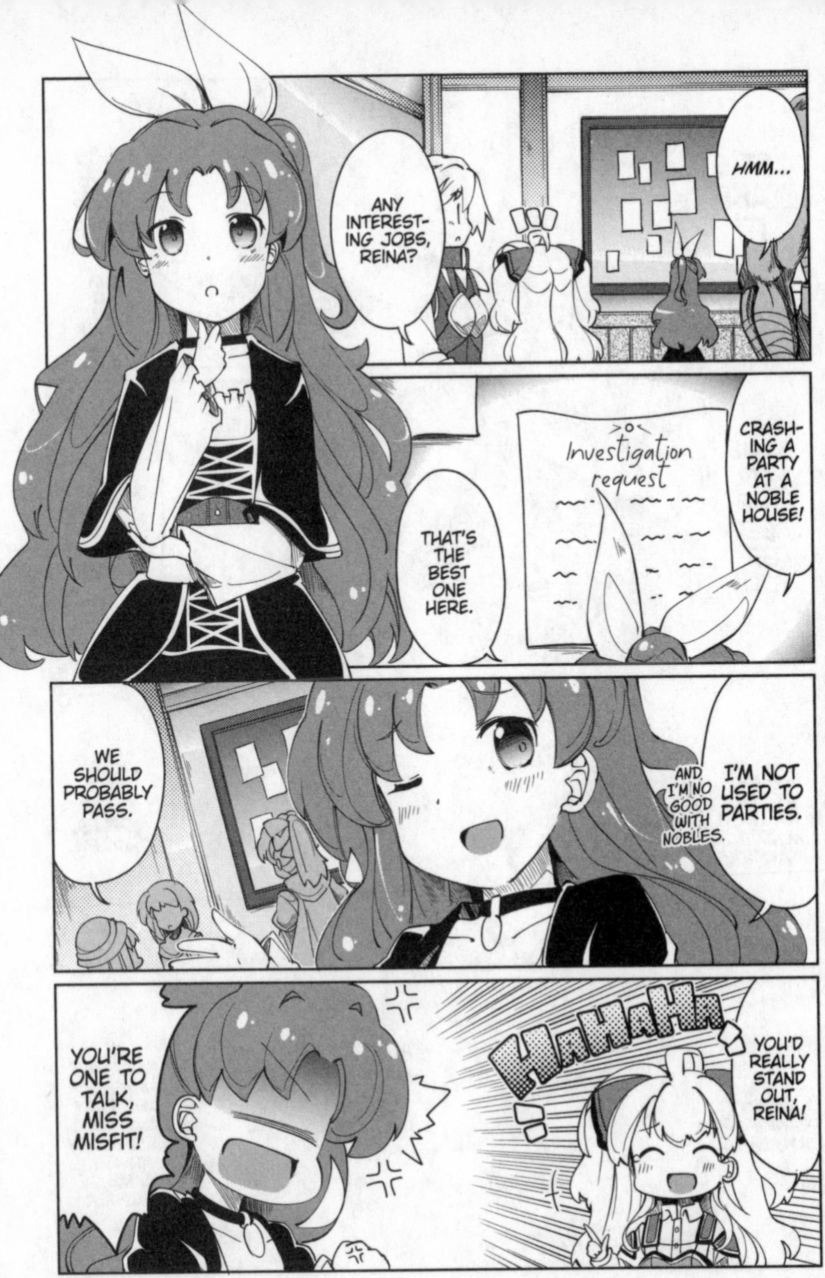
HMM...
ANY INTERESTING JOBS, REINA?
CRASHING A PARTY AT A NOBLE HOUSE!
Investigation request
THAT'S THE BEST ONE HERE.
I'M NOT USED TO PARTIES.
AND I'M NO GOOD WITH NOBLES.
WE SHOULD PROBABLY PASS.
YOU'D REALLY STAND OUT, REINA!
YOU'RE ONE TO TALK, MISS MISFIT!

Chapter 16

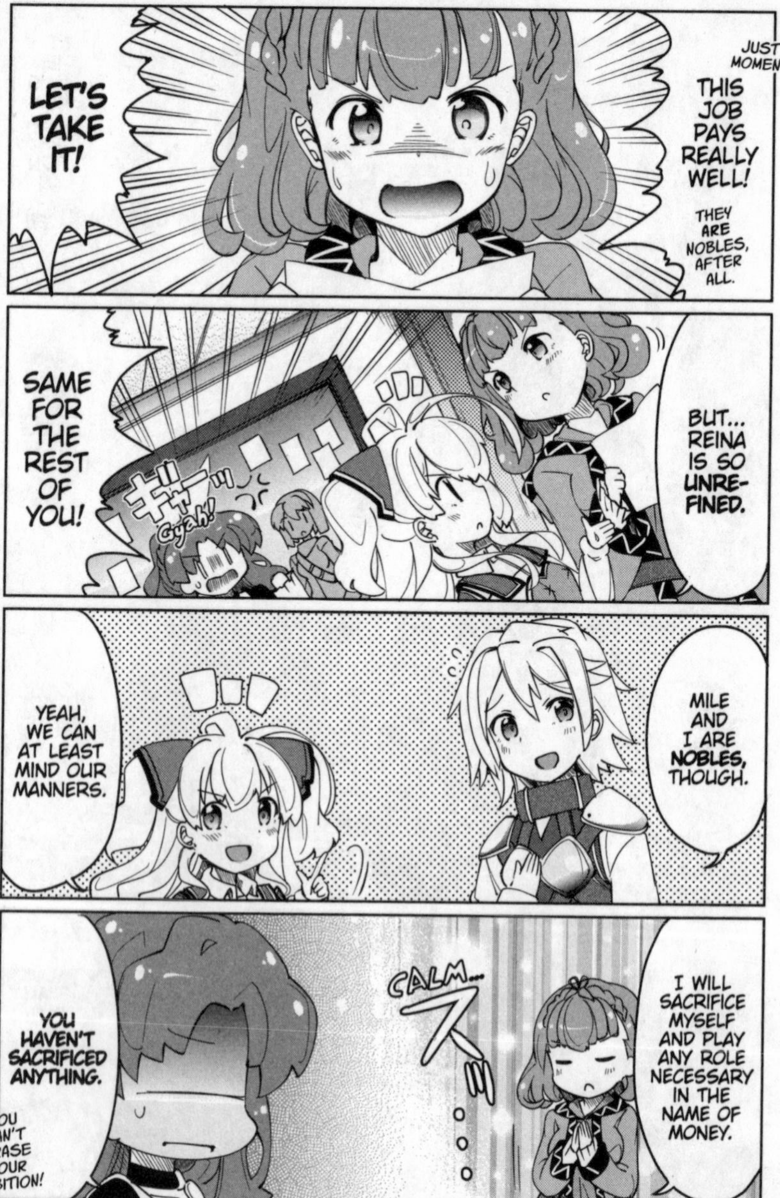
JUST A MOMENT!!
THIS JOB PAYS REALLY WELL!
THEY ARE NOBLES, AFTER ALL.
LET'S TAKE IT!
BUT... REINA IS SO UNREFINED.
ギャーッ
Gyah!
SAME FOR THE REST OF YOU!
MILE AND I ARE NOBLES, THOUGH.
YEAH, WE CAN AT LEAST MIND OUR MANNERS.
I WILL SACRIFICE MYSELF AND PLAY ANY ROLE NECESSARY IN THE NAME OF MONEY.
CALM...
YOU HAVEN'T SACRIFICED ANYTHING.
YOU CAN'T ERASE YOUR MBITION!

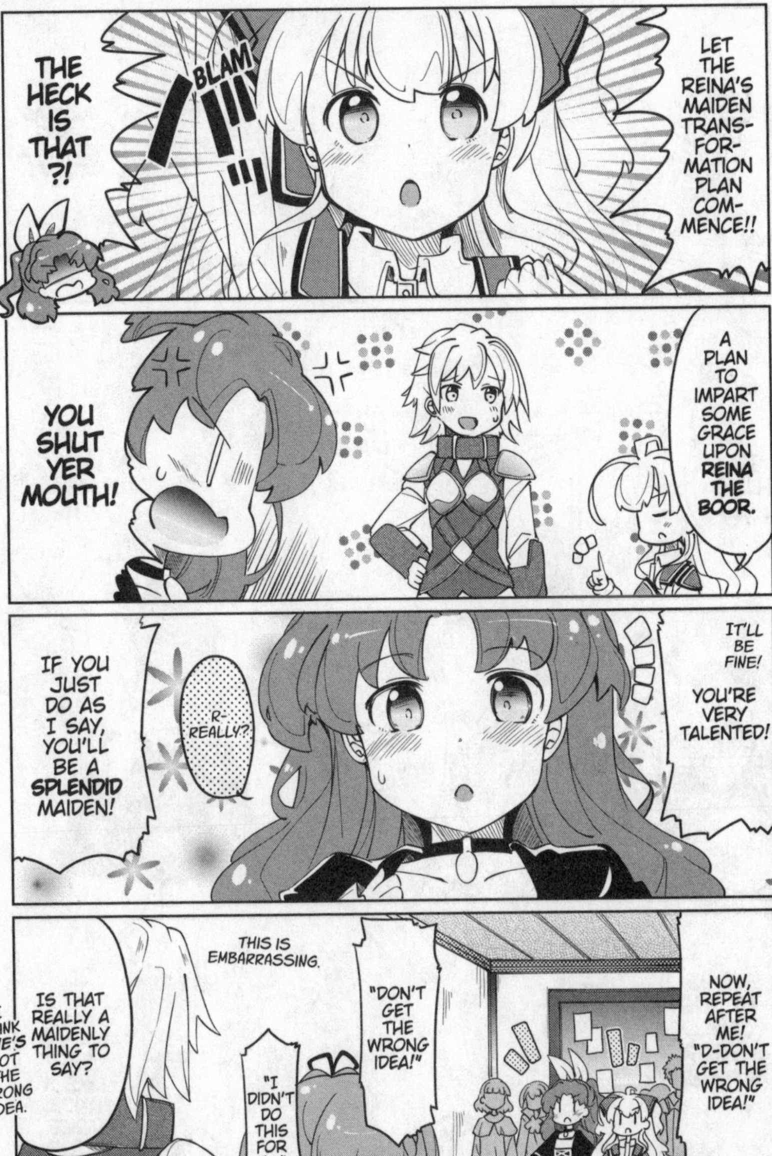
LET THE REINA'S MAIDEN TRANS-FOR-MATION PLAN COM-MENCE!!
BLAM
THE HECK IS THAT ?!
A PLAN TO IMPART SOME GRACE UPON REINA THE BOOR.
YOU SHUT YER MOUTH!
IT'LL BE FINE!
YOU'RE VERY TALENTED!
IF YOU JUST DO AS I SAY, YOU'LL BE A SPLENDID MAIDEN!
R-REALLY?
NOW, REPEAT AFTER ME! "D-DON'T GET THE WRONG IDEA!"
THIS IS EMBARRASSING.
"DON'T GET THE WRONG IDEA!"
"I DIDN'T DO THIS FOR Y--"
IS THAT REALLY A MAIDENLY THING TO SAY?
I THINK SHE'S GOT THE WRONG IDEA.

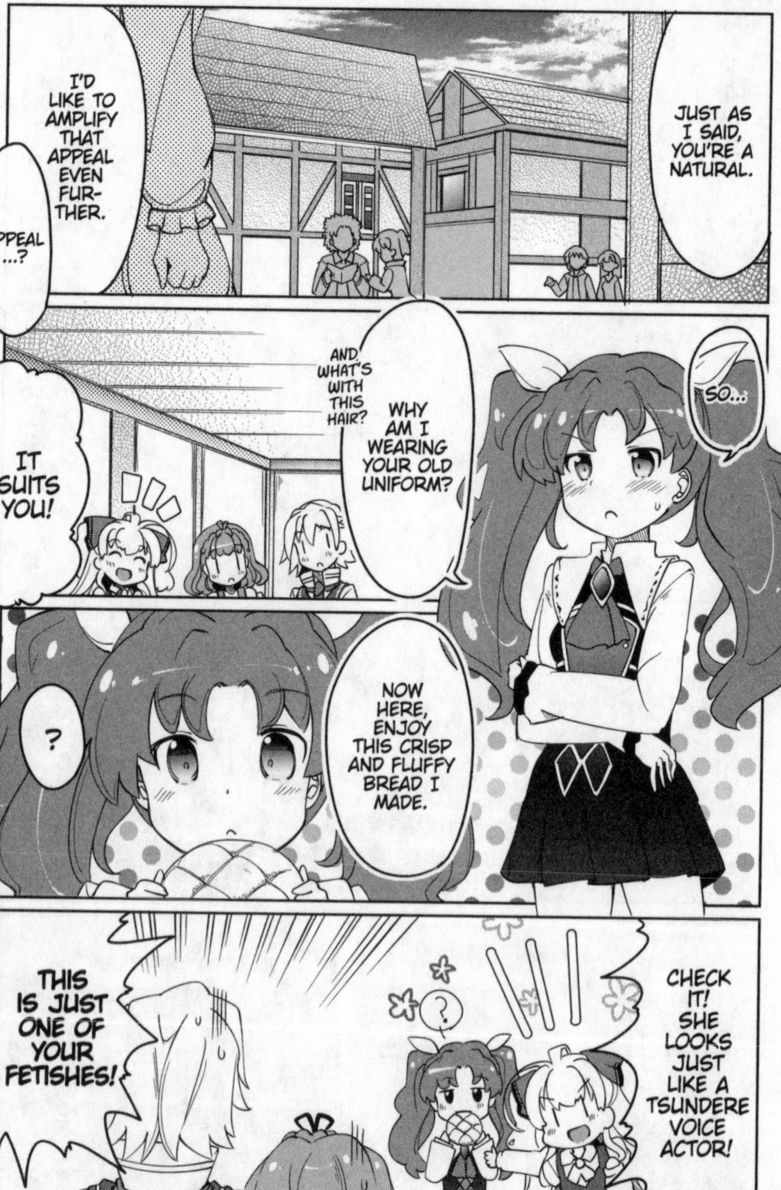
JUST AS I SAID, YOU'RE A NATURAL.
I'D LIKE TO AMPLIFY THAT APPEAL EVEN FUR-THER.
APPEAL ...?
SO...
WHY AM I WEARING YOUR OLD UNIFORM?
AND WHAT'S WITH THIS HAIR?
IT SUITS YOU!
NOW HERE, ENJOY THIS CRISP AND FLUFFY BREAD I MADE.
?
CHECK IT! SHE LOOKS JUST LIKE A TSUNDERE VOICE ACTOR!
?
THIS IS JUST ONE OF YOUR FETISHES!

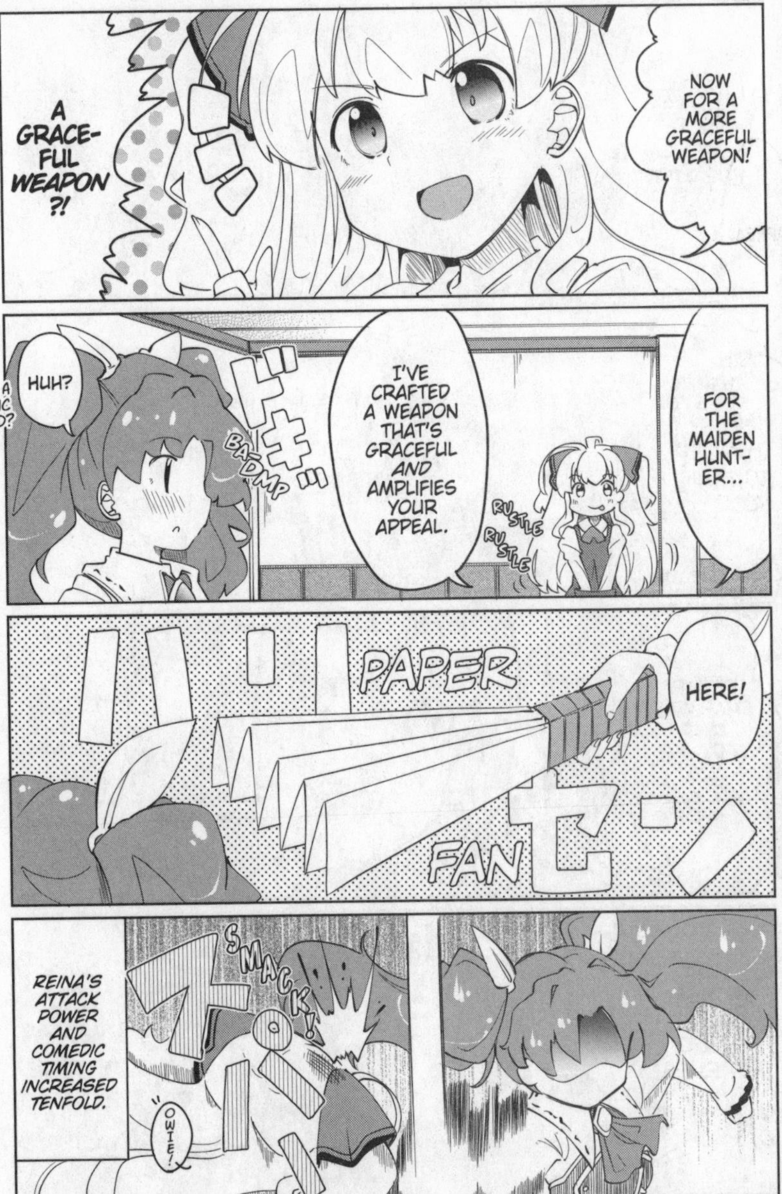
NOW FOR A MORE GRACEFUL WEAPON!
A GRACE-FUL WEAPON ?!
FOR THE MAIDEN HUNT-ER...
I'VE CRAFTED A WEAPON THAT'S GRACEFUL AND AMPLIFIES YOUR APPEAL.
RUSTLE RUSTLE
ドキッ
BA-DMP
HUH?
LIKE A MAGIC WAND?
HERE!
PAPER FAN
SMACK!
REINA'S ATTACK POWER AND COMEDIC TIMING INCREASED TENFOLD.
OWIE!

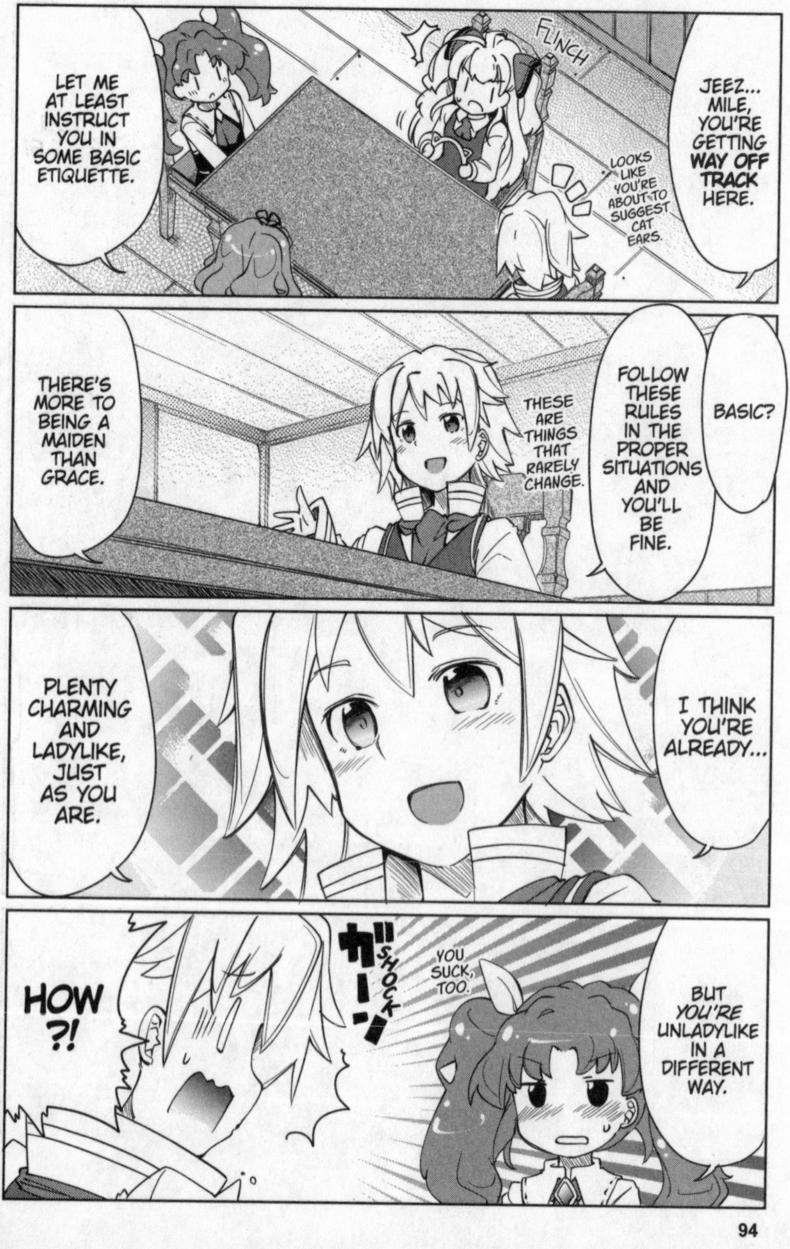
JEEZ... MILE, YOU'RE GETTING **WAY OFF TRACK** HERE.
FLINCH
LOOKS LIKE YOU'RE ABOUT TO SUGGEST CAT EARS.
LET ME AT LEAST INSTRUCT YOU IN SOME BASIC ETIQUETTE.
BASIC?
FOLLOW THESE RULES IN THE PROPER SITUATIONS AND YOU'LL BE FINE.
THESE ARE THINGS THAT RARELY CHANGE.
THERE'S MORE TO BEING A MAIDEN THAN GRACE.
I THINK YOU'RE ALREADY...
PLENTY CHARMING AND LADYLIKE, JUST AS YOU ARE.
BUT *YOU'RE* UNLADYLIKE IN A DIFFERENT WAY.
YOU SUCK, TOO.
ガーン SHOCK
HOW?!

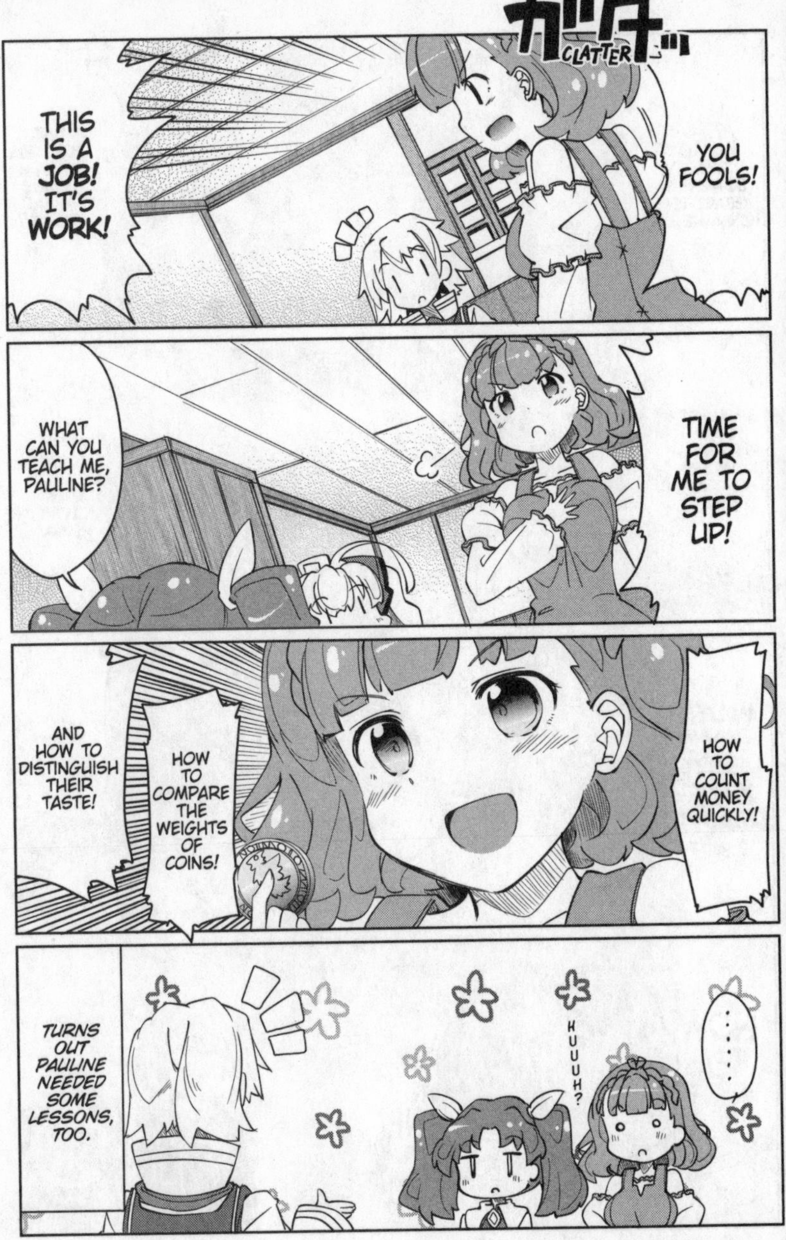
CLATTER
YOU FOOLS!
THIS IS A JOB! IT'S WORK!
TIME FOR ME TO STEP UP!
WHAT CAN YOU TEACH ME, PAULINE?
HOW TO COUNT MONEY QUICKLY!
HOW TO COMPARE THE WEIGHTS OF COINS!
AND HOW TO DISTINGUISH THEIR TASTE!
......
HUUUH?
TURNS OUT PAULINE NEEDED SOME LESSONS, TOO.

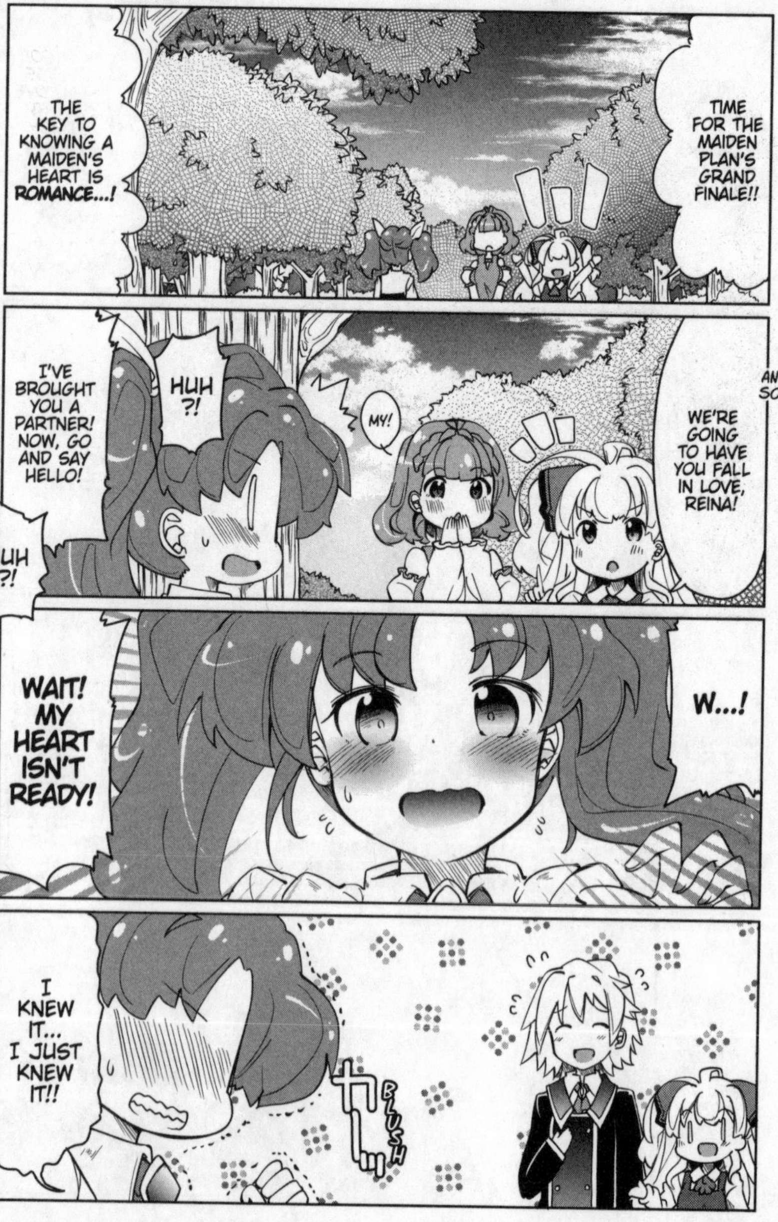
TIME FOR THE MAIDEN PLAN'S GRAND FINALE!!
THE KEY TO KNOWING A MAIDEN'S HEART IS ROMANCE...!
AND SO...
WE'RE GOING TO HAVE YOU FALL IN LOVE, REINA!
MY!
HUH ?!
I'VE BROUGHT YOU A PARTNER! NOW, GO AND SAY HELLO!
HUH ?!
W...!
WAIT! MY HEART ISN'T READY!
BLUSH
I KNEW IT... I JUST KNEW IT!!

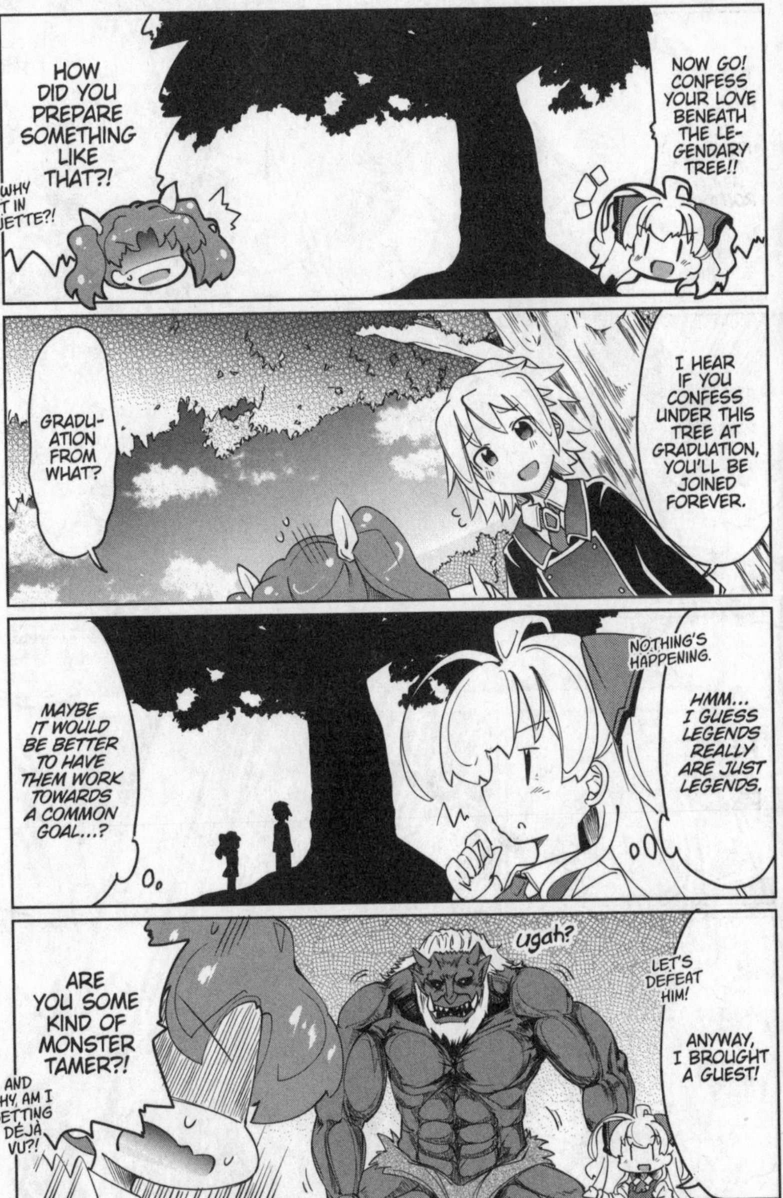
NOW GO! CONFESS YOUR LOVE BENEATH THE LE-GENDARY TREE!!
HOW DID YOU PREPARE SOMETHING LIKE THAT?!
AND WHY IS IT IN SILHOUETTE?!
I HEAR IF YOU CONFESS UNDER THIS TREE AT GRADUATION, YOU'LL BE JOINED FOREVER.
GRADU-ATION FROM WHAT?
NOTHING'S HAPPENING.
HMM... I GUESS LEGENDS REALLY ARE JUST LEGENDS.
MAYBE IT WOULD BE BETTER TO HAVE THEM WORK TOWARDS A COMMON GOAL...?
ANYWAY, I BROUGHT A GUEST!
LET'S DEFEAT HIM!
Ugah?
ARE YOU SOME KIND OF MONSTER TAMER?!
AND WHY, AM I GETTING DÉJÀ VU?!

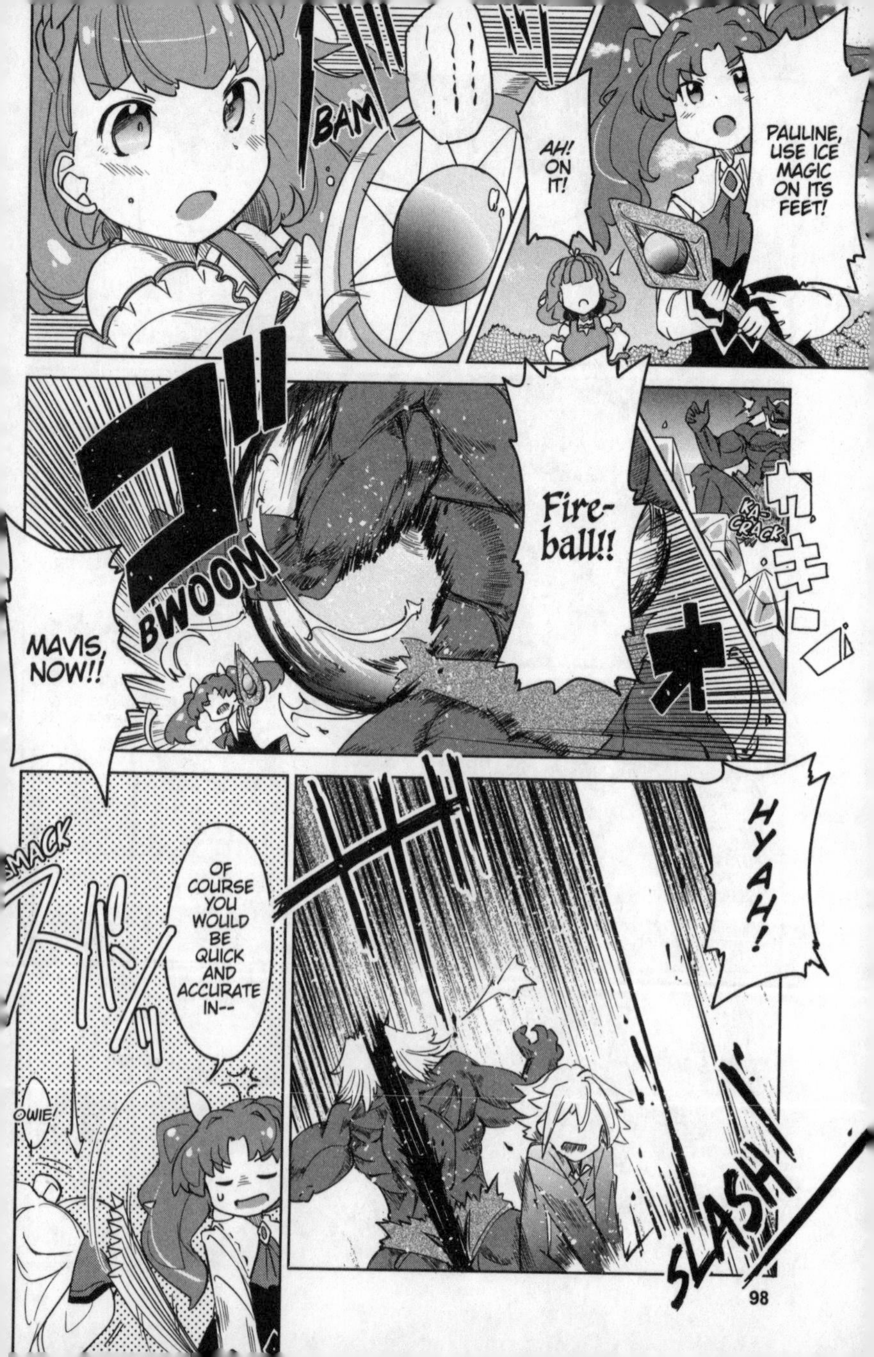
PAULINE, USE ICE MAGIC ON ITS FEET!
AH! ON IT!
BAM
KA-CRACK
Fire-ball!!
BWOOM
MAVIS, NOW!!
HYAH!
SLASH
OF COURSE YOU WOULD BE QUICK AND ACCURATE IN--
SMACK
OWIE!

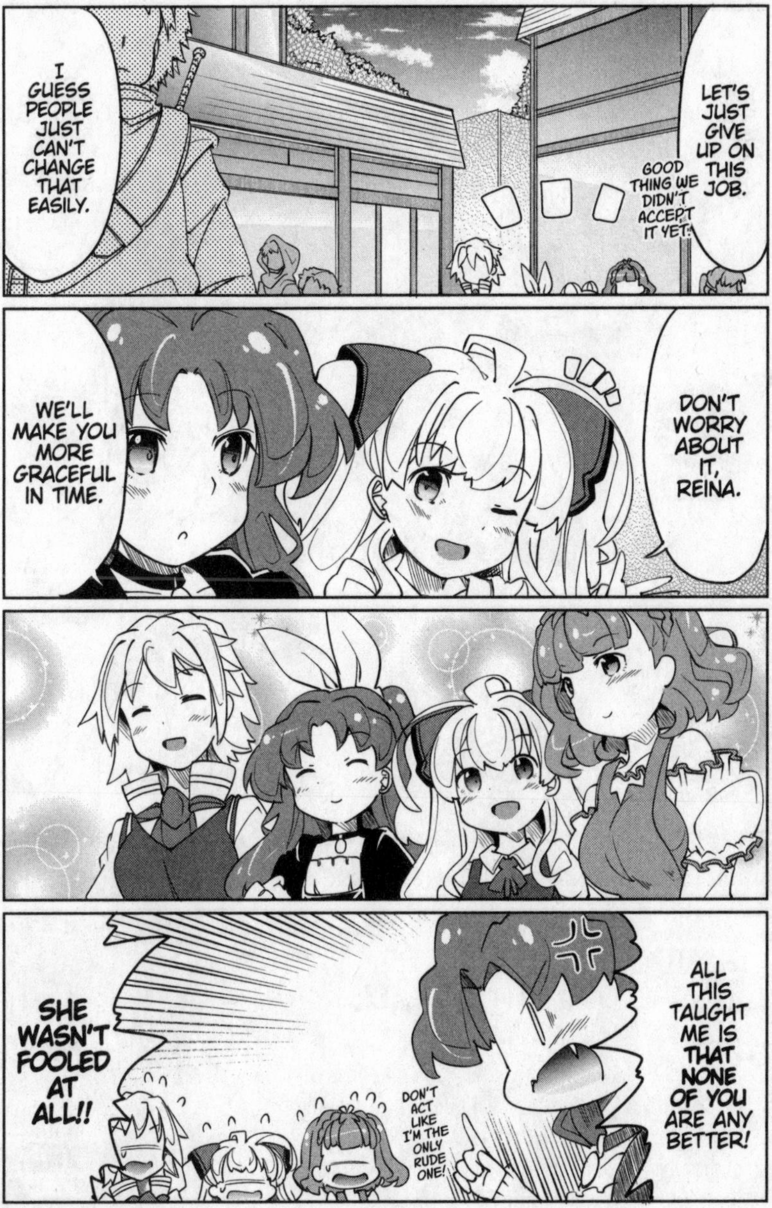
LET'S JUST GIVE UP ON THIS JOB.
GOOD THING WE DIDN'T ACCEPT IT YET.
I GUESS PEOPLE JUST CAN'T CHANGE THAT EASILY.
DON'T WORRY ABOUT IT, REINA.
WE'LL MAKE YOU MORE GRACEFUL IN TIME.
ALL THIS TAUGHT ME IS THAT NONE OF YOU ARE ANY BETTER!
DON'T ACT LIKE I'M THE ONLY RUDE ONE!
SHE WASN'T FOOLED AT ALL!!

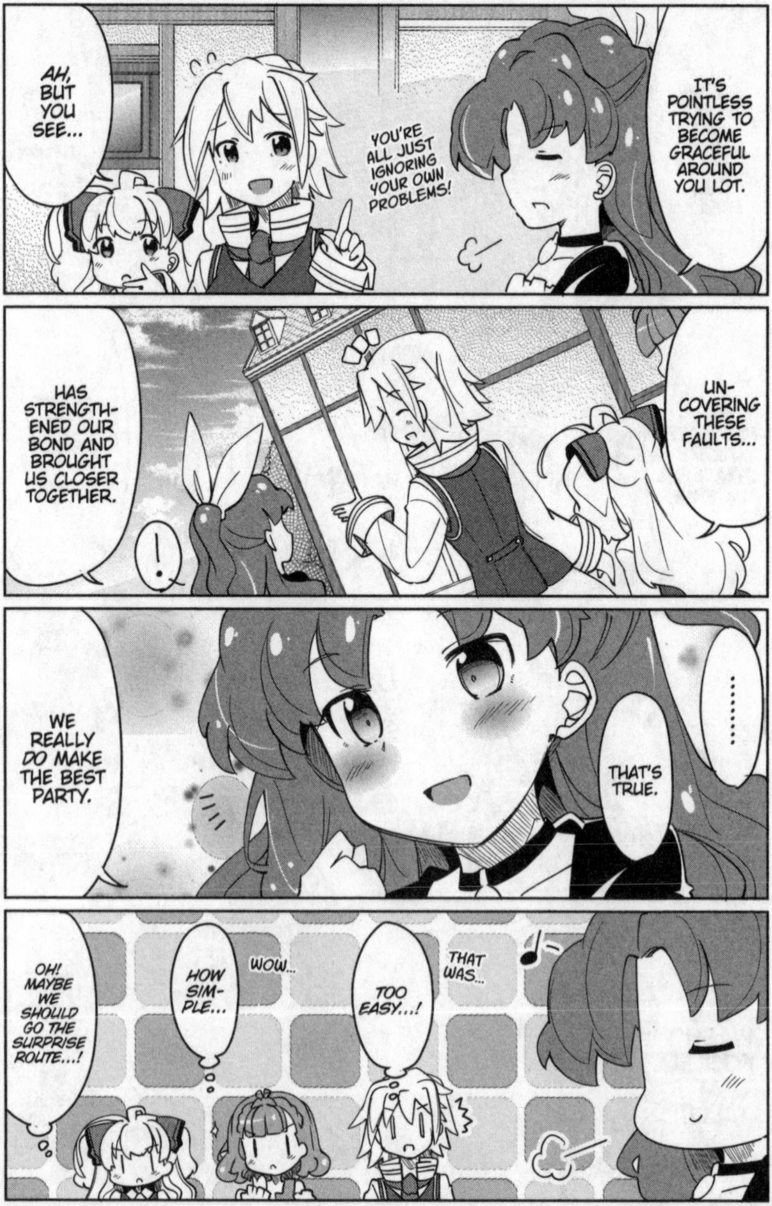
IT'S POINTLESS TRYING TO BECOME GRACEFUL AROUND YOU LOT.
YOU'RE ALL JUST IGNORING YOUR OWN PROBLEMS!
AH, BUT YOU SEE...
UN-COVERING THESE FAULTS...
HAS STRENGTH-ENED OUR BOND AND BROUGHT US CLOSER TOGETHER.
!
......
THAT'S TRUE.
WE REALLY *DO* MAKE THE BEST PARTY.
THAT WAS...
TOO EASY...!
WOW...
HOW SIMP-LE...
OH! MAYBE WE SHOULD GO THE SURPRISE ROUTE...!

Didn't I Say to Make My Abilities Average in the Next Life?!
EVERYDAY MISADVENTURES!

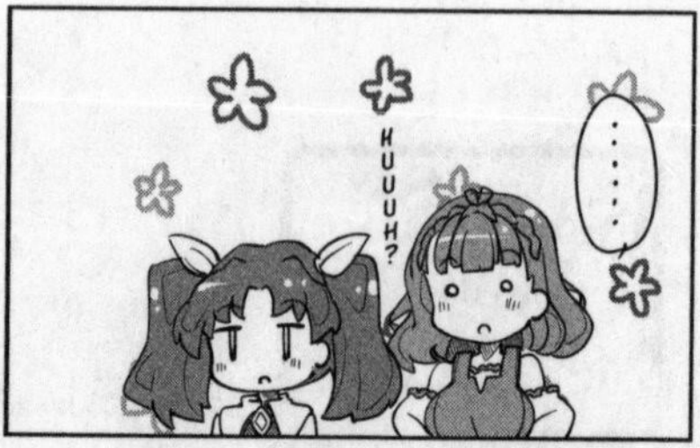

......
HUUUH?

Chapter 17

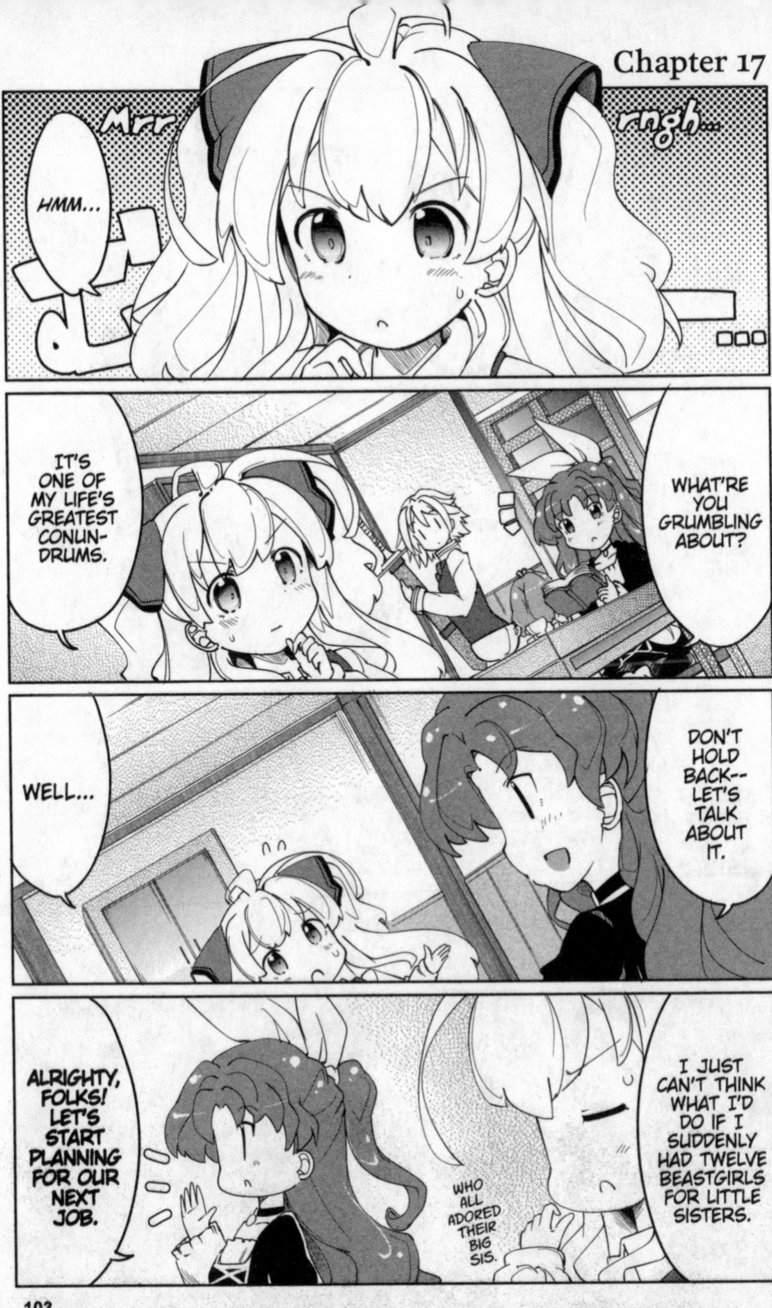
Mrr rngh...
HMM...
WHAT'RE YOU GRUMBLING ABOUT?
IT'S ONE OF MY LIFE'S GREATEST CONUNDRUMS.
DON'T HOLD BACK--LET'S TALK ABOUT IT.
WELL...
I JUST CAN'T THINK WHAT I'D DO IF I SUDDENLY HAD TWELVE BEASTGIRLS FOR LITTLE SISTERS.
WHO ALL ADORED THEIR BIG SIS.
ALRIGHTY, FOLKS! LET'S START PLANNING FOR OUR NEXT JOB.

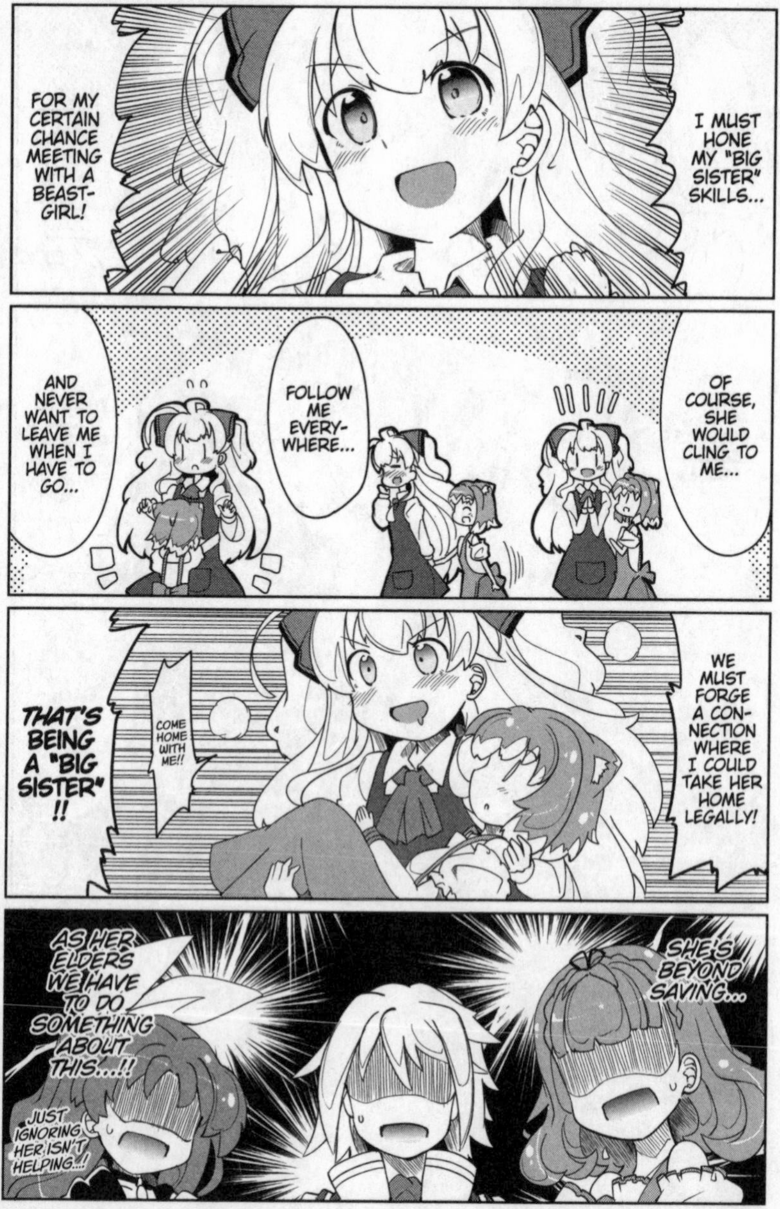
I MUST HONE MY "BIG SISTER" SKILLS...
FOR MY CERTAIN CHANCE MEETING WITH A BEAST-GIRL!
OF COURSE, SHE WOULD CLING TO ME...
FOLLOW ME EVERYWHERE...
AND NEVER WANT TO LEAVE ME WHEN I HAVE TO GO...
WE MUST FORGE A CONNECTION WHERE I COULD TAKE HER HOME LEGALLY!
COME HOME WITH ME!!
THAT'S BEING A "BIG SISTER"!!
SHE'S BEYOND SAVING...
AS HER ELDERS WE HAVE TO DO SOMETHING ABOUT THIS...!!
JUST IGNORING HER ISN'T HELPING...!

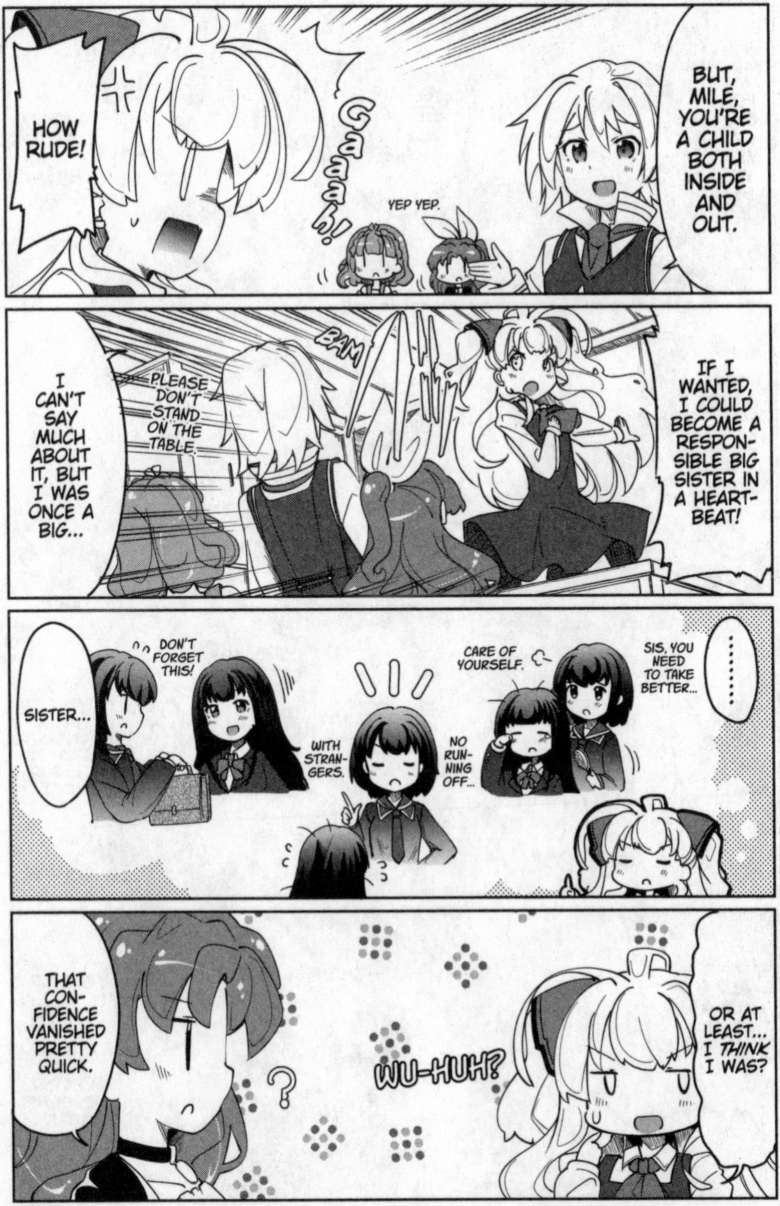
BUT, MILE, YOU'RE A CHILD BOTH INSIDE AND OUT.
YEP YEP.
Gaaah!
HOW RUDE!
IF I WANTED, I COULD BECOME A RESPONSIBLE BIG SISTER IN A HEARTBEAT!
BAM
PLEASE DON'T STAND ON THE TABLE.
I CAN'T SAY MUCH ABOUT IT, BUT I WAS ONCE A BIG...
......
SIS, YOU NEED TO TAKE BETTER...
CARE OF YOURSELF.
NO RUNNING OFF...
WITH STRANGERS.
DON'T FORGET THIS!
SISTER...
OR AT LEAST... I *THINK* I WAS?
WU-HUH?
THAT CONFIDENCE VANISHED PRETTY QUICK.

※*For more details, see the bonus story in Vol. 6 of the original novels.*

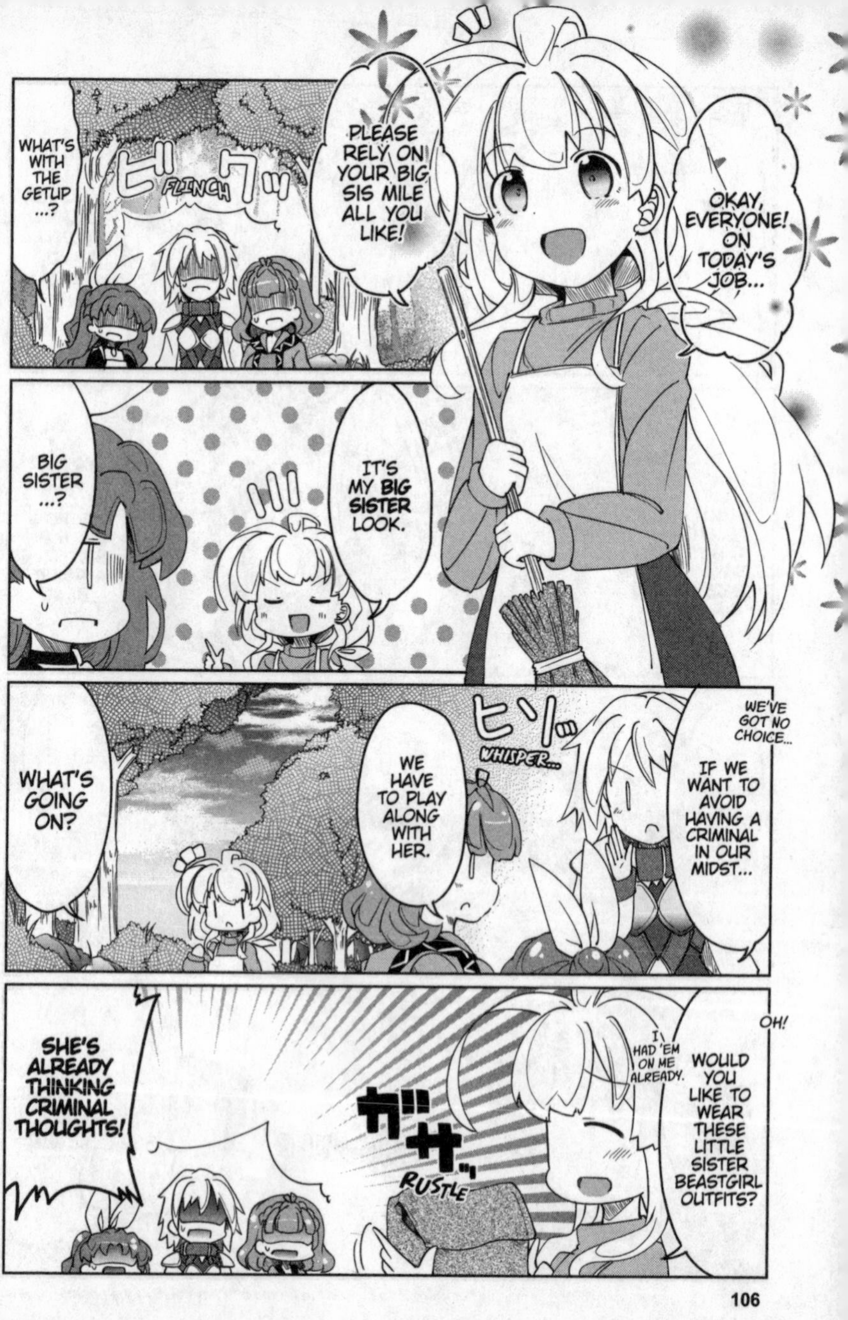
OKAY, EVERYONE! ON TODAY'S JOB...
PLEASE RELY ON YOUR BIG SIS MILE ALL YOU LIKE!
ビクッ
FLINCH
WHAT'S WITH THE GETUP ...?
IT'S MY BIG SISTER LOOK.
BIG SISTER ...?
WE'VE GOT NO CHOICE...
IF WE WANT TO AVOID HAVING A CRIMINAL IN OUR MIDST...
ヒソ
WHISPER...
WE HAVE TO PLAY ALONG WITH HER.
WHAT'S GOING ON?
OH!
I HAD 'EM ON ME ALREADY.
WOULD YOU LIKE TO WEAR THESE LITTLE SISTER BEASTGIRL OUTFITS?
ガサッ
RUSTLE
SHE'S ALREADY THINKING CRIMINAL THOUGHTS!

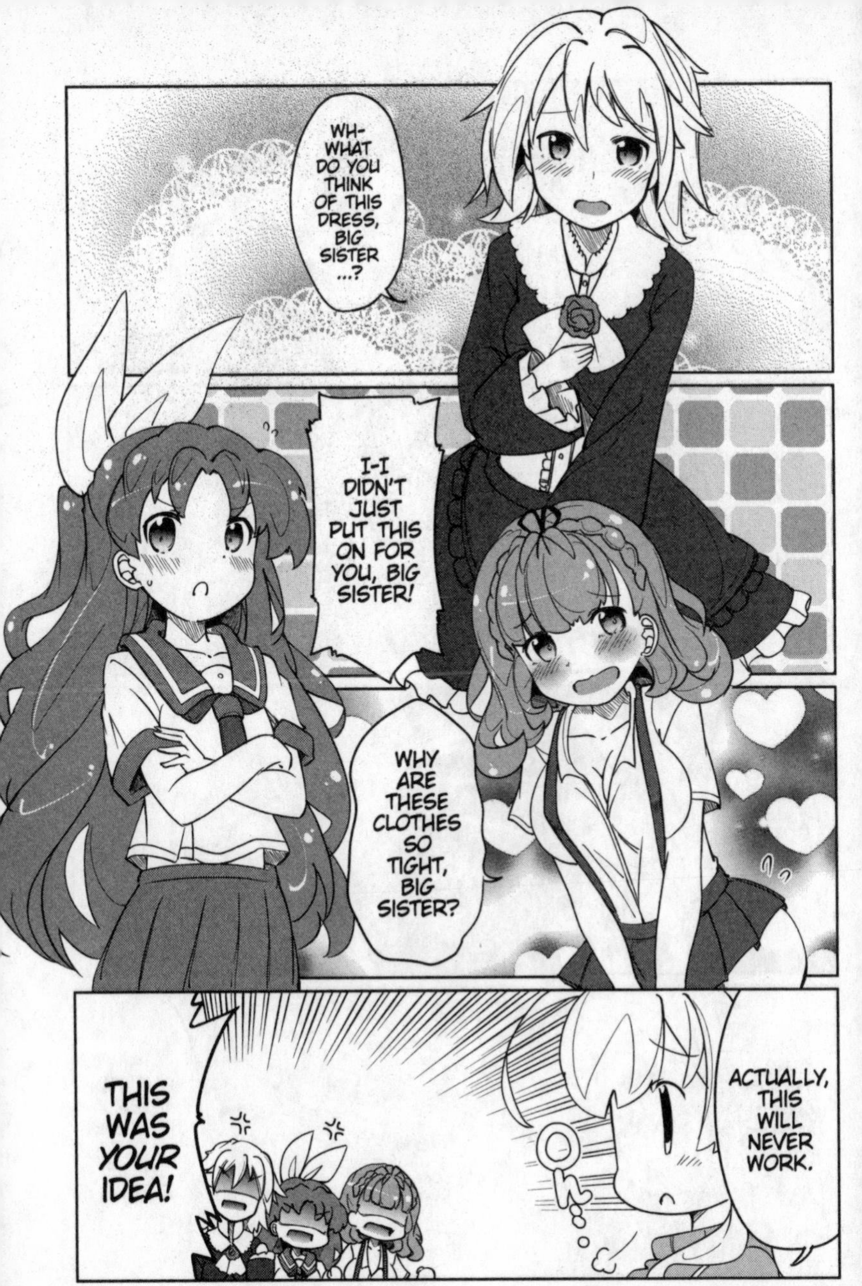
WH-WHAT DO YOU THINK OF THIS DRESS, BIG SISTER ...?
I-I DIDN'T JUST PUT THIS ON FOR YOU, BIG SISTER!
WHY ARE THESE CLOTHES SO TIGHT, BIG SISTER?
ACTUALLY, THIS WILL NEVER WORK.
Oh
THIS WAS *YOUR* IDEA!

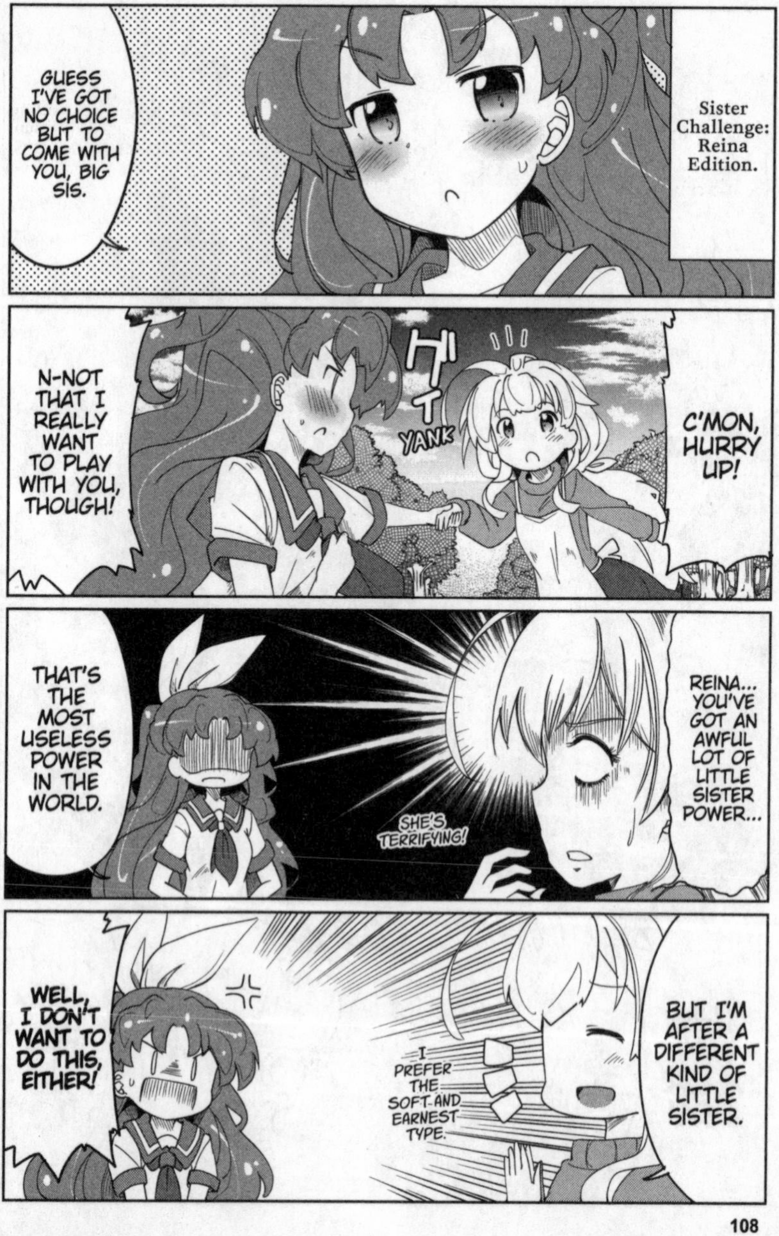
Sister Challenge: Reina Edition.
GUESS I'VE GOT NO CHOICE BUT TO COME WITH YOU, BIG SIS.
C'MON, HURRY UP!
グイ
YANK
N-NOT THAT I REALLY WANT TO PLAY WITH YOU, THOUGH!
REINA... YOU'VE GOT AN AWFUL LOT OF LITTLE SISTER POWER...
SHE'S TERRIFYING!
THAT'S THE MOST USELESS POWER IN THE WORLD.
BUT I'M AFTER A DIFFERENT KIND OF LITTLE SISTER.
I PREFER THE SOFT-AND-EARNEST TYPE.
WELL, I DON'T WANT TO DO THIS, EITHER!

LET ME FIX IT.

BIG SIS, YOUR HAIR IS ALL MESSED UP.

FWEH?

Pauline Edition.

YAY!

THE WEATHER IS LOVELY TODAY. LET'S HAVE A PICNIC.

WELL, I DO HAVE A LITTLE BROTHER, AFTER ALL.

HUH...? SO THEN, I'M...

WAIT A MINUTE-- THIS MAKES ME THE LITTLE SISTER!

THIS IS A COMPLETELY DIFFERENT TYPE OF SERVICE!!

FOR THE LITTLE SISTER SERVICE.

BUT IF YOU INSIST, THESE WILL BE THE FEES.

PLAYING WITH BIG BRO/SIS	1 SILVER
LAYING HEAD IN LAP	2 SILVER
SNUGGLING IN BED IN THE MORNING	3 SILVER
ADDITIONAL SERVICES	

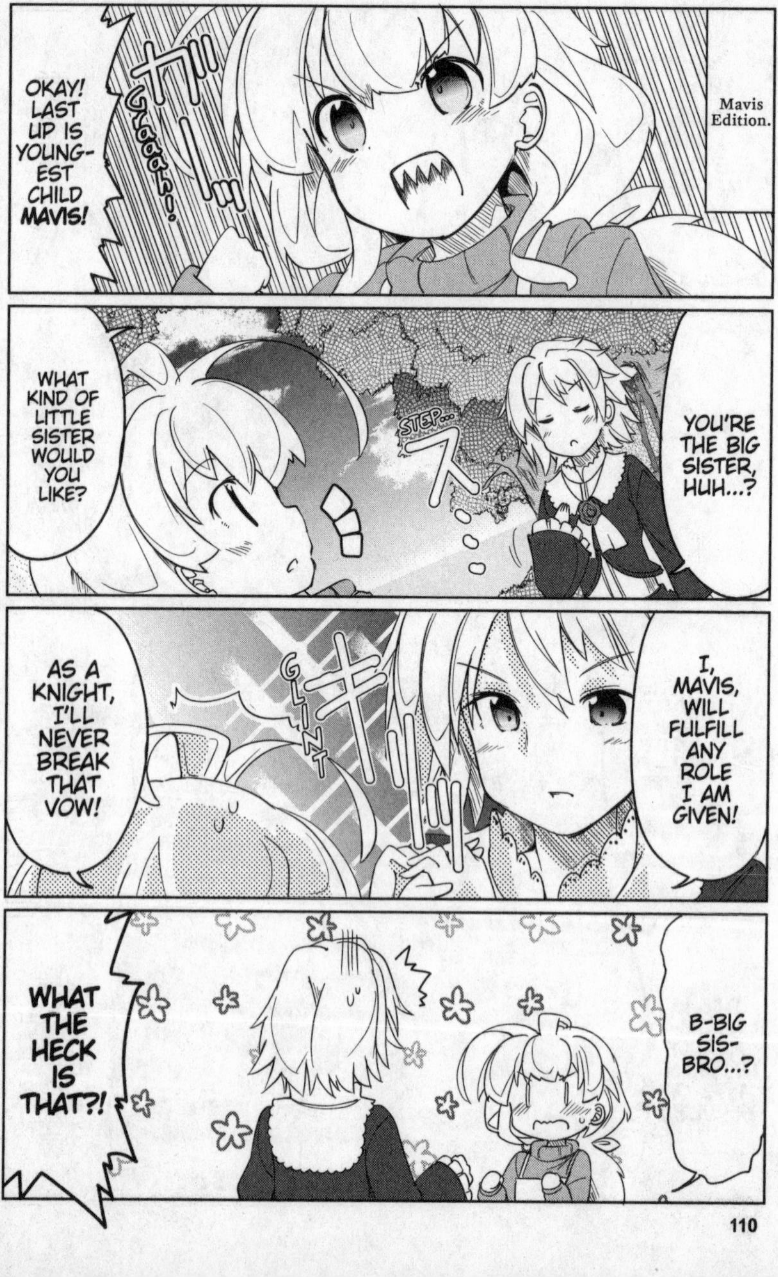
Mavis Edition.
OKAY! LAST UP IS YOUNGEST CHILD MAVIS!
Graaah!!
YOU'RE THE BIG SISTER, HUH...?
STEP...
WHAT KIND OF LITTLE SISTER WOULD YOU LIKE?
I, MAVIS, WILL FULFILL ANY ROLE I AM GIVEN!
GLINT
AS A KNIGHT, I'LL NEVER BREAK THAT VOW!
B-BIG SIS-BRO...?
WHAT THE HECK IS THAT?!

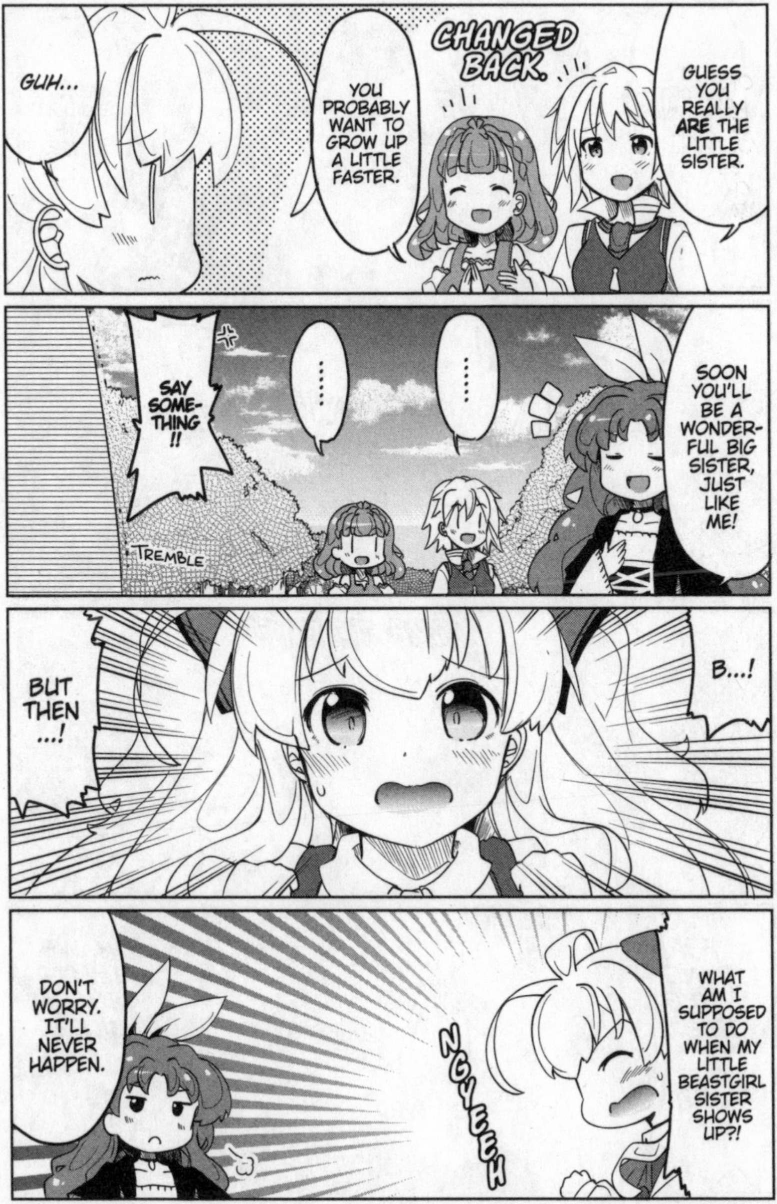
GUESS YOU REALLY ARE THE LITTLE SISTER.
CHANGED BACK.
YOU PROBABLY WANT TO GROW UP A LITTLE FASTER.
GUH...
SOON YOU'LL BE A WONDERFUL BIG SISTER, JUST LIKE ME!
......
......
SAY SOMETHING!!
TREMBLE
B...!
BUT THEN ...!
WHAT AM I SUPPOSED TO DO WHEN MY LITTLE BEASTGIRL SISTER SHOWS UP?!
NGYEEEH
DON'T WORRY. IT'LL NEVER HAPPEN.

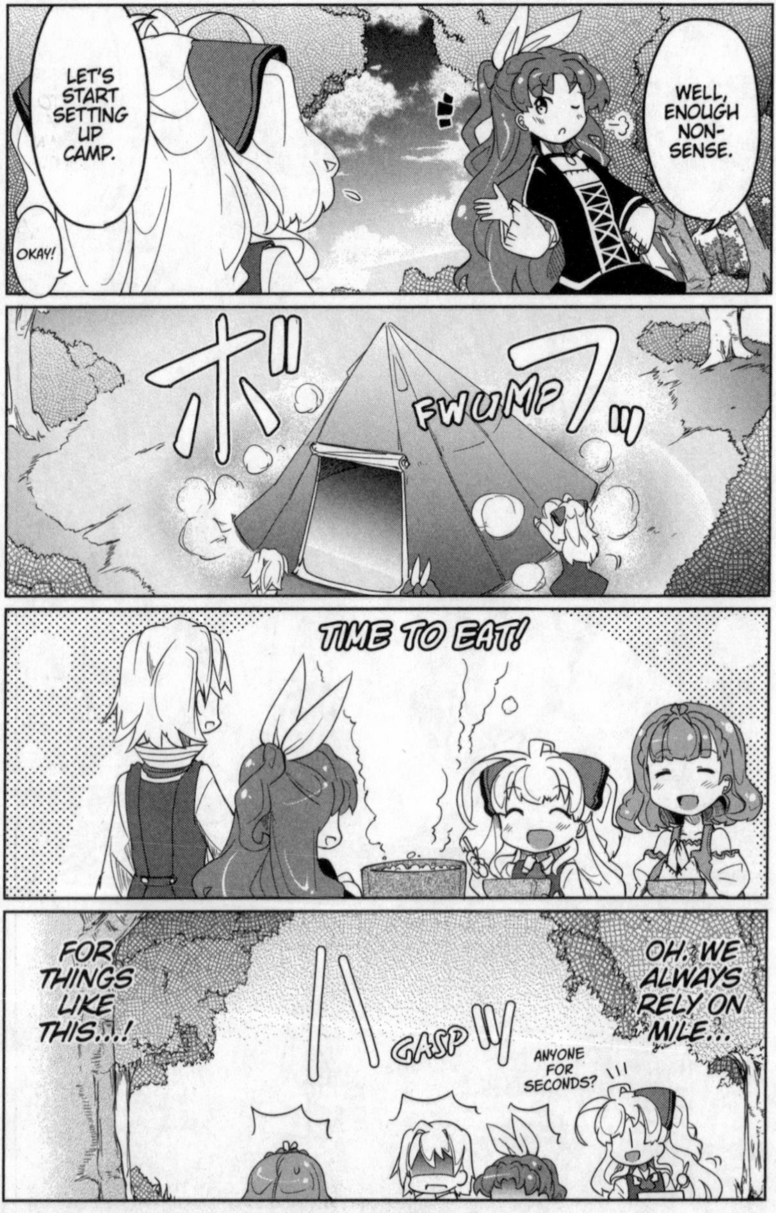
WELL, ENOUGH NON-SENSE.
LET'S START SETTING UP CAMP.
OKAY!
ボフッ
FWUMP
TIME TO EAT!
OH. WE ALWAYS RELY ON MILE...
FOR THINGS LIKE THIS...!
ハッ
GASP
ANYONE FOR SECONDS?

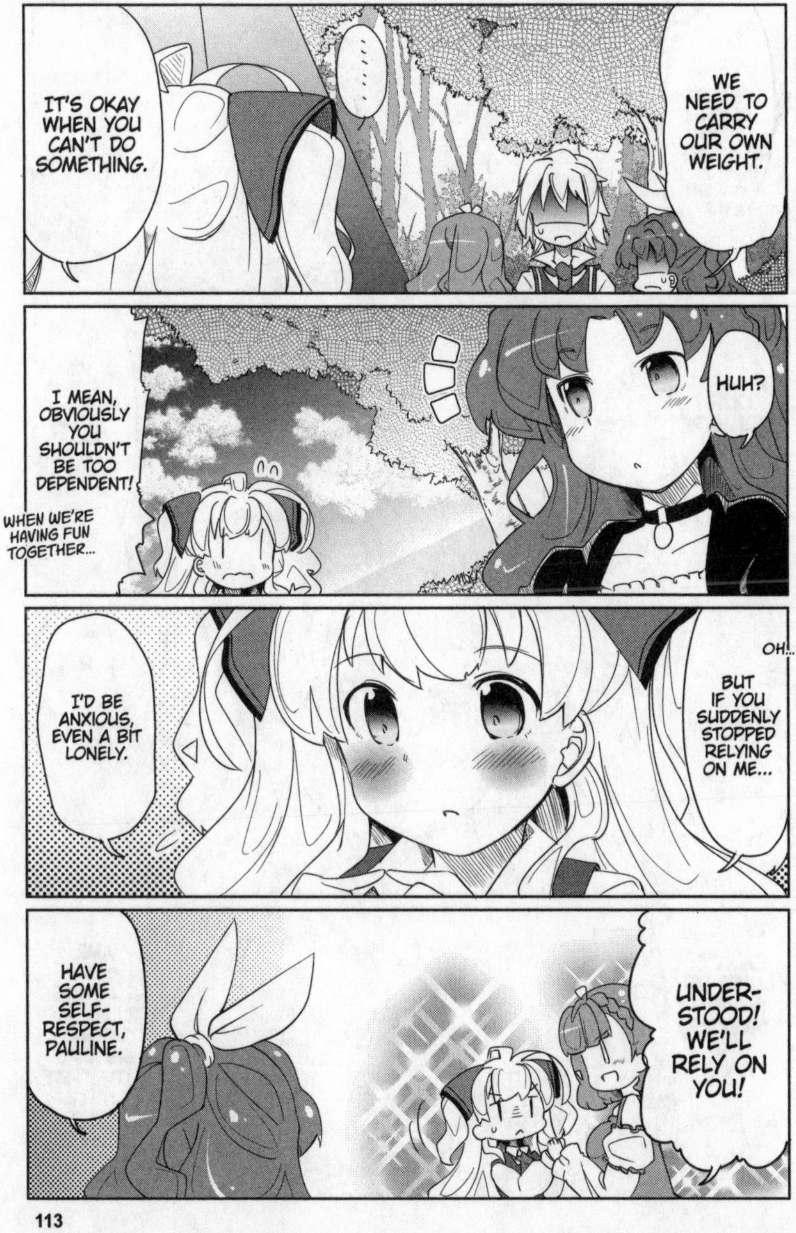
WE NEED TO CARRY OUR OWN WEIGHT.
......
IT'S OKAY WHEN YOU CAN'T DO SOMETHING.
HUH?
I MEAN, OBVIOUSLY YOU SHOULDN'T BE TOO DEPENDENT!
WHEN WE'RE HAVING FUN TOGETHER...
OH...
BUT IF YOU SUDDENLY STOPPED RELYING ON ME...
I'D BE ANXIOUS, EVEN A BIT LONELY.
UNDER-STOOD! WE'LL RELY ON YOU!
HAVE SOME SELF-RESPECT, PAULINE.

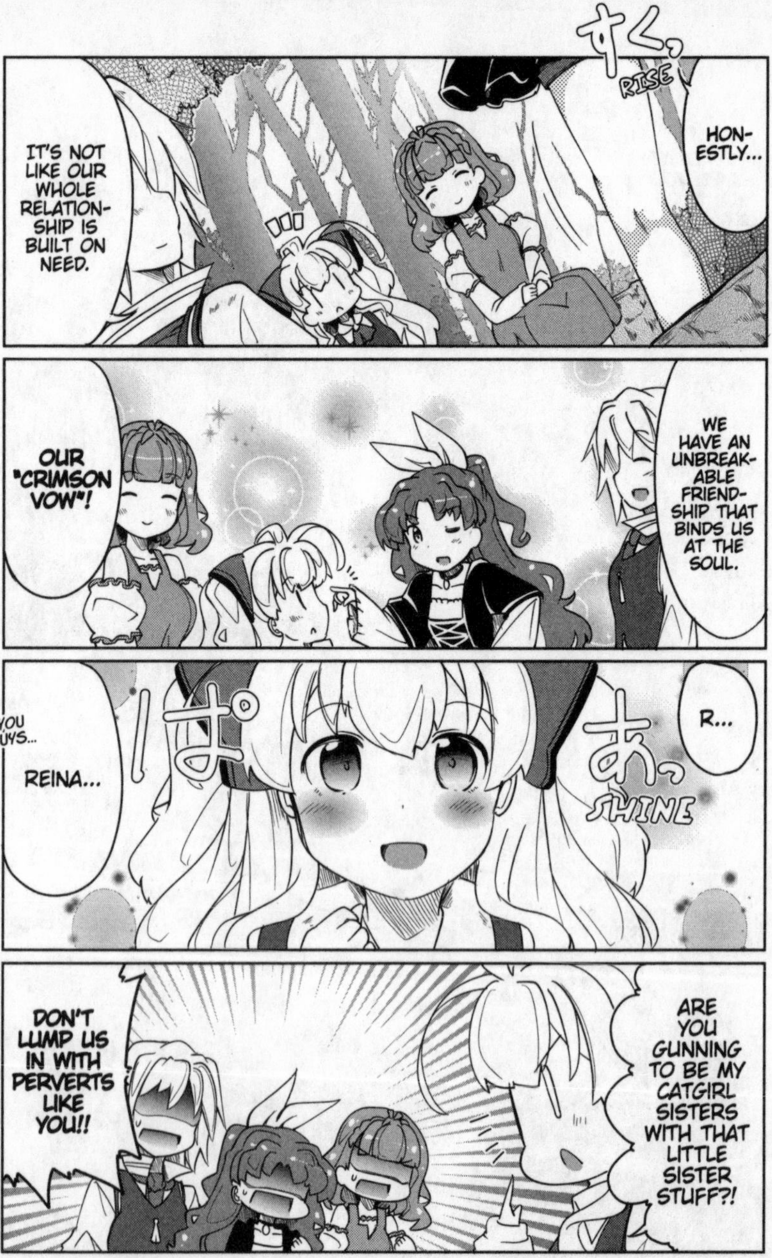
すく
RISE
HONESTLY...
IT'S NOT LIKE OUR WHOLE RELATIONSHIP IS BUILT ON NEED.
WE HAVE AN UNBREAKABLE FRIENDSHIP THAT BINDS US AT THE SOUL.
OUR "CRIMSON VOW"!
R...
ぱあっ
SHINE
REINA...
YOU GUYS...
ARE YOU GUNNING TO BE MY CATGIRL SISTERS WITH THAT LITTLE SISTER STUFF?!
DON'T LUMP US IN WITH PERVERTS LIKE YOU!!

Didn't I Say to Make My Abilities Average in the Next Life?!

EVERYDAY MISADVENTURES!

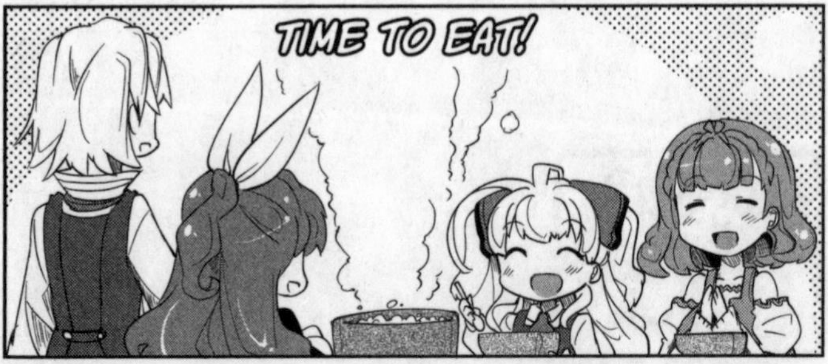
TIME TO EAT!

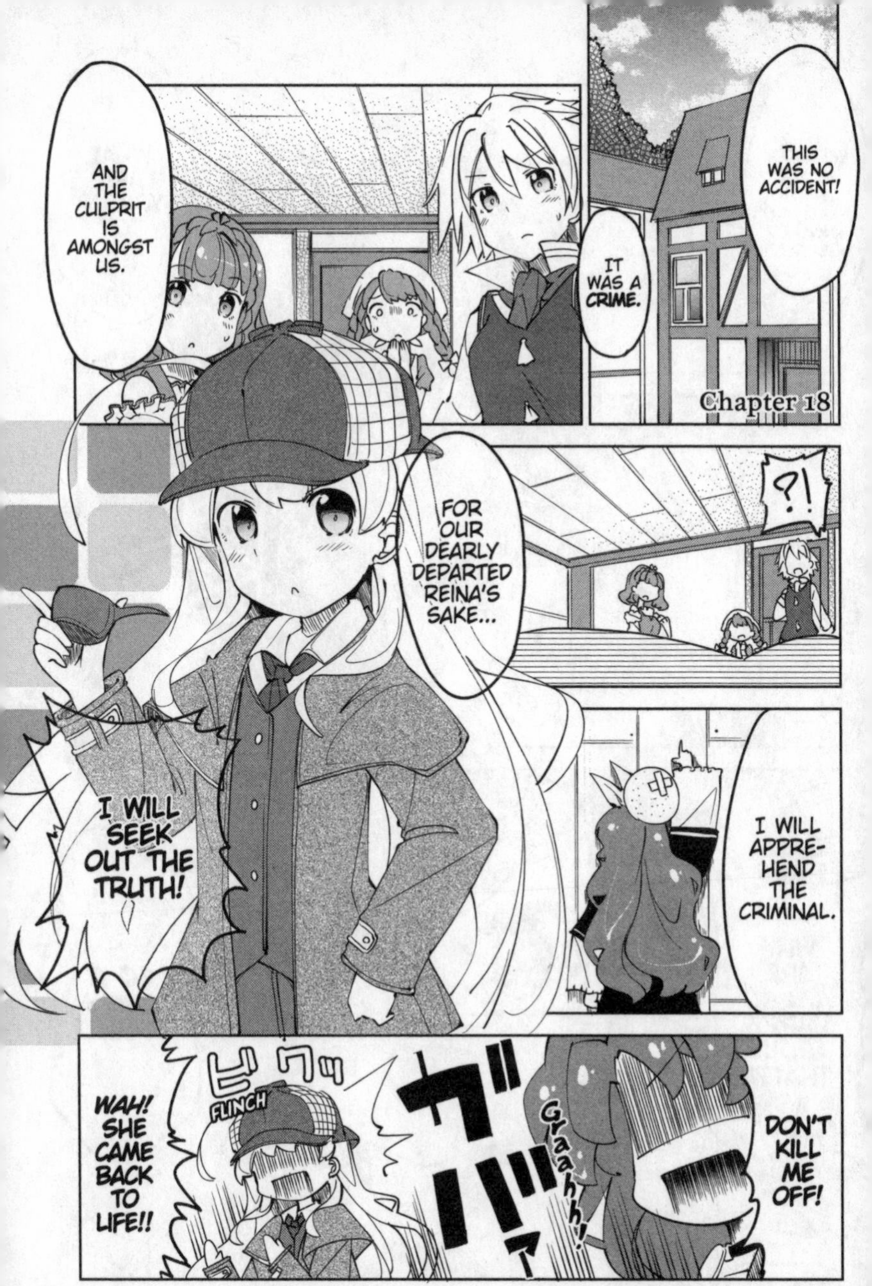
THIS WAS NO ACCIDENT!
IT WAS A CRIME.
Chapter 18
AND THE CULPRIT IS AMONGST US.
FOR OUR DEARLY DEPARTED REINA'S SAKE...
?!
I WILL APPREHEND THE CRIMINAL.
I WILL SEEK OUT THE TRUTH!
DON'T KILL ME OFF!
ヴバァ
Graahh!
ビクッ
FLINCH
WAH! SHE CAME BACK TO LIFE!!

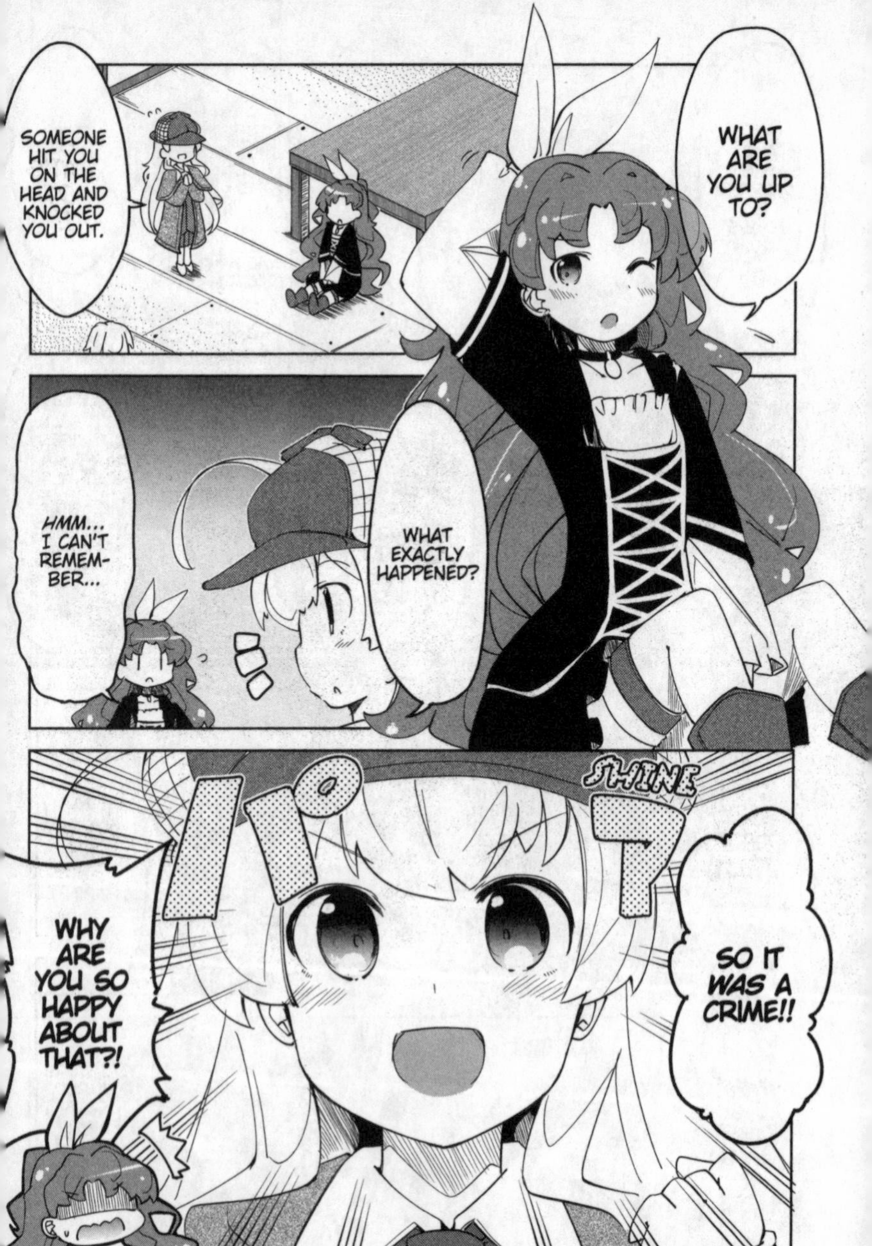
WHAT ARE YOU UP TO?
SOMEONE HIT YOU ON THE HEAD AND KNOCKED YOU OUT.
WHAT EXACTLY HAPPENED?
HMM... I CAN'T REMEMBER...
SHINE
SO IT WAS A CRIME!!
WHY ARE YOU SO HAPPY ABOUT THAT?!

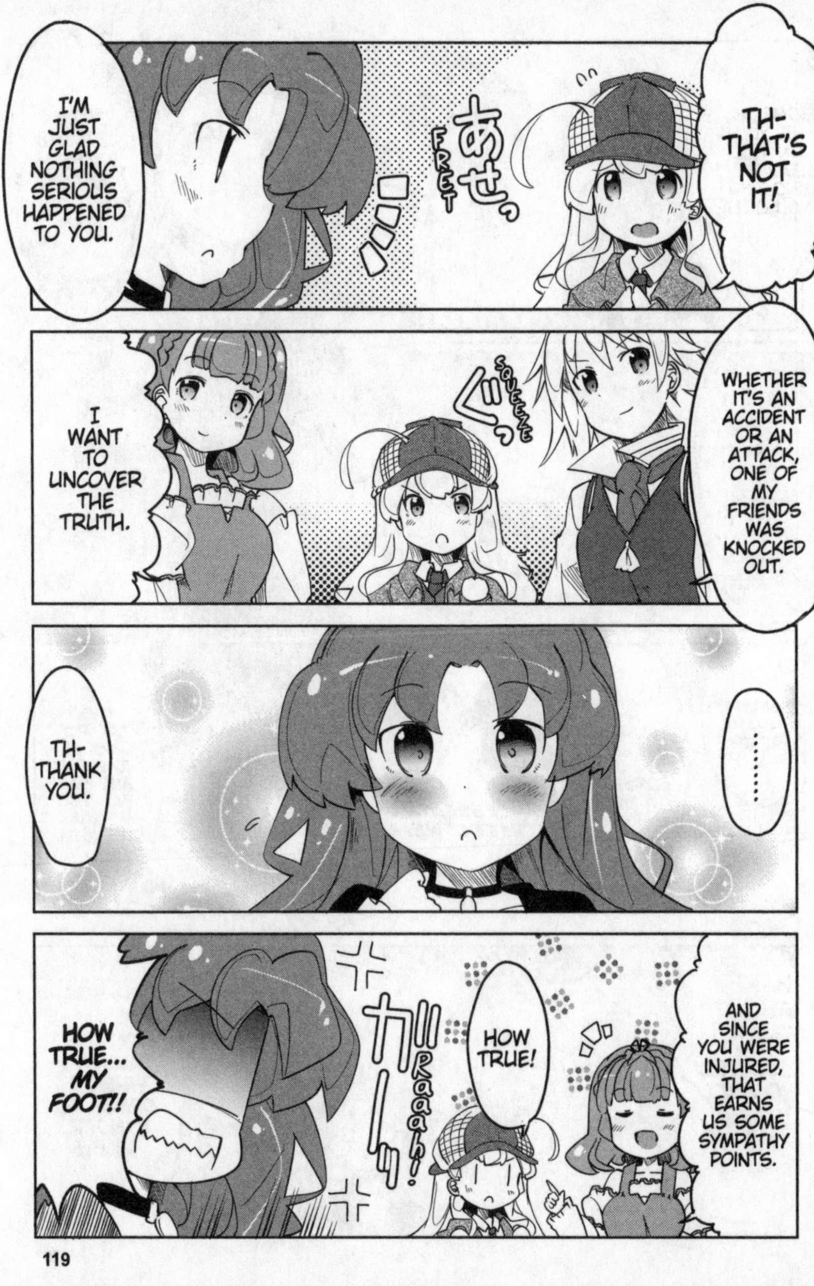
TH- THAT'S NOT IT!
あせっ FRET
I'M JUST GLAD NOTHING SERIOUS HAPPENED TO YOU.
WHETHER IT'S AN ACCIDENT OR AN ATTACK, ONE OF MY FRIENDS WAS KNOCKED OUT.
ぐっ SQUEEZE
I WANT TO UNCOVER THE TRUTH.
......
TH- THANK YOU.
AND SINCE YOU WERE INJURED, THAT EARNS US SOME SYMPATHY POINTS.
HOW TRUE!
カーッ RAAAH!
HOW TRUE... MY FOOT!!

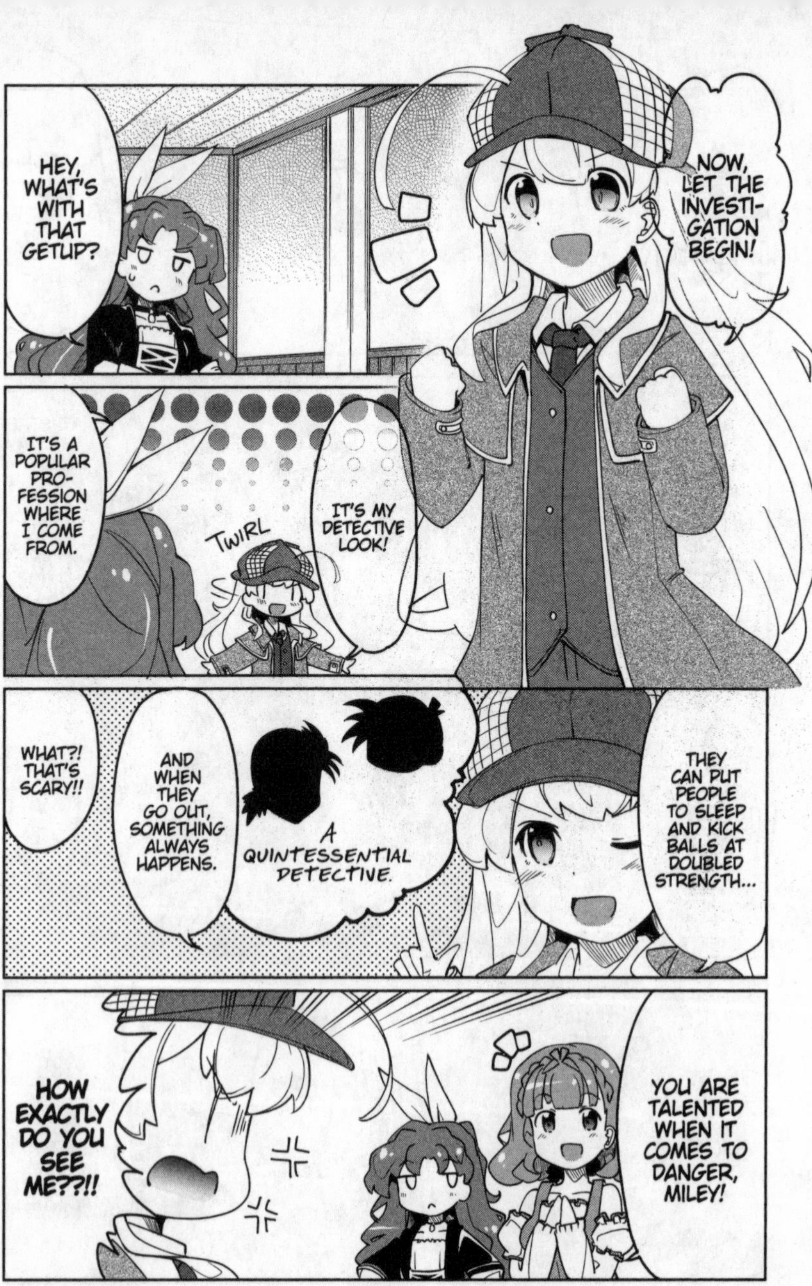
NOW, LET THE INVESTIGATION BEGIN!
HEY, WHAT'S WITH THAT GETUP?
IT'S MY DETECTIVE LOOK!
TWIRL
IT'S A POPULAR PROFESSION WHERE I COME FROM.
THEY CAN PUT PEOPLE TO SLEEP AND KICK BALLS AT DOUBLED STRENGTH...
A QUINTESSENTIAL DETECTIVE.
AND WHEN THEY GO OUT, SOMETHING ALWAYS HAPPENS.
WHAT?! THAT'S SCARY!!
YOU ARE TALENTED WHEN IT COMES TO DANGER, MILEY!
HOW EXACTLY DO YOU SEE ME??!!

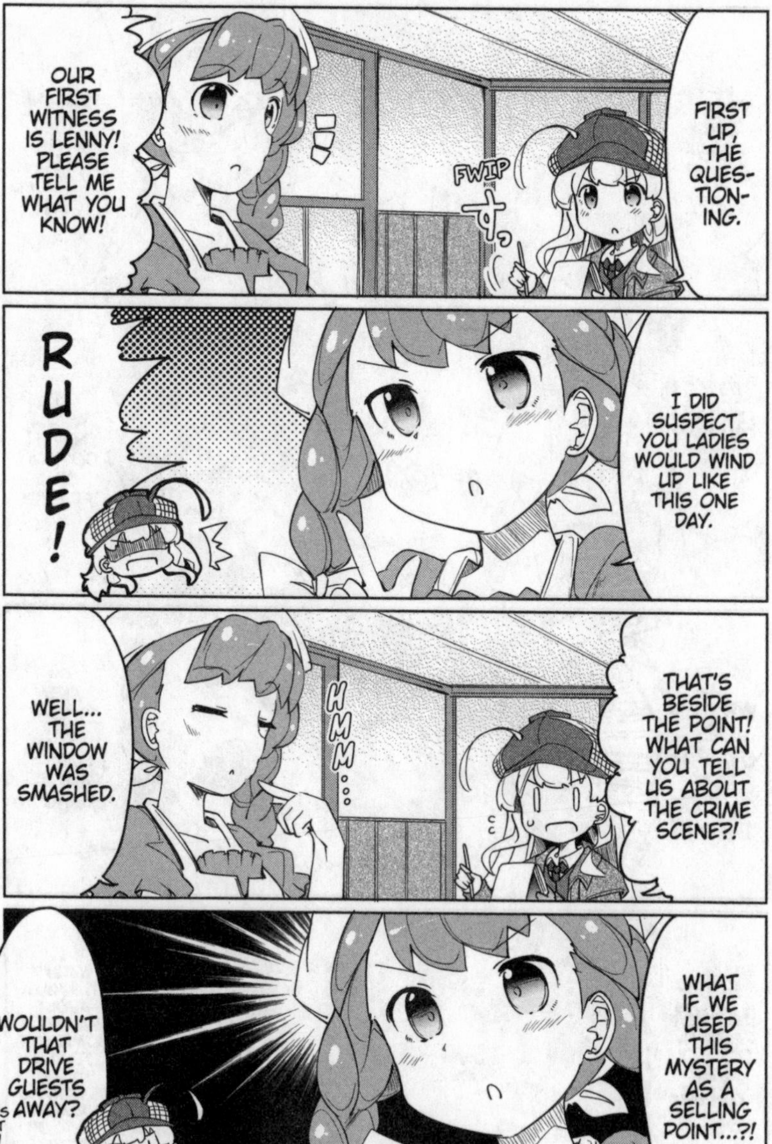
FIRST UP, THE QUESTIONING.
FWIP
OUR FIRST WITNESS IS LENNY! PLEASE TELL ME WHAT YOU KNOW!
I DID SUSPECT YOU LADIES WOULD WIND UP LIKE THIS ONE DAY.
RUDE!
THAT'S BESIDE THE POINT! WHAT CAN YOU TELL US ABOUT THE CRIME SCENE?!
HMM...
WELL... THE WINDOW WAS SMASHED.
WHAT IF WE USED THIS MYSTERY AS A SELLING POINT...?!
WOULDN'T THAT DRIVE GUESTS AWAY?
A MERCHANT'S HEART IS AN INDOMITABLE FORCE!

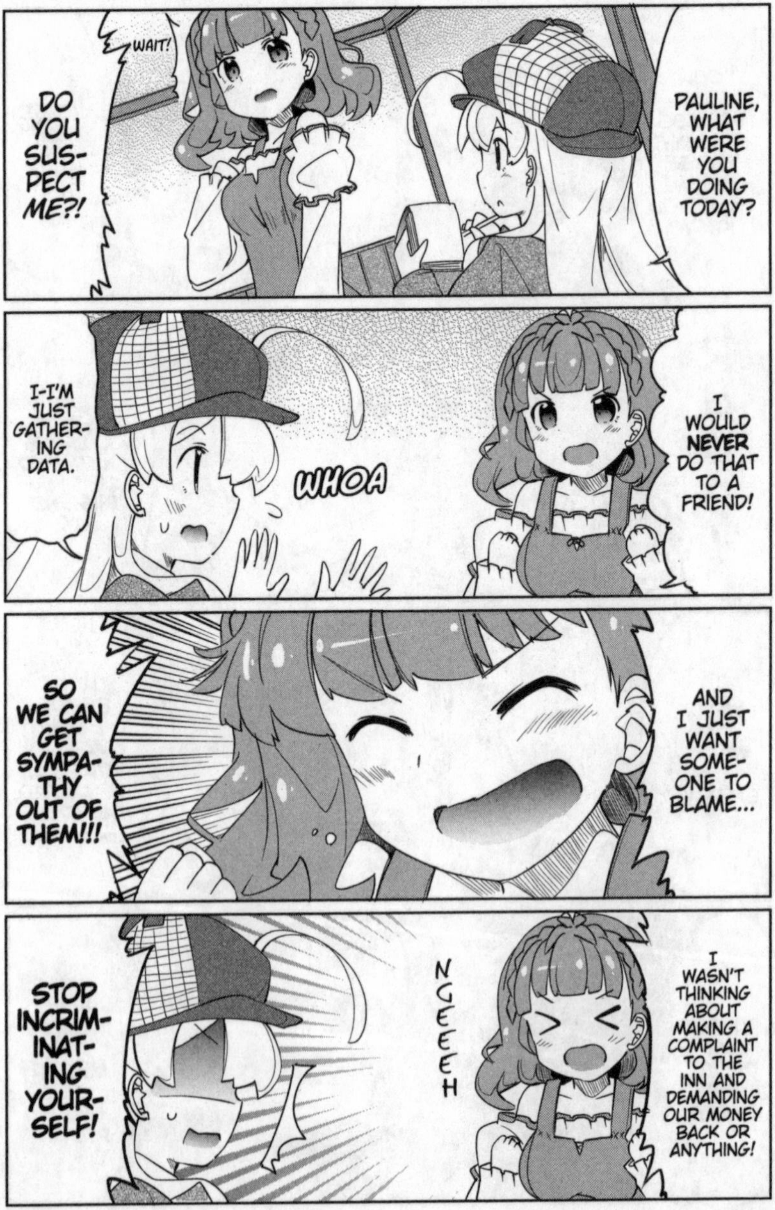
PAULINE, WHAT WERE YOU DOING TODAY?
WAIT!
DO YOU SUSPECT ME?!
I WOULD NEVER DO THAT TO A FRIEND!
WHOA
I-I'M JUST GATHERING DATA.
AND I JUST WANT SOMEONE TO BLAME...
SO WE CAN GET SYMPATHY OUT OF THEM!!!
I WASN'T THINKING ABOUT MAKING A COMPLAINT TO THE INN AND DEMANDING OUR MONEY BACK OR ANYTHING!
NGEEEEH
STOP INCRIMINATING YOURSELF!

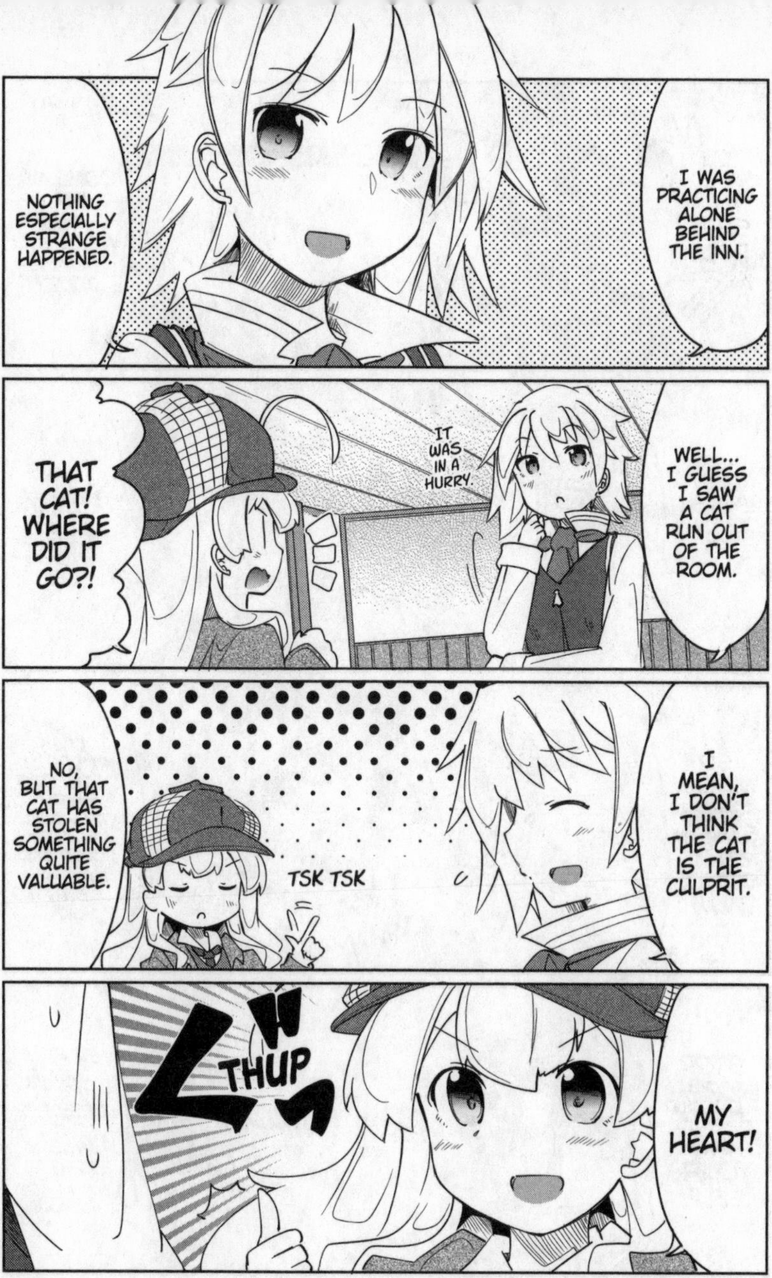
I WAS PRACTICING ALONE BEHIND THE INN.
NOTHING ESPECIALLY STRANGE HAPPENED.
WELL... I GUESS I SAW A CAT RUN OUT OF THE ROOM.
IT WAS IN A HURRY.
THAT CAT! WHERE DID IT GO?!
I MEAN, I DON'T THINK THE CAT IS THE CULPRIT.
TSK TSK
NO, BUT THAT CAT HAS STOLEN SOMETHING QUITE VALUABLE.
MY HEART!
THUP

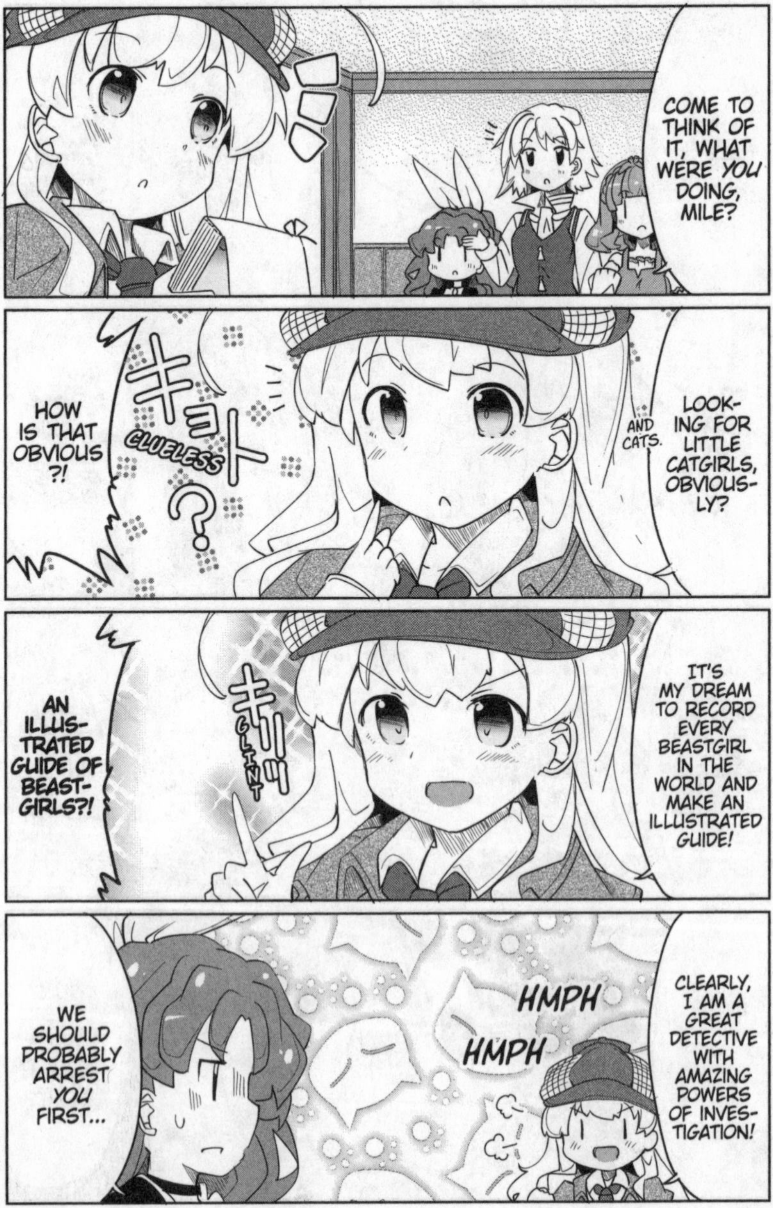
COME TO THINK OF IT, WHAT WERE *YOU* DOING, MILE?
LOOKING FOR LITTLE CATGIRLS, OBVIOUSLY?
AND CATS.
キョト
CLUELESS
HOW IS THAT OBVIOUS?!
IT'S MY DREAM TO RECORD EVERY BEASTGIRL IN THE WORLD AND MAKE AN ILLUSTRATED GUIDE!
キリッ
GLINT
AN ILLUSTRATED GUIDE OF BEASTGIRLS?!
CLEARLY, I AM A GREAT DETECTIVE WITH AMAZING POWERS OF INVESTIGATION!
HMPH
HMPH
WE SHOULD PROBABLY ARREST *YOU* FIRST...

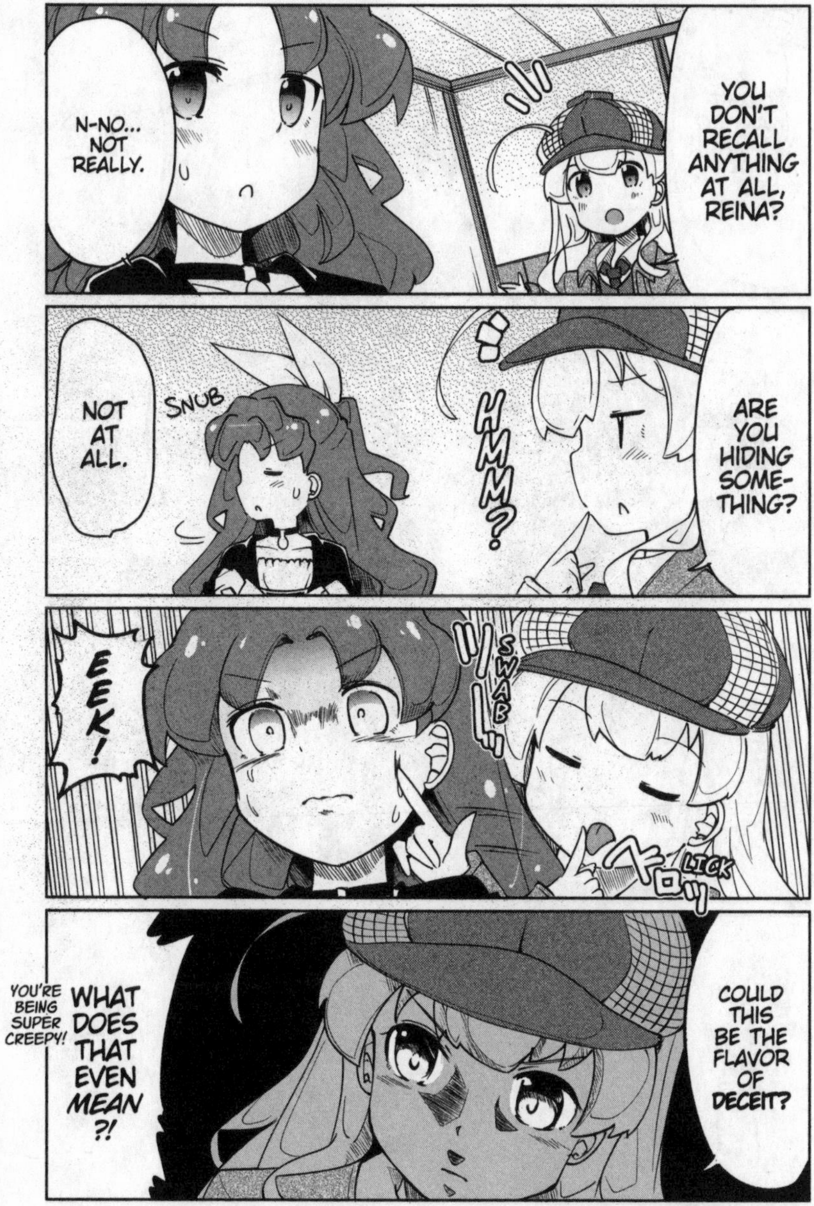
YOU DON'T RECALL ANYTHING AT ALL, REINA?
N-NO... NOT REALLY.
ARE YOU HIDING SOME-THING?
HMMM?
SNUB
NOT AT ALL.
LICK
SWAB
EEK!
COULD THIS BE THE FLAVOR OF DECEIT?
WHAT DOES THAT EVEN MEAN?!
YOU'RE BEING SUPER CREEPY!

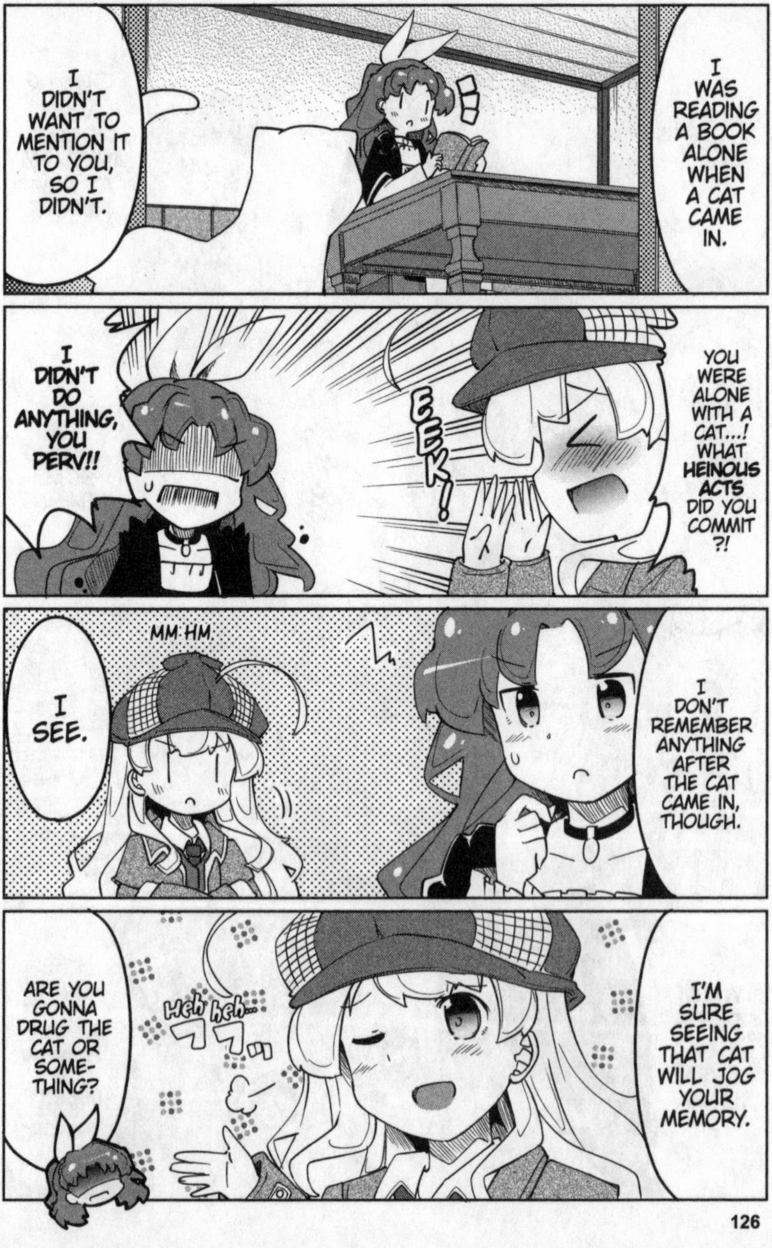
I WAS READING A BOOK ALONE WHEN A CAT CAME IN.
I DIDN'T WANT TO MENTION IT TO YOU, SO I DIDN'T.
YOU WERE ALONE WITH A CAT...! WHAT HEINOUS ACTS DID YOU COMMIT?!
EEK!
I DIDN'T DO ANYTHING, YOU PERV!!
I DON'T REMEMBER ANYTHING AFTER THE CAT CAME IN, THOUGH.
MM HM.
I SEE.
I'M SURE SEEING THAT CAT WILL JOG YOUR MEMORY.
Heh heh...
フフッ
ARE YOU GONNA DRUG THE CAT OR SOMETHING?

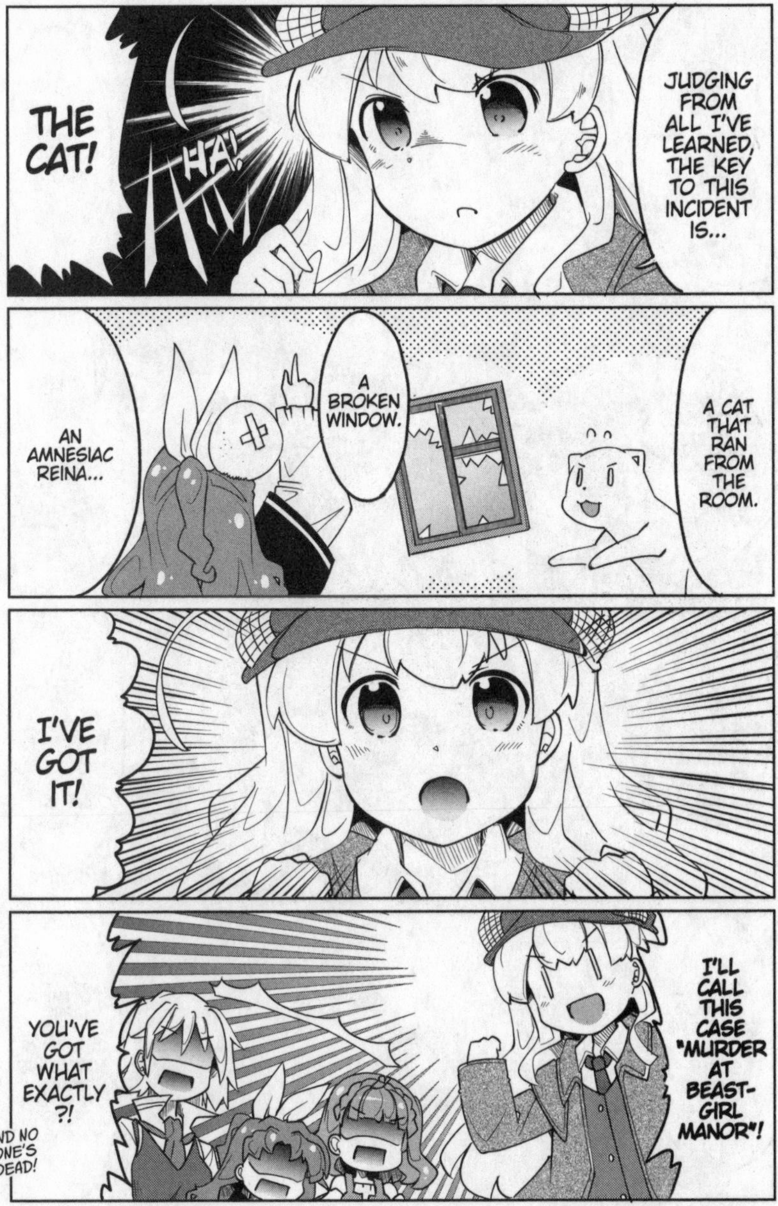
JUDGING FROM ALL I'VE LEARNED, THE KEY TO THIS INCIDENT IS...
HA!
THE CAT!
A CAT THAT RAN FROM THE ROOM.
A BROKEN WINDOW.
AN AMNESIAC REINA...
I'VE GOT IT!
I'LL CALL THIS CASE "MURDER AT BEAST-GIRL MANOR"!
YOU'VE GOT WHAT EXACTLY?!
AND NO ONE'S DEAD!

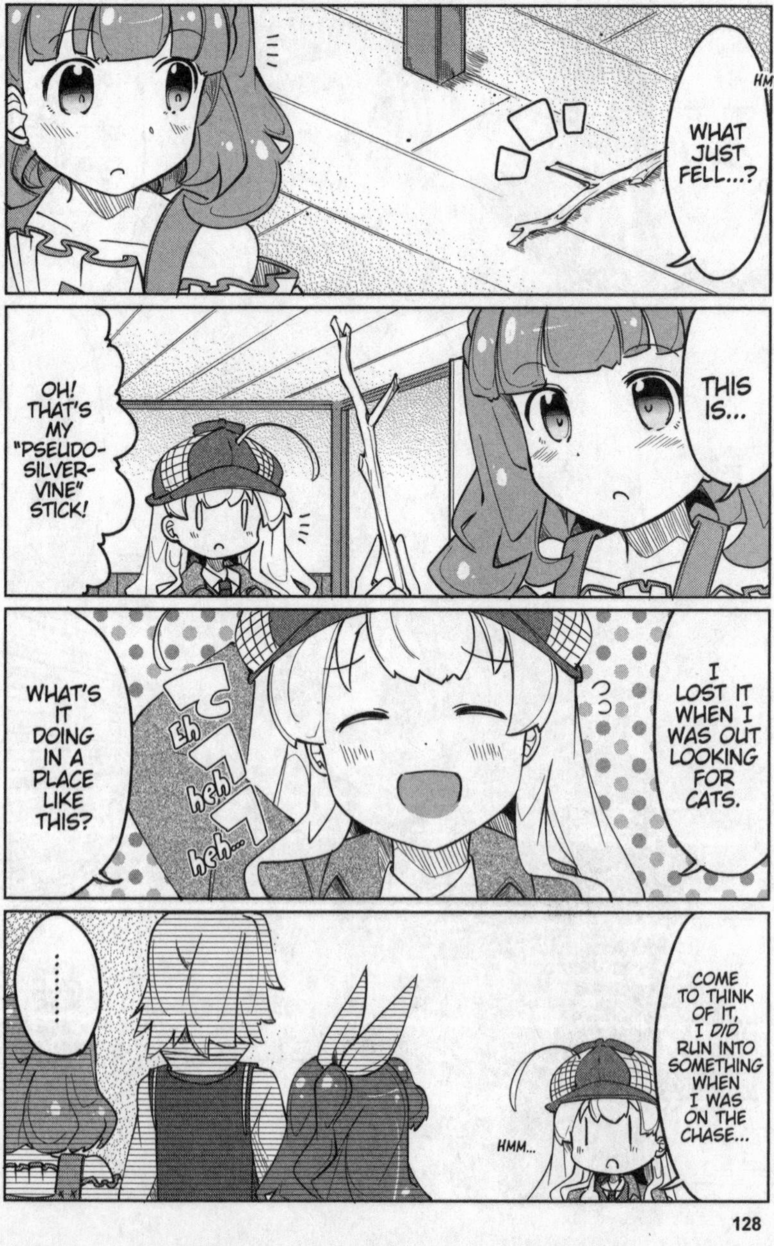
HM?
WHAT JUST FELL...?
THIS IS...
OH! THAT'S MY "PSEUDO-SILVERVINE" STICK!
I LOST IT WHEN I WAS OUT LOOKING FOR CATS.
Eh heh heh...
WHAT'S IT DOING IN A PLACE LIKE THIS?
COME TO THINK OF IT, I *DID* RUN INTO SOMETHING WHEN I WAS ON THE CHASE...
HMM...
......

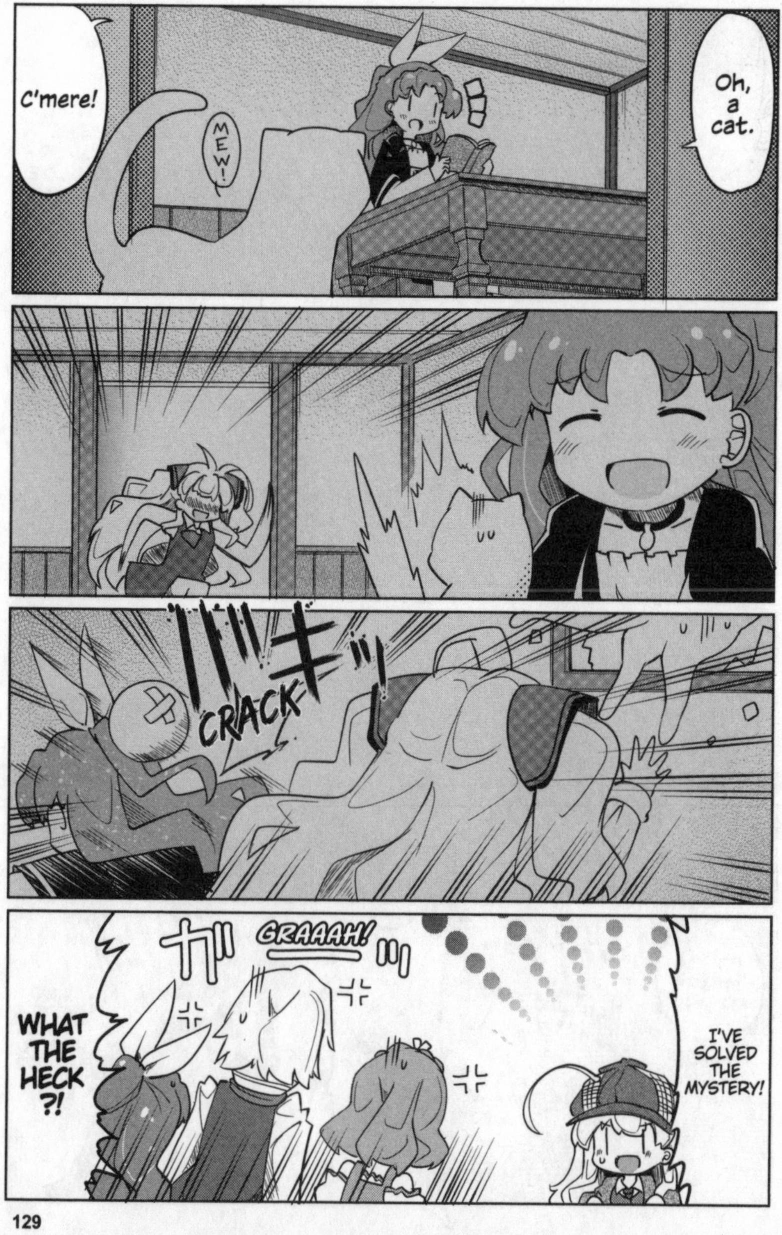
Oh, a cat.
MEW!
C'mere!
CRACK
GRAAAH!
I'VE SOLVED THE MYSTERY!
WHAT THE HECK ?!

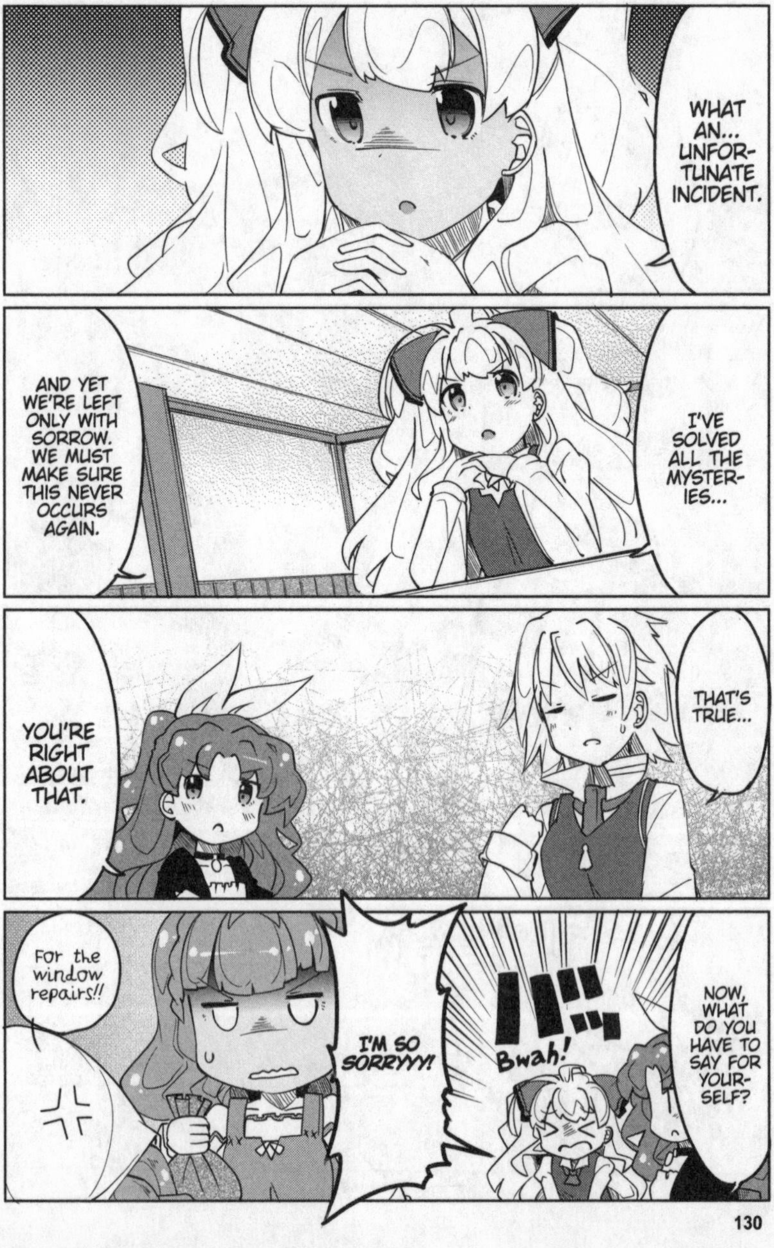
WHAT AN... UNFORTUNATE INCIDENT.
I'VE SOLVED ALL THE MYSTERIES...
AND YET WE'RE LEFT ONLY WITH SORROW. WE MUST MAKE SURE THIS NEVER OCCURS AGAIN.
THAT'S TRUE...
YOU'RE RIGHT ABOUT THAT.
NOW, WHAT DO YOU HAVE TO SAY FOR YOURSELF?
Bwah!
I'M SO SORRYYY!
For the window repairs!!

Didn't I Say to Make My Abilities Average in the Next Life?!
EVERYDAY MISADVENTURES!

Didn't I Say to Make My Abilities Average in the Next Life?!
EVERYDAY MISADVENTURES!

BONUS STORY
Didn't I Say to Make My Abilities Average in the Next Life?!

The Village Festival

"Oh? Looks like they're preparing for something."

"Yeah, probably a festival. This time of year, it'll be a wheat harvest festival or something."

The Crimson Vow had been hunting on their way back to the capital and decided to take a detour into the mountains where they discovered a small village of about thirty homes. The villagers were all gathering to build scaffolding and hang decorations. Reina seemed to have some idea of what was going on while Mile was clearly in the dark.

"Wow, you sure know a lot about this stuff, Reina."

"I traveled to many different villages with my father. When you're peddling, if you don't know a particular village's way of life, you won't know what goods to stock for sale. I have a firm grasp on this."

"I see."

"There's not much fun to be had in the countryside, so you see events like this more often than in larger towns. New Year's festivals, Thunder God festivals, Earth God festivals—all kinds. In town, we have the Goddess festival and the celebration of the King's birthday, but celebrations are a lot sparser than out in the country," Pauline explained.

This made sense to Mile. And then...

"Looks pretty fun. Let's go check it out!"

"Knew you'd say that..." sighed the other three.

They still had time before their deadline, and thanks to Mile's storage magic—her loot box, in which time did not pass—there was no danger of their spoils, well, spoiling. They knew what Mile was going to say before she said it; the two years they'd spent eating and sleeping together had taught them that much about her.

When the Vows stopped by the village elder's home to learn more, they discovered the festival was to be held the following day. Mile piped up:

"Can we join in, too?!"

"Knew you'd say that..." said the other three, in perfect unison.

There was a big difference between *checking something out* and *joining in*. The former implied an outsider observing, but the latter implied that they would be part of the festival.

"No, no—the food and drink will be brought by all the villagers to enjoy as a group. There's no way they'd let some freeloading passersby in on that."

Obviously not. It wasn't as though the villagers were inviting guests to the festival. It was a peaceful little celebration meant just for themselves. The decorations and refreshments would be provided by the villagers, paid for out of village funds, and they wouldn't be charging admission.

"Well, we can provide some refreshments, too! We've got all kinds of interesting foods, much more than we need for ourselves!"

With this, Mile pulled an enormous block of orc meat from her loot box.

"S-storage magic... Very well, you may join us!"

The village elder realized that the block of meat alone was much more than four girls could eat. Furthermore, there was no way such a cute young girl with storage magic could be hurting for money, so there was little chance they were criminals or posed any danger towards his poor, rural village. They could earn more than enough back in the capital without resorting to anything like that.

Plus, the elder thought, *having some cute girls here should liven things up...*

The day of the festival...

"Hey now, step right up! We've got ginger-fried orc and fried rock lizard! Teriyaki ocean fish and cockatrice kabobs!"

Using the stove, cooking implements, and ingredients from Mile's loot box, Mile and Pauline prepared several dishes. For the sake of everyone's safety and comfort, Mile had omitted any raw dishes like sashimi; mochi, which was a choking hazard for the elderly; and anything else that might be deemed suspect, focusing on dishes that might be uncommon in this area.

While Mile and Pauline were cooking, however, what were the other two up to?

"*Hah!*"

Clang clang!

"And just like that, one copper is cut into fourths!"

"*Whoooooaaaa!!!*"

Mavis was amusing the villagers with her old standard, the copper cutter. And Reina...

"Let's fire it up!!"

was doing a Fire Dance, a brand-new technique of hers.

To clarify, she was not twirling lit batons. Cramming in a skill like that overnight would have resulted in the whole area on fire, and the dancer herself covered in burns. Reina's Fire

Dance was more of a literal dancing fire, with flames swirling around her and forming various shapes.

When first attempting this under Mile's instruction, Reina had groused quite a bit. However, once she realized how effective the training would be in bolstering control of her fire magic, she became fired up (so to speak) and gave it her all.

"Pauline, we should probably have something to eat, too. I'll take care of our stall, so could you go gather up some of the dishes the villagers made?"

"On it. You hold down the fort here!"

Indeed, it would be silly of them to attend a festival and only eat the food they made themselves. They would provide the villagers with food and sample the food the villagers had provided. Naturally.

"Wow, you're so cool! The food and those performances were amazing!"

"Hey, are you really C-rank? You don't look it!"

The Crimson Vow took a break from their cooking and exhibitions to stuff themselves with the food Pauline had collected, rinsed down with fruit juice. The village children flocked around them, squawking, so Mavis decided to humor them. The others' mouths were too packed with food to reply.

"*Ha ha ha!* Is that so? We really *are* C-ranks, though."

"*Wooow,* we've never seen C-rank performers before!"

Pfft!

The other three spat at once—their mouths still full of food.

"*Ew,* that's nasty!"

"Sh-shut up! We ain't performers, we's *hunters!*"

"What's with that accent, Reina...?"

The four street performers—or rather, the Crimson Vow—each took their turn going around to sample other foods and watch other performances. They even pushed their way into a circle that was doing something like a Bon Festival dance after watching the locals for a bit. It was a fun, if a disorienting evening.

The next day...

"Your food and your performances were really amazing," said the village elder. "So, we'd love to have you at our next festival. Which Performers' Guild branch should we contact with our request?"

"That's enooooough!!!"

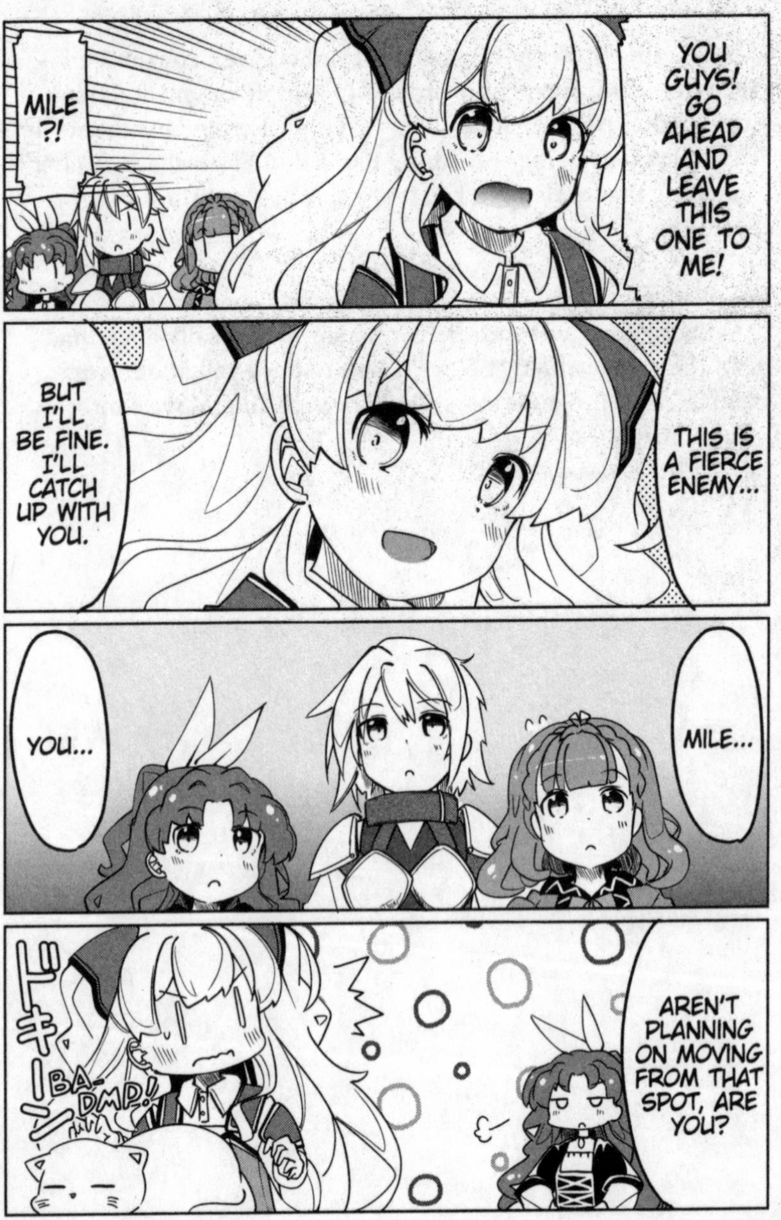
YOU GUYS! GO AHEAD AND LEAVE THIS ONE TO ME!
MILE ?!
THIS IS A FIERCE ENEMY...
BUT I'LL BE FINE. I'LL CATCH UP WITH YOU.
MILE...
YOU...
AREN'T PLANNING ON MOVING FROM THAT SPOT, ARE YOU?
ドキー
BA-DMP!

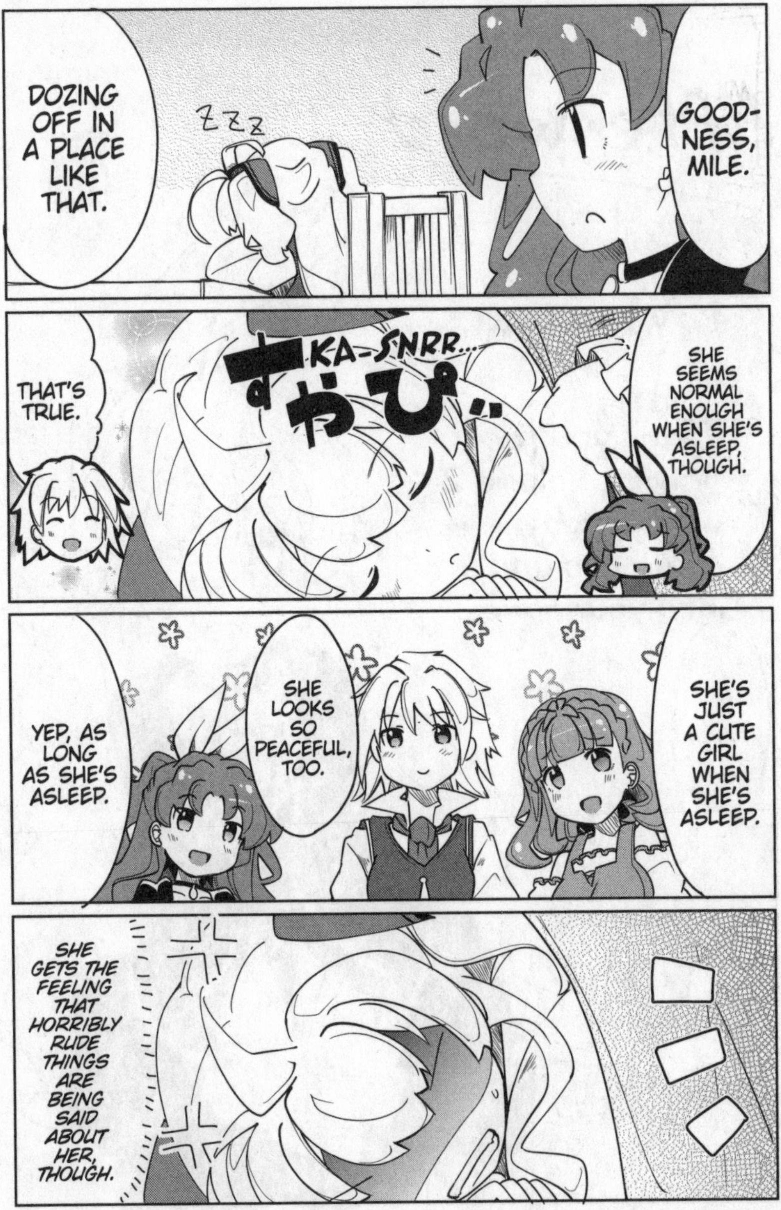
GOODNESS, MILE.
DOZING OFF IN A PLACE LIKE THAT.
Z Z Z
SHE SEEMS NORMAL ENOUGH WHEN SHE'S ASLEEP, THOUGH.
KA-SNRR...
THAT'S TRUE.
SHE'S JUST A CUTE GIRL WHEN SHE'S ASLEEP.
SHE LOOKS SO PEACEFUL, TOO.
YEP, AS LONG AS SHE'S ASLEEP.
SHE GETS THE FEELING THAT HORRIBLY RUDE THINGS ARE BEING SAID ABOUT HER, THOUGH.

Afterword

Hello,
I'm Yuki Moritaka.

Thank you for bringing Volume 2 of Everyday Misadventures into your home.

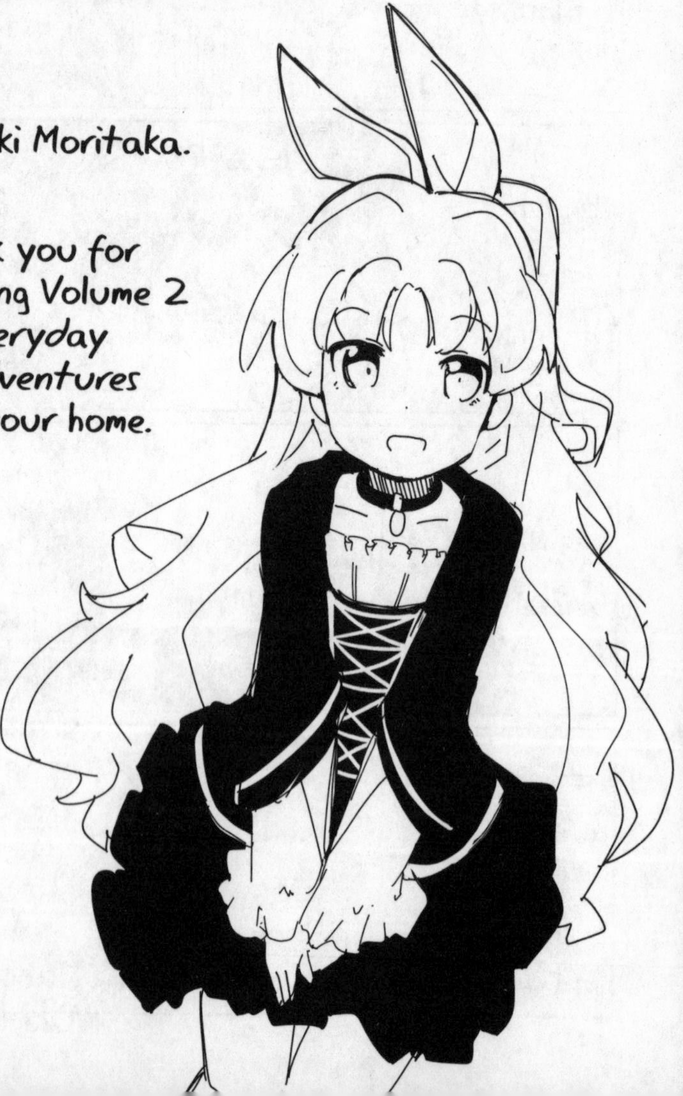

I'm so grateful for these opportunities to imagine and draw everyday episodes of the Crimson Vow's life. I always have a blast!

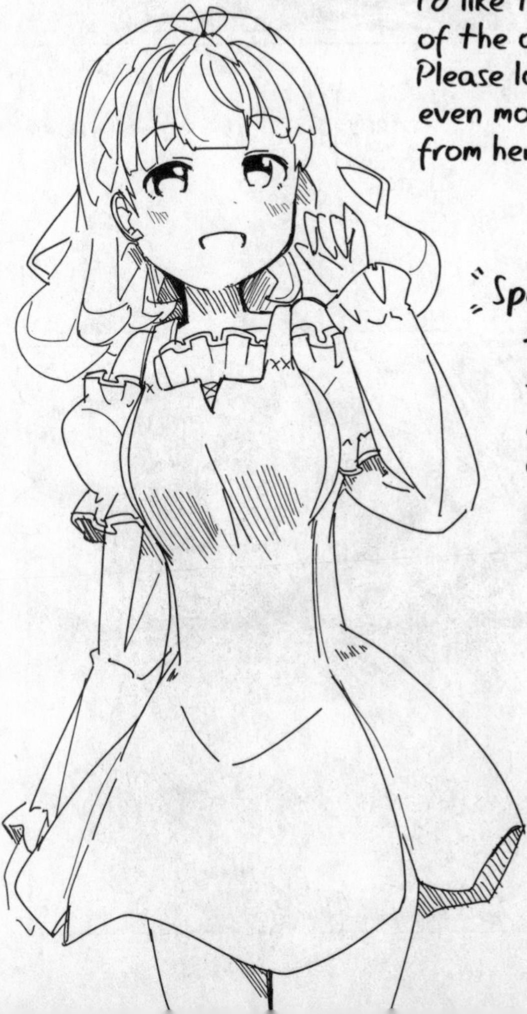

I'd like to draw more of the other characters! Please look forward to even more Misadventures from here on out.

"Special Thanks"

Thank you to the editor, designer, and all other parties for your help.

And to the readers, for reading this far.

March 2020
Yuki Moritaka

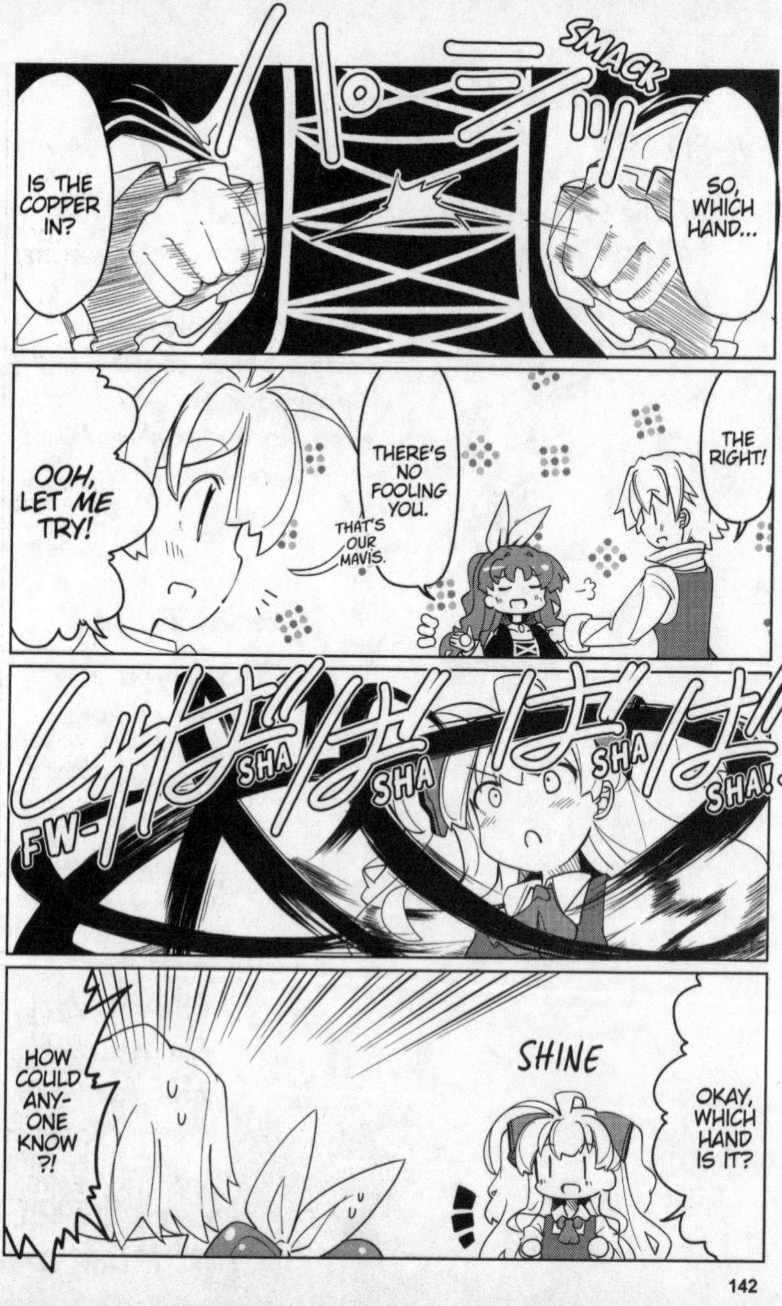
SMACK
SO, WHICH HAND...
IS THE COPPER IN?
THE RIGHT!
THERE'S NO FOOLING YOU.
THAT'S OUR MAVIS.
OOH, LET ME TRY!
FW-
SHA
SHA
SHA
SHA!
OKAY, WHICH HAND IS IT?
SHINE
HOW COULD ANY-ONE KNOW ?!

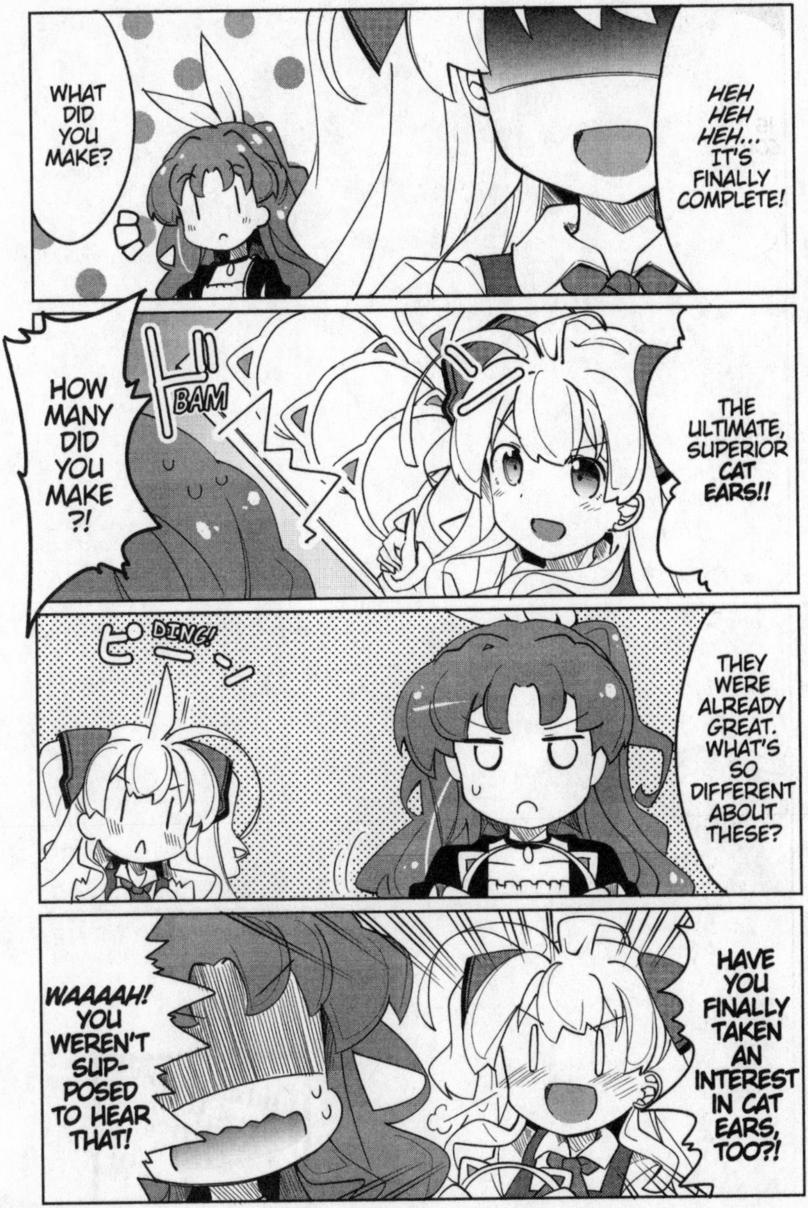
HEH HEH HEH... IT'S FINALLY COMPLETE!
WHAT DID YOU MAKE?
THE ULTIMATE, SUPERIOR CAT EARS!!
BAM
HOW MANY DID YOU MAKE?!
THEY WERE ALREADY GREAT. WHAT'S SO DIFFERENT ABOUT THESE?
DING!
HAVE YOU FINALLY TAKEN AN INTEREST IN CAT EARS, TOO?!
WAAAAH! YOU WEREN'T SUP-POSED TO HEAR THAT!

Didn't I Say to Make My Abilities Average in the Next Life?!
EVERYDAY MISADVENTURES!